LIBER SPIRITUUM

A COMPENDIUM OF WRITINGS ON ANGELS AND OTHER SPIRITS IN MODERN MAGICK

Liber Spirituum

A Compendium of Writings on Angels & Other Spirits in Modern Magick

ADAM P. FORREST
EDITOR

AZOTH PRESS™

2016

Contents

⁜

Opening
a Book of Spirits

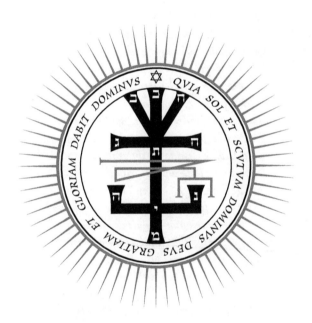

Adam P. Forrest

Adam P. Forrest serves, along with Chic and Tabatha Cicero, as a Chief Adept of the Hermetic Order of the Golden Dawn, an office he has filled for more than 30 years. He is a priest of the Hermetic Fellowship, and, along with Isidora Forrest, a founding steward of that organization. He has been a ceremonial magician since he was a teenager and chalked his first Magic Circle and Triangle in the loft of an unused barn back in Tennessee. He is a Bakchos priest of Dionysos, and has also served as a priest of Hermēs-Thōth, Apollōn, Hekatē-Persephassa, Jēsous-Osiris, and his own Higher and Divine Genius. At the request of Israel Regardie, he contributed a ritual of evocation to The Complete Golden Dawn System of Magic *(Falcon Press, 1984). He has been a regular contributor of articles, rituals, and illustrations to the* Golden Dawn Journals. *He also contributed his translations of two of the Orphic Hymns to* Written in Wine: A Devotional Anthology for Dionysos *(Bibliotheca Alexandrina, 2008). He is by vocation a magus and priest, and by profession a graphic designer, illustrator, editor, and writer, and lives in the Pacific Northwest with his wife, Isidora, and an ancient black cat.*

‡

Opening
a Book of Spirits

PIRITS STAND AT—or very, very near—the centre of Magic. For to my mind the most profound gift that experience in Magic bestows is the ability to see—and for many Magicians, even to travel—beyond the veil that separates our physical world from the non-physical reality that lies behind it. And, far luckier than Dorothy, when we look behind that veil, we don't find just another refugee from black-and-white Kansas. We find that even the Technicolor wonders of Oz are just the bare beginning, for world upon world stretches away beyond that veil. Worlds that are vast, diverse, enchanting, initiating, illuminating, and *inhabited*.

The inhabitants of those worlds are Spirits.

De Dicto / De Re as axioms.

Generally, when I and many other Magicians use the term to describe those otherworldly dwellers, we mean something along the lines of "noncorporeal entities." It is most often a general term, and can refer to a wide array of discarnate beings, from elementals to angels, from ghosts to Gods. "Spirits" translates a range of words in the languages of the Western Occult Traditions, commonly including Greek *daimones, daimonia,* and *pneumata*; Hebrew *ruchoth*; Latin *spiritūs, genii,* and the loanwords *dæmones* and *dæmonia*; and Egyptian *akhu* or *aakhu,* and sometimes *baiu* and *kau*.

Some use the term to refer specifically to sapient beings, that is, entities with a rational mind comparable to or greater than the human mind. However, there is a better term for this, which is the Latin *intelligentiæ,* "intelligences," and its equivalents in Greek and Hebrew, *noes* and *sekhalim*. By retaining the wider meaning for "spirits," the word can usefully encompass the broadest diversity of otherworldly beings which the Magical skryer and traveller may encounter, including those creatures which seem to be more mentally akin to birds and beasts and insects.[1] The Greek word *daimōn* has always been capable of this wider meaning, Homer for instance using it regularly to refer to the Olympian Gods, though it came to also have the specific meaning of a lower class of spirit, and this meaning became standardized in early Christian discourse, as part of the campaign (inherited from the radical monotheism of late Judaism) of classifying all spiritual beings other than the Christian God and His Angels as deceptive evil spirits. However, terms for spirit remained capable of application to the Divine even in exclusionary monotheistic theology, for the *Ruach ha-Qodesh*, *Hagia Pneuma*, or *Spiritus Sanctus* still needed to be named.

Of course, as any Magician knows, there are many individual types of spirits. The Pagan Neoplatonic Theurgist Iamblichos long ago discussed the categories of spiritual beings that he classed among the "Superior Kinds," the beings who serve as links in the Great Chain of Being between the human and the Divine; he itemized Souls, Heroes, Daimones, Archons, Angels, Archangels, and Gods, leading ultimately to the transcendent One. In Judaism, the Angels are divided into various hosts or choruses, such as the Seraphim, Kerubim, Chashmallim, and Tarshishim. In the spiritual cosmology of the grimoires, we find spirits divided into Goetic and Theurgic spirits, into celestial and fallen Angels, into spirits of the elements, planets, and the zodiacal signs, and many other categories.

And then there are familiar spirits. In preparing this volume, I thought back over my long-term, familiar relationships with spirits through the years, and was both startled and amused to realize that I have had a longer close relationship with some few spirits—and the Archangel Raphael came particularly to mind—than I have had with any of my incarnate human friends, including my wife, whom I have known and loved for 40 years. Familiar human friends, lovers, and associates in this mobile age often find themselves being separated by relocations to other regions and even other continents, but one's familiar spirits (other than, by definition, *terroir*-infused *genii loci*) remain just as close regardless of one's terrestrial address.

On the other hand, there are certainly Spirits with whom I have shared my Magical life for a time and then moved on: by way of comparison, think of professors with whom you studied a subject for several semesters, specialists with whom you treated a medical issue for a time, coaches who helped you develop a skill through a

---

1. There is also the special case of the spirits associated with the system of the Qemeyoth or Magic Squares preserved by Agrippa and others. In that instance, *dæmonium* (a diminutive of the word *dæmon*) is used for a particular class of entity distinguished from and specifically identified as less than an *intelligentia*. Bearing this classification in mind, some Magi have encountered these *dæmonia* of the Magic Squares as "Blind Forces," having not actual but only potential rationality until the ritual interaction with an evocator formulates what may be described as an *ad hoc* mentality for the dæmonium appropriate to a particular Working. These seem like a sort of Astral planetary golem, in many ways. —APF

particular stage, and even acquaintances with whom you pursued what turned out to be a passing interest or a one-off project.

But there are also the ultimate classes of familiar spiritual beings: one's personal Deity or Deities, and for many of us, there is also the Higher and Divine Genius or the Holy Guardian Angel[2] with Whom to come into communion. Iamblichos made an attempt to describe the impact of regular exposure to higher spiritual entities on human beings, and many modern practitioners can attest to the reality of that influence. One hallmark of the relationship with the Higher and Divine Genius is that it leads to an expansion of both mind and heart. During my first sustained interaction with my Genius back in the 1980s, I was managing a cinema with a large group of teenaged employees, and some of them later told me that they had been very curious about my private life that spring, because they were sure I had fallen deeply in love. They were certainly correct. And then there are the Gods. My chief personal Deity for the last dozen years or more has been the God Dionysos, and under His influence, I experienced a condition in which I was separated by just an instant's concentration from being immersed in a state of bliss at any time during the day or night. When this condition had endured for more than a year, I remember asking some of my Magical companions for their opinions, "So, is this permanent? Am I just a blink away from ecstasy for the rest of my life?" Alas, the answer was no; after about two and a half years, the shores of that blissful state began to gently recede.

So we know what Spirits are; now what is a *Book* of Spirits? In the Magical traditions set down in the grimoires, we encounter two types of Books of Spirits. The first is an intimate personal resource, a catalogue compiled by the practicing Magus of the Spirits he has encountered, along with their seals, sigils, descriptions, and all the information he has gleaned from his interactions, so that he may rely on it to build his relationship with those spirits as his Work proceeds. The second type is a less personal catalogue, a listing made available to the student Magician, supposedly by a master of the art, of spirits whom the aspiring evocator may wish to attempt to summon in the future. The most familiar surviving example of this second type of Book of Spirits is the one incorporated into the *Goetia* of the *Lemegeton*.

Having been granted the privilege of editing this first offering from Azoth Press, I wished to orchestrate a book that would have some characteristics of both types of grimoric *Libri Spirituum*, focusing on the communication between human Magi and Spiritual Beings. To do that, we have taken advantage of our current circumstances, perhaps unique in the history of the Western Magical Tradition,

---

2. Those two being for some synonymous names for a single entity, and in the understanding and experience of others, two distinct beings. —APF

of having a significant number of experienced, practicing Mages[3] willing to write about not only their technical expertise but also their personal experience in Magical Operations with Spirits, and of living in a culture where neither censorship nor other overt forms of persecution stand as a bar to publishing that information for the benefit of students.

In our first contribution, John Michael Greer admits us to the halls of the temples and lodges where humans and Spirits work together to further the Great Work, in "The Place of Mingled Powers: Spiritual Beings in the Magical Lodge."

Next, Aaron Leitch addresses the crucial concept of familiar spirits, and shares some of his own experience with long-term Spiritual engagement in "Patrons and House Gods: Building Lifelong Relationships with Your Spiritual Guardians."

Chic Cicero and Tabatha Cicero introduce us to the Golden Dawn's Inner-Order Z-2 Formula of Evocation, and provide a fascinating example of the formula's application to the calling of an Archangel in "The Evocation of Metatron: A Golden Dawn Z-2 Ritual."

Jake Stratton-Kent leads us on an exploration of the importance of "The Prayer for Success," a particular invocation recurring in the Solomonic grimoires, and reveals that the catalogue of names in the prayer is a true invocation of a group of particular Spirits to be called upon repeatedly to aid the Magician in his or her Work. He also demonstrates how much may be learned by a determined and well-informed examination of the sometimes unfamiliar names in such a catalogue.

M. Isidora Forrest grants us a rare window into the personal Work of a veteran Adept performing an extended Operation in "Lay Thy Tongue Upon My Heart: Forty Days of Ritual Communion Between a Pagan Adept and the Archangel Raphael Tipherethel."

Frater Ashen Chassan (Bryan Garner) then shares the particulars of his experience with one of the most useful grimoric operations performed with the cooperation of evoked spirits: the creation and charging of magical talismans. He sets out his approach to several different types of grimoric talismans and the evocations necessary to charge them in "Substance Through Spirit: A Reflection on Magical Evocation and Talisman Construction."

---

3. Ever since I first began to study Magic, I have used—and continue to use—the word 'Magician' to describe a practitioner, and I originally thought it was the only directly-related word we had in English. But it has always bothered me a bit, as it has two problems. First, the word carries the unavoidable baggage of rabbit-infested headwear and of diverting assistants pretending to be sawn in half. Second, it seems to me a somewhat ordinary word for an extraordinary vocation; it says by its form that a Magician is to the Magical arts and sciences simply as a technician, an electrician, or a politician is to the technical, electrical, or political arts and sciences. A few years ago, I realized that there has been for centuries an excellent though obscure English word deriving by the usual process from the Greek *Magos* and the Latinized *Magus*: Mage. I think that we should reclaim this direct, elegant, and potent monosyllable from obscurity. —APF

Next, Jeffrey S. Kupperman shows us how truly ancient Magical Operations—in this case Theurgic invocations of the Gods following the teachings of the great Neo-platonic teacher Iamblichos—continue to be viable Magical Workings in the 21st century, and presents a new Theurgic Ritual to commune with the God Apollo in *"Kalein tous Theous:* Divine Invocation in the Late Neoplatonic Tradition."

Scott Michael Stenwick rounds out our *Liber Spirituum* by sharing the insights gained from his own study and practice while providing us with the tools and techniques to expand our Magical practice to include the Angels of that greatest of Magical Circles, the celestial Zodiac, in "Evoking Zodiacal Angels."

The traditional instructions for the grimoric *Book of Spirits* inform the Mage that seals and sigils are key to both the talismanic and referential functions of the book. The seal of the individual Spirit is to be included with each entry, and Seals of Solomon are to be placed in the front and back of the book to consecrate and indeed to seal and contain the contents. To that end, in the design of the present volume, a talismanic seal has been placed on the cover page of each article in *Liber Spirituum*. In the cases where a pentacle or seal is central to the article, a form of that has been employed; in the remaining articles, a talismanic seal appropriate to the content has been created in the style of those found in manuscripts of the *Key of Solomon*. There are many versions of the Seals of Solomon, and the one to be found in the front and back of this book is one employed in varying forms in a range of Solomonic texts going back at least to the *Heptameron seu Elementa Magica*. The versicle surrounding it here is from *Psalm* 17:8 (16:8 in the Vulgate and related translations), invoking the grace of Divine sanctuary in the beautiful metaphor, "Under the Shadow of Thy Wings." In the back of our *Liber Spirituum* (the front, were this a Hebrew book), the versicle is in the original Hebrew of the *Psalm: Be-Tzel Kenapheikha*; in the front, in the Latin of the Vulgate translation: *Sub Umbra Alarum Tuarum*. The Latin has a particular resonance for many modern Magi as it is part of the closing salutation of the Rosicrucian *Fama Fraternitatis*, and—often abbreviated to *S∴V∴A∴T∴*—it shares the Latin initials of the four Virtues of the Adept: *Scire, Velle, Audere, Tacere* ("To Know, To Will, To Dare, To Keep Silence"). Another Seal of Solomon stands watch at the entry to this introduction. Versions of it occur in various MSS of the *Key of Solomon* as well as in the *Calendarium Naturale Magicum*. The encircling versicle in this formulation is from the Latin rendering of *Psalm* 84:11 (83:12 in the Vulgate), which translates as "For the Lord God is a Sun and a Shield; the Lord will give Grace and Glory." In the original Hebrew, "Grace and Glory" is *Chen ve-Kavod*, and Qabbalists know that *Chen* (חן) is an acronym which unfolds by Notariqon into *Chokhmah Nistarah*, "The Secret Wisdom," while *Kavod* refers to the Glory of the Divine, which is beheld in the Beatific Vision that is the transformative goal of the *Sworn Book of Honorius*.

Finally, I would like to offer just a few words about the editorial conventions employed in this anthology. I have not standardized the method of representing Hebrew words in the Roman alphabet, but allowed it to vary among the different contributors, as the spelling of Hebrew-derived words and particularly of names may be meant by the writer to convey particular cultural nuances. For example, spelling the Archangelic name כסיאל as *Cassiel* rather than *Kassiel* may convey that the writer is using the name not in terms of its Hebrew origins or Qabbalistic developments, but specifically as it occurs in the rites of certain Latin and French grimoires.

The footnotes to be found in several of the articles are the work of the individual authors, with the exception of those initialed APF, which are my own additional notes contributed to hopefully clarify a point or provide a further reference for the reader. Of course, the authors of the articles are innocent of any perceived errors in notes with those telltale initials.

Our esteemed authors, while sharing a rare identity as Magi in the Western tradition, nonetheless represent a diverse array of backgrounds and training. Bearing in mind then that their students and devoted readers who have followed one or more of them to this anthology may not be deeply familiar with another branch or form of Western Magic represented here, the references have been standardized as much as possible to include information on the earliest publication of cited works, to allow readers to more easily place the sources in at least a chronological context.

With that, O kindred spirit, I bid you welcome to this Book of Spirits and to the company of the magical men and women who have written it for you.

Adam Forrest
The Hallows
Feast of Carnevale
9 February 2016

The Place of Mingled Powers

Spiritual Beings in the Magical Lodge

JOHN MICHAEL GREER

John Michael Greer currently serves as the Grand Archdruid of the Ancient Order of Druids in America. He is the author of more than thirty books on a wide range of subjects, including Paths of Wisdom: Cabala in the Western Tradition *(Llewellyn, 1996);* Inside A Magical Lodge: Group Ritual in the Western Tradition *(Llewellyn, 1998);* The Art And Practice Of Geomancy: Divination, Magic, and Earth Wisdom of the Renaissance *(Weiser, 2009);* The Druid Grove Handbook: A Guide to Ritual in the Ancient Order of Druids in America *(Lorain Press, 2011);* The Gnostic Celtic Church: A Manual and Book of Liturgy *(Lorian Press, 2013); and* After Progress: Reason and Religion at the End of the Industrial Age *(New Society Publishers, 2015). With Christopher Warnock, he translated* The Picatrix: The Occult Classic of Astrological Magic *(Adocentyn Press, 2010–11). He is also the editor of the new edition of Israel Regardie's* The Golden Dawn: The Original Account of the Teachings, Rites, and Ceremonies of the Hermetic Order *(Llewellyn, 2016). He lives in Cumberland, Maryland, an old red brick mill town in the north central Appalachians, with his wife Sara. You may follow his blogs at* The Well of Galabes: Reflections on Druidry, Magic, and Occult Philosophy *(galabes. blogspot.com) and* The Archdruid Report: Druid perspectives on nature, culture, and the future of industrial society *(thearchdruidreport.blogspot.com).*

✢

The Place of Mingled Powers

Spiritual Beings in the Magical Lodge

 AGIC IS IN LARGE PART a solitary practice, but mages, like other human beings, are social primates. Group workings of various kinds thus have a long-established place in magical lore. The world's magical traditions, diverse as they are, have an equal diversity of structures for group work, and a fair sample of that diversity is on display in the contemporary occult scene.

The modern magical tradition has made a distinctive contribution to that diversity. By "modern magic"—as distinct from older systems such as classical, medieval, and Renaissance magic on the one hand, and postmodern magical systems such as chaos magic on the other—I mean the tradition that took shape in the wake of Éliphas Lévi's *Dogme et Rituel de la Haute Magie* (*"Doctrine and Ritual of High Magic,"* 1856)[1] in Europe, the Americas, and Australasia, and kept its place as the predominant form of occultism on those continents until it was elbowed aside by the rise of popular Neopaganism in the late twentieth century. When operative mages in that tradition worked together, they normally did so in the context of a magical lodge.

Even today, when the tradition just described is only one of many options for the operative mage, lodge methods are still part of the common practice in a great many corners of the magical scene. Those methods are not always well understood even by those who practice them, and one aspect of the magical lodge particularly prone to confusions just now is the role of spiritual beings in magical lodge work. That's a crucial dimension of the system, for human beings are not the only participants in a properly functioning magical lodge. When a magical lodge functions as it should, it becomes a place of mingled powers where the Seen and the Unseen work together at common tasks.

---

1. Badly Englished by A.E. Waite and retitled *Transcendental Magic*—Waite could never settle for a good title when he could think of a boring one instead. See Éliphas Lévi, *Transcendental Magic*, trans. Arthur Edward Waite (London: George Redway, 1896); a less pompous and turgid translation of this occult classic is badly needed.

The Magical Lodge

The magical lodge itself is a complex phenomenon with a long history. I hope my readers will not be too bitterly disappointed, though, if I mention that the history in question didn't originate in the mystery temples of the Nile, the lamaseries of the Himalayas, the sun temples of lost Atlantis, or any of the other exotic and untraceable homelands to which occultists of an earlier day assigned it. The Neopagan habit of backdating freshly minted traditions to the distant past via undocumented "grandmother stories" is nothing new; a century ago, magical lodges and occult traditions did the same thing with even more panache, manufacturing origin stories going back millennia in which Egypt, Atlantis, Lemuria, and the like routinely played an important part.[2] All this is great entertainment, but it has little if anything to do with history.

The historical origins of the magical lodge are more prosaic, though not without interest. In Europe during the Middle Ages, religious organizations of laymen called confraternities were a common form of social organization. The confraternities early on evolved a distinctive way of managing their regular meetings, with a presiding officer sitting on the side of the room opposite the door, a second officer near the door whose duties included controlling access to the meeting and maintaining discipline, and the members sitting on the two remaining sides of the room, facing one another across the floor. As confraternities developed their own initiation rituals and other ceremonial activities, the open floor became a blank slate onto which any desired pattern might be drawn—in many cases, quite literally, with chalk, charcoal, and red clay serving as writing media that could be scrubbed away after the ceremony was done.

This same set of practices passed over into the craft guilds of the high Middle Ages, most of which started out as religious confraternities focused around reverence to patron saints. Among the guilds that absorbed the confraternity system and added to it were the stonemasons. Because their work required them to travel to job sites far from home and identify themselves as trained craftsmen to the master mason in charge, the stonemasons developed passwords and signs of recognition; their initiation rituals were more complex than average, and their involvement with church building brought them into contact with the rich medieval lore of symbolism and sacred geometry, much of which found its way into the stonemasons' rituals and traditions.

Those borrowings were probably responsible for the survival of the stonemasons' guild when the Middle Ages gave way to what historians awkwardly call the Early

---

2. See, as one example out of many, Dion Fortune, *Esoteric Orders and their Work* (Wellingborough, Northamptonshire, UK: Aquarian Press, 1987 [First ed. London: Rider & Co., 1928]), pp. 23–29.

Modern period, and the medieval economic system of local guilds serving local markets was swept aside by the first wave of mercantile capitalism. Beginning in Scotland in the 17th century, and spreading from there, educated gentlemen began to join stonemasons' lodges as "accepted members"—"honorary members" would be the equivalent modern term—and their influence gradually transformed what had been a medieval craft guild into the modern institution of Freemasonry.

It's almost impossible to overstate the influence of Freemasonry on modern Western occultism. For more than two centuries, from around 1750 to the cultural convulsions of the 1960s, if you were a male occultist in Europe or North America, you were probably also a Freemason—and if you happened to be female, your chances of belonging either to a Masonic auxiliary or to one of the irregular branches of Masonry that admit women to membership were not small. By that channel among others, the practices and habits that Freemasonry inherited from its medieval ancestry were picked up enthusiastically by occultists and imported wholesale into most branches of Western occultism.

At first, though, that inheritance was used purely as an educational and instructional framework. The earliest occult lodges in the 18th century borrowed the toolkit of lodge ritual and organization more or less intact from Freemasonry; their rituals included plenty of occult symbolism but the actual practice of operative magic was carried on by initiates on their own time. It was in the second half of the 19th century, after Éliphas Lévi popularized ritual magic, that lodge workings in occult orders started to make room for magical practices in the initiation rituals themselves. The Hermetic Order of the Golden Dawn was the most famous of the magical lodge organizations that resulted from that creative fusion, but it was far from the only example.

The Magical Mesocosm

Enthusiastic adaptation of lodge rituals and forms to new purposes was not limited to the magical scene of the time. An astonishing range of organizations, from labor unions and insurance cooperatives to ethnic societies and youth groups, borrowed the lodge template either from Freemasonry or from one of a handful of less famous organizations descended from medieval guilds and confraternities, such as the Odd Fellows.[3] The sheer popularity of the lodge system in popular culture added to its attractiveness to occultists and operative mages, but there were other excellent

---

3. My collection of old lodge rituals includes, among others, one from the Daughters of Norway, which was an ethnic heritage organization; one from the Ladies Auxiliary of the Amalgamated Transit Workers Union, which was exactly what the name suggests; and one from the Woodmen of the World, which was an insurance cooperative. All of these, and many more, use the standard lodge system, complete with initiation rituals.

reasons why for more than a century, the vast majority of occult traditions in the Western world ended up using that particular toolkit and no other.

One of those reasons is far more significant than is often recognized: magical lodges are usually part-time phenomena. Most magical lodges don't have the financial resources to buy or lease their own buildings, and even those that do rarely have meetings more often than once a week. The constant flow of ritual and practice that takes place in a monastery or a temple is a very rare thing in Western occultism. That imposed two requirements for magical lodges. First, they had to use a generic space for their purposes; second, they had to be able to turn that generic space into fully charged and activated sacred space in short order whenever they wanted to do an initiation or any other kind of ritual working.

Those requirements had a profound impact on the structure of initiation, because people realized very quickly that the same processes that allow you to turn an empty lodge room into a magically charged sacred space in a single ritual working will also allow you to turn an ordinary candidate into a magically empowered initiate in a single ritual working. Thus you'll find that in the great majority of initiation rituals in our Western tradition, the opening ritual for each degree has very close structural similarities to the initiation ritual of that degree.

This led the occult lodge tradition into very deep waters. The Hermetic doctrine of macrocosm and microcosm, the mirroring of the universe in the individual human being and vice versa, is of course one of the standard concepts of Western occultism. What the participants in magical lodges realized, though, is that those are two terms of a three-term relationship. Between the macrocosm and the microcosm, the universe and the individual, stands the mesocosm—literally, the middle universe—which reflects both the macrocosm and the microcosm. That's what a magical lodge becomes when it's opened with the proper ceremony. It's a mirror of the macrocosm, representing the entire universe in miniature. It's also a mirror of the microcosm, representing every aspect of the individual in expanded form.

The advantage there is the advantage that always comes in magic when you move from a twofold to a threefold relationship. Put any two things in relationship with one another and they polarize; they become a pair of opposites; and that opposition, that polarization, fixes the volatile and locks both ends of the binary into place. If you want to build on that foundation, you have to bring in a third factor: it's with the triad, Binah the Great Mother, that the abstract becomes manifest and creation happens. In the same way, macrocosm and microcosm can polarize one another, but there's always the risk of fixation, of stuckness. Bring in the mesocosm and things start to move; having fixed the volatile, you volatilize the fixed, and transmutation becomes possible on many different levels.

This happens in any form of magical work. One of the great discoveries that came out of the evolution of the occult lodge tradition in the 18th and 19th centuries is precisely that occultists had been working with mesocosms all along. Consider the medieval sorcerer in his magic circle, sword in one hand and grimoire in the other, conjuring demons by the mighty names of God. The magic circle is a mesocosm; it represents the entire universe in symbolic form, with its four quarters, the divine names and the working tools of the art representing the powers of the cosmos, and chaos and old night pressing close around the periphery; it also represents the sorcerer himself, the four quarters and innate powers of his own body, mind, and spirit.

Among other things, this is one way to understand how magic works. The macrocosm reflects the microcosm, and vice versa, but when you create a mesocosm between them, the static condition of reflection becomes a flowing process that allows magical changes to occur. You start with the mesocosm reflecting the macrocosm and microcosm, but then the macrocosm and the microcosm reflect the mesocosm; when you change things in the mesocosm, corresponding changes reflect outward to the macrocosm, and inward to the microcosm. If you constellate an influence through a ritual in your magical mesocosm; that same influence reflects in both directions and constellates itself in your inner and outer life. As between, so above, and so below.

The Outer Lodge

The first step in any magical lodge working is thus the preparation of the space, the formulation of the mesocosm on outer and inner levels alike. Since magical lodges are part-time phenomena, this has to be done every time the lodge is opened; the lodge can't simply be consecrated once and for all, and left at that. Fortunately, the standard methods of magical lodge work provide effective tools to do what needs to be done.

The vast majority of magical lodge rituals are designed to be performed in a completely generic space. Those readers who have been inside a lodge hall of any kind, no matter what organization it serves, already know the design, as shown in Figure 1. The basic structure is a rectangular space with chairs along the sides, a seat for the presiding officer on one end, a seat for the secondary officer on the other, a door and an officer to guard it, and an altar that can be put at the center of the space.

The basic structure, in turn, is subject to almost limitless variations. Additional officers can be added, and assigned to stations anywhere in the lodge hall. Additional furnishings can be brought in, and distributed with equal freedom. A floor cloth or carpet marked with appropriate emblems can be used to divide the lodge space into symbolic regions. Veils can be set up across the hall, dividing it more dramatically. At the furthest end of ritual complexity are those lodges in which a smaller enclosed space—a chamber, a vault, the tomb of Hermes or Merlin or Christian

Rosycross—is set up somewhere in the lodge hall and becomes the focus of the ritual work.

In the great majority of cases, though, the only variations to the space are those that can be set up and taken down in a half hour or so. Unless the lodge has enough resources to afford a building of its own, and these are very much an exception, the whole kit and caboodle is designed to be packed away in a closet between lodge meetings. Setting up the lodge furnishings thus serves as an effective prelude to setting up the lodge on a more magical level.

The procedure here is just as standardized as the basic lodge architecture itself. The presiding officer makes sure that the doors are closed and everyone present is already an initiate, and a banishing ritual may be performed; a litany recounts the symbolism of

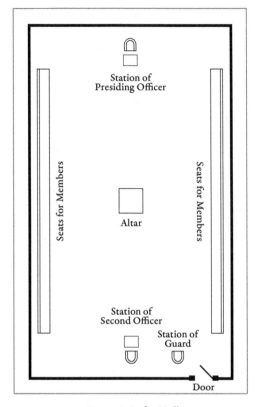

Figure 1. **Lodge Hall**

the degree and the names and duties of the officers; an invocation calls on whatever spiritual force presides over the working; and then the lodge is formally declared open. Ritual designers have plugged almost every conceivable variation into this framework, but it still works out to the same process. First, the mesocosm is set apart from the world around it; second, the symbolic patterns and stations are established and reinforced in the collective consciousness of the lodge and in the minds and wills of each person present; third, a spiritual influence is called down into the waiting receptacle; finally, by an act of will, the mesocosm is made complete and the work begins.

In an ordinary non-magical lodge, this is done in an entirely exoteric way, without any conscious magical technique involved. That has certain advantages, since in a fraternal lodge the effect of the ritual doesn't depend on the magical prowess of the initiators, and of course it also happens that people who've been doing lodge ritual for long enough end up practicing magic without ever quite realizing that that's what they're doing. I've been astonished more than once by the head of magical steam that some old men and women without a trace of occult training can build up when they're working a lodge ritual they love, and doing it for the three thousandth time. In an occult lodge, though, the same thing is done consciously, and whatever set of inner tools a given tradition provides can be brought to bear on the process of charging the hall.

The mesocosm concept mentioned earlier is crucial in this process. The lodge as mesocosm represents the universe, and it also represents the candidate in an initiation, as well as every other individual in the lodge. The presiding officer of the lodge represents the divine power presiding over the universe, and also represents the higher self or guardian angel of the individual, the reflection of the divine in the sphere of the self. Each of the other officers of the lodge represent a power of the cosmos and a factor in the individual psyche. Each piece of lodge furnishing represents an aspect of the universe and of the self. When the officers take on their roles consciously and mediate the energies they represent, the work has noticeably more impact, and the more skilled they are at handling magical energies, the more pyrotechnic the results can be.

The Inner Lodge

The lodge space itself also undergoes transformation in this process, from a blank slate to a map of the cosmos and the self. Every traditional initiation ritual divides up the lodge hall into areas corresponding to different aspects of the universe, which are also different aspects of the individual. For example, the lodge may be divided up into five zones—the four material elements in the four quarters and the element of spirit in the center. It might be divided into two zones of darkness and light, with the place of balance at the central altar. The whole Cabalistic Tree of Life, or some part thereof, may be mapped onto it; alternatively, some other map of the symbolic cosmos can be used in the same way. As the opening ritual proceeds, each section of the lodge room is charged with the appropriate influence; the officers begin mediating the appropriate forces, and the mesocosm is readied for work.

All this is done whenever a magical lodge opens. It can also be done with equal effectiveness by an individual mage working in the privacy of his or her own home. This was another of the discoveries that came out of the fusion of the lodge tradition with magical practice in 18th and 19th century Europe. Since the same magical mesocosm can be constructed in a solitary ritual as in a magical lodge meeting, magical lodges learned to teach their initiates simplified versions of the opening and closing ritual as a basic magical practice; among the many effects of this habit is that the initiates in question became intimately familiar with the magical work required to open and close the lodge, and thus generally did a better job in practice.

The furthest extension of this sort of thinking was pioneered by the Hermetic Order of the Golden Dawn in the 1890s, though it's been borrowed by a variety of other magical lodges since that time. Just as the opening and closing ceremony can be converted into an opening and closing ritual for solitary use, rituals of initiation and other group rituals can also be converted into solitary rituals for practical and spiritual magic.

The rituals the Golden Dawn derived from its Neophyte grade ceremony are the most famous examples of this conversion process.[4] Those rituals have fielded a certain amount of criticism over the years on the grounds that there are simpler ways to get the same results. This is true only if "the same results" are limited to the practical goals of the ceremonies. In the Golden Dawn curriculum, the "Z-2 rituals" also serve as ways to train adepti to fulfill certain key functions in Golden Dawn temple ceremonies. Many other magical lodges rely on a similar kind of multitasking in their training systems, using bits of lodge ritual as elements of individual work for training purposes even when a simpler approach might seem more practical.

The opening ceremony, though, is the most commonly repurposed element of magical lodge practice, and for good reason. This is the ceremony that defines the magical space in which a lodge will accomplish its work, and the powers and potencies that will assist the lodge in its labors are called into operation. In a great many magical lodge systems, these powers include gods, angels, and spiritual beings of various kinds: the nonhuman inhabitants of the magical mesocosm.

Spiritual Beings

In this essay as elsewhere, I treat spiritual beings as real, conscious, intelligent entities who have an existence independent of the human mind. I'm aware that this is a controversial stance in some parts of the magical community just now. A substantial number of mages these days prefer a cosmology in which human beings are the only real, conscious, intelligent entities around, and gods, angels, spirits, and the like are purely imaginary forms called into being by the human mind and will. That's certainly one way of understanding the cosmos; philosophically speaking, it's impossible either to prove or to disprove the objective existence of spiritual beings—but the two options are not interchangeable. Important issues ride on the distinction.

It so happens that for wholly personal reasons, I find a universe chock-full of real, conscious, intelligent spiritual beings with whom I can interact far more interesting and appealing than a universe that's simply an echo chamber for my ego. If, as many chaos magicians like to claim, the universe is whatever we will it to be, then it's as reasonable for me to will a universe crammed with spirits as it would be for someone else to will one in which spirits have no independent existence. By almost

---

4. Israel Regardie, *The Golden Dawn: An Account of the Teachings, Rites, and Ceremonies of the Order of the Golden Dawn* (St. Paul, MN: Llewellyn, 1982 [First ed. Chicago: Aries Press, 1937–1940]), vol. 3, pp. 152–276.

any other theory—and in particular, by the standard occult theory that underlies modern magic—things are considerably more straightforward: according to that latter theory, spiritual beings exist, and much of the work of the operative mage takes place in interaction with them.

All this is relevant to the work of the magical lodge, because most magical lodge systems derive from occult traditions that affirm the reality of spiritual beings, and nearly all such systems include direct or indirect interactions with such beings as part of the work done in a magical lodge. It would certainly be possible to construct an effective magical lodge ritual in which impersonal spiritual influences play the critical roles in the work, and I wouldn't be surprised to learn that such rituals exist, but that isn't the standard approach in magical lodges working in the modern magical tradition.

There are any number of ways to classify spiritual beings, and none of them are exact. For our present purposes, it's sufficient to note three very general classifications which are also the three basic roles that spiritual beings fill in most magical lodge workings, and in fraternal lodges as well. For simplicity's sake, we'll call them deities, powers, and creations.

Deities

In the sense meant here, deities are primary spiritual powers whose influence pervades every aspect of the work of a lodge. In the oldest lodges and proto-lodges that have left detailed ritual texts, the deity who presided over meetings and rituals was the Christian god, and ordinary religious practices such as prayer were used to invoke him in the opening ceremony and at various points during lodge workings. That remains the case in regular Freemasonry, which includes prayers to the god of the Bible in its lodge opening and closing rituals; a great many other fraternal lodges do the same thing. In magical lodges, the options are considerably broader; the god of the Bible is still very much an option, as a glance at Golden Dawn lodge rituals will demonstrate,[5] but he stopped being the only game in town a very long time ago.

Philosophers and theologians of many traditions have kept up a centuries-long debate about what differentiates deities from other classes of spiritual beings, but their quarrels can be left aside for our present purpose. What matters within the four walls of a magical lodge is that the entities I'm describing as deities are not localized in space. Once a deity is invoked in a magical lodge, all the activities of the lodge take place in the deity's presence, and so long as care is taken to maintain a satisfactory relationship, under his or her blessing and protection as well. What is

---

5.   See, for instance, Regardie, *op. cit.*, vol. 2, pp. 46–47.

required to keep such a relationship in good order depends, of course, on the deity in question; what will maintain good relations with Jehovah, for example, is not necessarily going to further a working relationship with Bacchus, or vice versa.

When designing a magical lodge, or for that matter choosing to be initiated into one, it's well to be sure that the deity invoked in its workings is of a nature congenial to the work to be done. It's at least as important, though, to be sure the deity is congenial to the initiates of the lodge, and vice versa. There's a certain wry amusement to be gotten from watching a magical lodge go through the motions of invoking a deity whom none of the lodge members reverence and some actively detest, but effective magic rarely comes out of such exercises. Deities are conscious entities, not vending machines, and trying to extract things from them by the equivalent of dropping in a quarter and pushing a button is not a good idea.

Powers

In the sense meant here, powers are spiritual beings whose powers are localized in space in an open magical lodge. The classic example, familiar to most operative mages these days, are the elemental archangels who are invoked in the Lesser Ritual of the Pentagram. Whether or not archangels occupy specific points in space, on the head of a pin or otherwise, may be left to the theologians; all I mean here by "localized" is that, within the space established by the ritual, it's possible to face toward Raphael and away from Gabriel, or vice versa. Different points in or around the lodge hall are assigned to different powers, who are evoked in those locations by one or another of the standard magical means.

Powers called into a magical lodge working can be evoked into various portions of empty space, into specific items of lodge furniture, or into members of the lodge. Various kinds of mediumship have long played a role in magical lodges. In some lodges, for example, it's standard to have a lodge officer who goes into trance in lodge ritual and serves as a mouthpiece for a specific spiritual being, or a series of such beings. In other lodges, officers make contact with specific powers assigned to their offices and stations, and consciously mediate those powers when the lodge is working ritual.

There are risks involved in this latter process. In some branches of the Hermetic Order of the Golden Dawn, officers used to go to great lengths to protect themselves from being obsessed by powers behind the godforms they mediated in ritual. In other branches of the tradition, to be sure, the danger of obsession and the resulting inflation of the ego does not seem to have been taken seriously enough! After the original Golden Dawn blew itself to pieces in 1900–1903, a good many magical lodges took the hint, and had their officers mediate energies without the added challenge of being overshadowed by a conscious entity. The tool of choice for this work was usually a creation.

Group Minds

These, finally, are spiritual beings who are brought into existence by the work of a magical lodge, as distinct from those who exist independently of the lodge and who thus have to be invoked or evoked. Some creations come into existence automatically, as a product of certain phenomena familiar to students of the inner side of human social interaction; others are deliberately constructed by magical means.

The automatic creation most often used in magical lodge work is the group mind or collective personality.[6] Any group of human beings united by a shared emotion, even temporarily, generates a group mind, which feeds the emotional state that creates it back into the psyches of its creators. Mob violence and the behavior of crowds display the group mind at its most basic level; an operative mage with well-developed magical senses can learn a great deal about group minds by observing the crowds at a football game, a rock concert, or any other venue where people habitually check their minds at the door and surf the waves of emotion.

The same thing in a more controlled and directed fashion plays an important part in the magical lodge tradition and its work. The opening ritual in a magical lodge, or for that matter a fraternal lodge, is among other things a way of calling up shared emotional states among the members of the lodge, and thus building and feeding a group mind. That process has a feedback component; the shared emotion builds the group mind, which then elicits more of the shared emotion from the lodge members. This is a very powerful tool, but it can also backfire spectacularly; those readers who have watched a magical working group disintegrate in an unstoppable spiral of pointless bickering have seen that latter effect at work.

Artificial Spirits

Two kinds of deliberately constructed creations are commonly used in magical lodge systems. Interestingly, the one that gets most of the discussion is the less common of the two—though a census would be impossible, lodge secrecy being what it is, fewer than half of the traditional magical lodge rituals I know of make use of the type in question. This is what is often called an "artificial elemental," a constructed spirit assigned a specific station and task in a magical lodge.

The term's a misnomer—artificial beings of this sort can be considerably more or less intelligent than elemental spirits are generally held to be, and need not have any connection at all with whatever set of elements a magical tradition happens to use. "Artificial spirits" would be a more accurate term, or possibly "magical robots"—the

---

6. See Dion Fortune, *Applied Magic* (Wellingborough: Aquarian Press, 1987. [First ed. London: Aquarian Press, 1962. Compiled from articles originally published in the *Inner Light Magazine*, 1927–1940]), pp. 21–27, and *Sane Occultism* (Wellingborough: Aquarian Press, 1987 [First ed. London: Rider & Co., 1929]), pp. 58–62.

latter because, at least to start with, created beings of this kind tend to carry out their assigned functions with mechanical precision.

This is their great strength; their great weakness, and one of the two reasons many magical lodge systems don't use them, is that they only have as much strength as the lodge members put into them. This is not the case with powers, and even more emphatically not the case with deities; both these categories of spiritual being have their own sources of power, while artificial spirits do not. Like battery-powered devices, they need to be recharged at intervals.

The second difficulty with artificial spirits is more complex. In the long run, artificial spirits, group minds, and most other creations tend to display what might as well be called the "Frankenstein effect"—that is, they start to behave like independent entities with their own wills and concerns, perhaps in harmony with the purposes and intentions of the lodge, perhaps not. It's a neat problem in magical theory whether creations sprout minds of their own, whether independent spiritual beings take over the energetic form in a manner similar to obsession, or whether some other process might be involved.

Whatever explanation turns out to be the right one, though, the fact of the matter remains: most creations are unstable, and can become problematic in unpredictable ways, while deities and powers are much more reliable to work with. This is the second reason why most traditional magical lodge rituals rely on deities and powers rather than creations, and when creations are unavoidable—for example, the group mind of the lodge, which comes into being whether it's wanted or not—a deity is invoked to indwell the group mind and make sure it behaves itself.

One instructive exception to this rule is the second form of creations commonly found in magical lodges: the use of creations by lodge officers as a way of mediating magical energies in ritual. Here the Frankenstein effect is kept in check by a novel use of the principle of obsession: the created forms are obsessed by the lodge officers who wear them, rather than vice versa, and this functions very effectively to keep the forms from being obsessed by anyone or anything else. The act of mediation does tend to have an impact on the consciousness of the mediating officer, molding it in the direction of whatever influence the form embodies. For this reason, it's standard practice to have the officers of the lodge rotate from one position to another at regular intervals to avoid personality imbalances.

Interacting with Spiritual Beings

Operative mages around the world have figured out any number of ways to interact with spiritual beings and involve them in magical workings. In lodge workings based on the modern magical tradition, only two of them have seen much use, and one of those—trance mediumship—is used by a minority of lodges. In most lodge systems, the work is done by the method that the Golden Dawn papers call "scrying in the spirit vision" and Carl Jung called "active imagination."

There are good practical reasons for this choice of methods. Most other approaches to making contact with spiritual beings would pose real challenges if practiced in a lodge. Conjuring spirits to visible appearance, for example, is a lengthy and cumbersome operation. This also usually requires burning large amounts of dittany of Crete or some other materializing incense, which risks setting off smoke alarms and can cause trouble with the landlord as well.

Conjuring spirits into a mirror or scrying crystal is less cumbersome, but would limit contact with the spiritual beings to those members of the lodge who have the particular talent of mirror or crystal scrying, and the need to look back and forth from the mirror or crystal and the lodge room would be a source of distraction. By contrast, the use of the imagination as a vehicle for contact with spiritual beings allows everyone in the lodge to participate in the contact, so long as they have done the necessary training.

Modern popular culture disparages the human imagination—it's telling that in contemporary usage, the word "imaginary" is treated as a synonym for "unreal." As Henry Corbin pointed out in his classic essay "Mundus Imaginalis," however, the imagination can function as a valid mode of cognition; there is a crucial difference, in Corbin's phrasing, between the imaginal and the merely imaginary.[7] Given systematic training along the lines taught in traditional occult schools, the imagination becomes an organ of perception and action in the *mundus imaginalis*, the realm of images and similitudes that modern magical traditions generally call the astral plane. Trained mages can construct forms in that realm, but they can also experience forms that they do not create; they can also participate with spiritual beings in the construction of forms as a means of mutual communication.

A Practical Example

It's easier to understand how these factors work in practice through an example. I've chosen to use a fictional one, to avoid squabbles over territory. Magical lodge traditions vary widely in the fine details of technique; the methods described below are among the more common, and provide a convenient overview of some of the available options.

The lodge, let's say, is working a Grail ritual along the lines sketched out by the late Jessie Weston in *From Ritual to Romance*. The cosmology and symbolism on which the lodge is based is Gnostic, or more exactly that curious fusion of

---

7. Henry Corbin, "Mundus Imaginalis, or the Imaginary and the Imaginal," in *Swedenborg and Esoteric Islam: Two Studies*, trans. Leonard Fox [from « Mundus imaginalis ou l'imaginaire et l'imaginal », Cahiers internationaux du symbolisme 6, Bruxelles, 1964] (West Chester, PA: Swedenborg Foundation, 2006).

Gnostic spirituality and fertility cult found in the Naassene Document and reflected in the rituals that Weston believed formed the original background of the Grail legends.[8]

The deities invoked to preside over the working are the Gnostic Christ, Iesseus Mazareus Iessedekeus, who is also Attis and Adonis, and the Moirothea, the mother of the four Gnostic luminaries and of all living things, who is also Cybele and Aphrodite. The powers evoked to govern the four elemental quarters are the four luminaries, Daueithe in the east ruling air, Harmozel in the south ruling fire, Oroiael in the west governing water, and Eleleth in the north ruling earth.[9]

There are three lodge officers—the Master in the east, the Warden in the west, and the

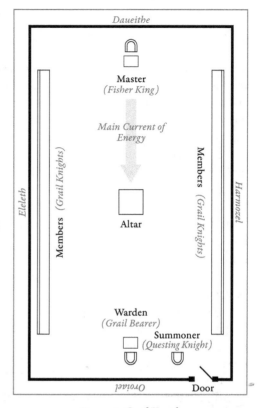

Figure 2. **Grail Temple**

Summoner beside the door—and each of them has a created form as a structure for mediating the energies of the ritual: the Master uses the form of the Fisher King, the Warder of the Grail Bearer, and the Summoner of the Questing Knight. In each degree of initiation, an additional created form is prepared for the initiate. There is also a created form used by every member of the lodge who does not hold an office in any given ritual: this is the image of a Grail Knight in armor.

All the members of the lodge, in the course of their training, have practiced invoking the Christ, the Moirothea, and the four luminaries in daily ritual workings, and have meditated at length on the symbolism and structure of the ritual as well as the teachings that underlie it. The members who sit along the sides of the lodge in

---

8. Jessie Weston, *From Ritual to Romance* (Gloucester, MA: Peter Smith, 1983 [First ed. Cambridge: The University Press, 1920]), pp. 149–163.

9. I have used the *Gospel of the Egyptians* as a source here; see Bentley Layton, *The Gnostic Scriptures: A New Translation* (Garden City, New York: Doubleday, 1987), pp. 105–120.

any given working aren't there as spectators; they have their own created forms to maintain, and they also build and maintain the imaginal forms through which the officers move, assist the officers in their magical work, and in initiations, put the appropriate created form on the candidate and keep it in place through the working. Their effort is an important ingredient in the success of the working.

Just before the lodge meets, the Master enters the hall, makes sure all the lodge furnishings are in place, and then advances to the west of the altar. His responsibilities include establishing and maintaining a good relationship with the deities and powers that work with the lodge; on the basis of that relationship, using a set of standard ritual forms, he invokes the Christ and the Moirothea, calling on them to be present during the working. He then faces each of the quarters and evokes the four luminaries, again using a standard ritual form, and asks and receives their help in the work of the lodge. He then advances to his station in the east, sits in his chair, takes on the form of the Fisher King, and with the help of the deities and powers, establishes the imaginal forms and energy flows that define the lodge in its inner dimension. (One such pattern, the primary flow of energy between the Master's station and the altar, is shown in the diagram.)

Meanwhile, the other members of the lodge are preparing themselves for the work. When the Master has finished his work, he goes to the door and signals the others to join him. The two remaining officers take their stations, take on their respective forms, and invoke the Christ and the Moirothea. The other lodge members then file into the lodge and take their places along the sides of the hall, where they take on their created forms and add their efforts to the imaginal structures the Master has created.

At this point the opening ceremony begins. The opening ceremony in a magical lodge serves an assortment of different functions, but one of them is the formal invocation of the deities and evocation of the powers who will be adding their influences to the efforts of the lodge members in the working. While the invocation and evocation rituals will be performed by one or more of the lodge officers, all the lodge members participate in the work inwardly. By the end of the opening ritual, the presence and conscious cooperation of the deities and powers should be clearly sensed by everyone present.

The work of the lodge then takes place within the space thus prepared and empowered. If the lodge is performing an initiation, the deities and powers will be called upon to add their powers to the efforts of the lodge members to awaken one or more centers in the subtle body of the initiate, or bring about whatever other transformation might be central to the initiation process. If the lodge is performing a seasonal ritual, the deities and powers will be called on to do much the same thing on a macrocosmic scale. The spiritual beings involved in lodge work, in other words, are not merely abstractions or symbols; they are active presences whose efforts make a clearly perceptible contribution to the success of the lodge work.

When the work of the lodge is done, the closing ceremony is performed. Like the opening, this has multiple functions, but one important element is thanking the spiritual beings who have participated in the work of the lodge, licensing the powers to depart in the traditional manner, and clearing the imaginal structures from the lodge hall, returning it to its former status of blank slate onto which some other set of patterns can be drawn at need. The mingled powers are allowed to return to their proper places, until the magical mesocosm of the lodge is formed again by its incarnate and discarnate participants.

References

Corbin, Henry. "Mundus Imaginalis, or the Imaginary and the Imaginal," in *Swedenborg and Esoteric Islam: Two Studies*, trans. Leonard Fox. West Chester, PA: Swedenborg Foundation, 2006.

Fortune, Dion. *Applied Magic*. Wellingborough, Northamptonshire: Aquarian Press, 1987.

—, *Esoteric Orders and their Work*. Wellingborough, Northamptonshire: Aquarian Press, 1987.

—, *Sane Occultism*. Wellingborough, Northamptonshire: Aquarian Press, 1987.

Greer, John Michael. *Inside a Magical Lodge*. St. Paul, MN: Llewellyn Publications, 1998.

Layton, Bentley. *The Gnostic Scriptures: A New Translation with Annotations and Introductions*. Garden City, New York: Doubleday, 1987.

Lévi, Éliphas (A.-L. Constant). *Dogme et Rituel de la Haute Magie*. Paris: G. Baillière, 1854.

—, *Transcendental Magic*, trans. Arthur Edward Waite. York Beach, ME: Weiser Books, 1972.

Regardie, Israel, *The Golden Dawn: An Account of the Teachings, Rites, and Ceremonies of the Order of the Golden Dawn*. St. Paul, MN: Llewellyn, 1982.

Weston, Jessie. *From Ritual to Romance*. Gloucester, MA: Peter Smith, 1983.

✝

Patrons and House Gods

Building Lifelong Relationships with Your Spiritual Guardians

Aaron Leitch

AARON LEITCH has been a scholar and a spiritual seeker for nearly three decades. He is a member of the Hermetic Order of the Golden Dawn, the Gentlemen of Jupiter, and the academic Societas Magica. His writings cover a variety of fields including Enochiana, ancient Middle Eastern religion and mythology, Solomonic mysticism, Hermeticism and alchemy, Wicca and Neopaganism, the Hermetic Order of the Golden Dawn, Thelema, angelology, Qabalah, African Diaspora religions, and hexcraft and hoodoo folk traditions. He is the author of Secrets of the Magickal Grimoires: The Classical Texts of Magick Deciphered *(Llewellyn, 2005),* The Angelical Language, Volume I: The Complete History and Mythos of the Tongue of Angels and Volume II: An Encyclopedic Lexicon of the Tongue of Angels *(Llewellyn, 2010), and* The Essential Enochian Grimoire: An Introduction to Angel Magick from Dr. John Dee to the Golden Dawn *(Llewellyn, 2014). He has contributed to several anthologies, including* At the Crossroads *(Scarlet Imprint, 2012),* Commentaries on the Golden Dawn Flying Rolls *(Kerubim Press, 2013), and* The Holy Guardian Angel *(Nephilim Press, 2014), and is the editor of* Ritual Offerings: Feeding Your Spirits, Empowering Your Magick *(Nephilim Press, 2014). You may follow his blog at* Ananael: The Secrets of Wisdom *(aaronleitch.wordpress.com), and visit his website at* The Aaron Leitch Homepage *(kheph777.tripod.com).*

✢

Patrons and House Gods

*Building Lifelong Relationships
with Your Spiritual Guardians*

HERE IT COMES TO Western occult literature, I would say there is nothing quite so popular as the spirit catalog. These litanies of spiritual entities originated almost as soon as Western culture had discovered the secrets of making paper; the old grimoires with their catalogs of angels and demons have a history as old and rich as the spread of the Bible among the masses. It would appear the very moment it became possible to write down and share our experiences with and descriptions of our culture's spiritual creatures, we did so—to the tune of thousands of hand-written manuscripts.

The spirit catalog comes in many forms, showcasing any number of spiritual entities (angelic or demonic depending on the text) and what tasks they can accomplish for the magician. A lot of the spirits' functions tend to repeat (more on this later), but different spirits will tend to specialize in specific skills: invisibility, divination, attacking enemies, generating friendships, healing, protection, giving familiars, etc., etc.

Perhaps the most famous example of such a text is the Goetia of Solomon, with its list of 72 demons and their special functions. Other grimoires present their own similar chthonic hierarchies, such as the *Grand Grimoire*, *Grimoirum Verum*, *Testament of St. Cyprian*, the Faustian *Harrowing of Hell*, the *Book of Oberon*, and the latter portions of the *Book of Abramelin*. It is perhaps less common (yet not difficult) to find such lists populated with celestial angels and what they can do for you. Examples can be found in the *Arbatel*, the *Heptameron*, the *Grimoire of Armadel*, the *Almadel of Solomon*, the *Pauline Art*, Dr. John Dee's Enochian journals and the talismans in the *Key of Solomon the King* to name only a few. In some cases the angelic texts are less specific, giving functions for entire groups of angels rather than individual entities, though this is hardly always true.

What might be less obvious to the student is how these same texts have influenced our own modern systems of occultism. For example, when I entered the Neopagan community in the early 1990s, it was considered standard practice for novices to begin their practice by "finding a Patron God and/or Goddess." This consisted of consulting books like *The Witches' God* and *The Witches' Goddess* by Janet and Stewart Farrar, each of which present long lists of historical deities and what natural forces they represent. In other words: a spirit catalog from which many young Neopagans at the time chose which gods they would work with and for what purposes. Sadly, such choices were too-often based upon which deity seemed the "coolest"—the most attractive to the individual—at the time. Today's young pagans might still consult those books, though they are more likely to first encounter similar lists offered by countless websites dedicated to Pagan basics.

Meanwhile, when new grimoires are created, they are often catalogs of spirits as well—entirely new spirits despite the fact there are hundreds of existing entities already named in our Western systems. (And thousands upon thousands if you count the legions of unnamed spirits.) It turns out the market for whom such new grimoires are written have already studied or directly worked with the most popular existing spirits and want "something new."

Of course, the original spirit catalogs are also still available and are still consulted by some modern occultists. However we will see in what follows how—in all of these examples—today's aspirants may not be using the catalogs in the way they were originally intended. To our minds, such lists make it appear the spirits are all equally available to be "called up" at any time depending on our needs at the moment. (I call this "summon-demand-banish", which I will explain later.) Or, at the extreme other end of the spectrum, some very intrepid souls assume a grimoire intends for us to summon each and every angel or demon listed in its pages as part of a larger initiatory process.

However, I will here argue in favor of a third option, falling somewhere between these two extremes: I will offer some evidence the methods of our Western occult predecessors, though not blatantly spelled out in the grimoires, were of a more devotional bent. That is to say, regardless of the existence of the catalogs, their authors actually intended for us to establish contact with very few spirits—maybe even, in some cases, just one—and spend a lifetime building a working relationship with them.

In doing this, they would have been more in line with the ancient pagan methods of establishing house gods within the home, of the acquisition and keeping of familiar spirits, or even the consecration of a priest or prophet to a specific tutelary deity. All of these reflect a more shamanic and devotional approach to the spirit world: a witch's home is not populated with the hundreds or thousands of deities and spirits available in her tradition. Instead she has only a few, maybe even only one or two, through whom she works all of the magick she or her clients could possibly need. If she runs into a problem her spirits can't fix, she can then take steps to contact a new spirit (usually with the help of one of her existing familiars), or just refer the client to a fellow shaman who already knows the right spirits.

By contrast, modern neopagans and magicians all too often have homes populated with no deities or spirits whatsoever. This is not to suggest they do not work with gods or familiars, but they often lack the altars and offerings to the spirits one would see in, say, the home of a Santero. Rather than establishing permanent physical bases for a few useful spirits, and making those spirits a part of their families and daily lives, they are often satisfied to simply refer to books and call whatever spirit seems most useful. In my opinion, this is perhaps the least effective manner of working with spiritual entities.

In the following essay, I will take a look at the shortcomings of the modern "summon-demand-banish" method of working with the spirits and then offer some anecdotal evidence from my own experiences with the devotional route, specifically establishing altars to various archangels and deities in my home (aka "house gods"). It is my hope this will serve to illustrate the advantages such spiritual relationships can bring with them.

Spirit Catalogs or Take-Out Menus? (Summon-Demand-Banish)

First let's take a look at the 20th century (though the trends began in the late 19th century), a time when science and materialism reigned supreme, where magick was reduced to either a form of psychology (à la Regardie and Crowley) or some kind of energetic technology not yet understood by science (à la Bardon). Most of the Western "old magick" lay dormant and forgotten; though some credit must be given to the neopagans (especially very early in that movement) who sought old folk spells wherever they could uncover them. Beyond that, most magick was derived from the masonic-influenced lodge systems like the Golden Dawn and Thelema. The old ways were largely dismissed as outdated historical curiosities—a superstitious form of magick we had "evolved beyond."

Those occultists with a more romantic frame of mind might appropriate some of the grimoires' talismans, maybe a magick circle, perhaps even a conjuration or two. Yet, these were always employed via modern (post-nineteenth century) lodge-style methods such as the use of pentagram and hexagram rituals, formal hall openings, complimentary color schemes, vibration of words of power, masonic-style regalia and scepters, etc.[1] The original medieval and renaissance tradition behind the grimoires was unknown and largely unsought.

---

1. See Donald Michael Kraig's *Modern Magick* (St. Paul, Minn.: Llewellyn Publications, 1988), or Konstantinos' *Summoning Spirits* (St. Paul, Minn.: Llewellyn Publications, 1988).

This situation created a very unfortunate relationship between modern Western magicians and the indigenous spirits of our culture. As we cherry-picked the grimoires for the bits of information we thought might be useful to our own systems (or, in the case of goetia, anything we thought might shock our friends), it was a pretty sure bet the spirit catalogs were going to catch our eye. It was convenient to have these wonderful lists of ancient spirits—quite often with sigils included—and exactly what they could do for us. However, there was little to no interest in exploring these complex hierarchies of spiritual beings, to learn where the spirits came from, who they were and what relationships they had to one another, and to us. The spirit catalogs were not recognized as important glimpses into an older occult tradition, but instead became order-menus similar to what one finds in a fast-food restaurant. It was only necessary to scan through the lists until you found a spirit that could do what you desire, then work with it according to your own tradition.

That occultists of the time saw little problem with this isn't surprising, as the then-popular view was that spiritual entities were not objective persons, but merely convenient names and symbols made up by the ancients to represent natural forces they couldn't understand. From the psychological perspective, the gods, angels and spirits are just projections of man onto nature, reflections of our selves in the mirror of the universe, and tools we can use to manipulate our mental states. Aleister Crowley's "Initiated Interpretation of Ceremonial Magick" is a much-lauded analysis of books like the *Goetia*, describing the spirits, their names and their sigils as formulas that stimulate specific portions of the human brain. According to this view, there simply are no "persons" in the spirit catalogs to get to know.

This gave rise to what I call the "summon-demand-banish" formula: whenever you have a need, you look up the spirit whose function can serve you, summon it, demand it help you, then banish it away, likely to never call upon it again. Then, the next time you have a need, you return to the catalog to find whichever spirit can do that job, summon it, make your demand and banish. And repeat...

I simply cannot overemphasize how detrimental this has been to Western occultism and our relationship with the spirits of nature. How would you feel, for example, if a stranger called you to his house, ordered you to tend his yard, then locked you outside without another word? No offer of payment or equipment to do the job. In the long run, the guy doesn't even acknowledge that you really exist! Would you get to work for him despite all of this? I wouldn't; yet this is exactly what our modern attitudes toward the spirits have resembled.

Believe it or not, the western grimoires may themselves share a portion of the blame for this approach to the spirits. The concept of the Solomonic spirit catalog seems to have developed from one of the tradition's foundational texts, the *Testament of Solomon*. Therein, we indeed see the eponymous king systematically summoning a long list of demonic entities, binding each to his will. This lore passed into the grimoires, and we find it for example at the heart of the *Goetia*, where King Solomon is again depicted as having summoned all 72 of its spirits to seal them into a brass vessel. With this kind of mythological backing, it is no wonder occultists would seek to emulate Solomon by binding every demon (or, at least, as many as possible) from a given list of names.

However, in attempting to apply Solomon's mythos to our own practices, we have overlooked two important details. First, King Solomon is King Solomon, a powerful ancestral figure and mythological master, similar in that way to Moses or Christ. Much as we are encouraged to emulate the example of the latter two figures, we are never expected to part a sea or turn water into actual wine. They were the masters, the god-like heroes who could accomplish any miracle whatsoever. Likewise, of course King Solomon is depicted as summoning and binding to his will every single ruler and sub-ruler of hell, no matter how many thousands there may be; that's why he's the king. Yet, as with Moses and Christ, it is unlikely any of us were expected to pull off quite the same feats.

Secondly, note that Solomon in our examples (*Testament* and *Goetia*) is not, in fact, operating as one would expect of a Solomonic magician. He is not summoning the denizens of hell in order to reveal the future, find lost items, gain love and honor, bring money, destroy enemies, etc. Instead, he is acting more in line with a traditional exorcist: in the *Testament* summoning and binding a series of demons who are responsible for the ills of mankind, while in the *Goetia* apparently wishing to imprison the rulers of hell on general principles. In the *Testament*, he does put the spirits to work building the Temple, but does not employ them toward any of the usual grimoiric goals. In the *Goetia*, he does nothing more than trap them in a vessel and toss it into the sea. As a point of fact, the story ends with the Babylonians—who appear to be the villains of the story—fishing the vessel out of the water, releasing all the spirits, and employing one of them for divination purposes.

Taking these points together, it would seem we Solomonic magicians are not operating in harmony with our king so much as in spite of him. We're following in the footsteps of the Babylonians in the *Goetia*, releasing the spirits so we can put them to work toward our own ends. Of course, I say this somewhat tongue in cheek, but it serves to illustrate that we are not intended to copy Solomon in our practices by conjuring and binding an endless list of greater and lesser spirits. More like the Babylonians, we should seek the one spirit (or a few spirits) in the list that can work with and for us on a regular basis.

Therefore, even though Solomon is depicted as summoning large numbers of entities, I suggest the "fast food menu" approach to spirit-work is a modern misinterpretation of the old legends. However, this does leave us to question exactly how the spirits were approached by occultists before the twentieth century. After all, didn't they compile the spirit catalogs in the first place? And didn't they have to use a "summon-demand-banish" method in order to accomplish that?

The answer is no, they did not.

Spirit Catalogs—Finding Your Patron(s) Among the Crowd

First of all, these lists of spirits are hardly ever unique to a single text; they tended to circulate among occultists, and appear (in slightly different forms) in many manuscripts. Unlike today, our occult forefathers did not have access to wonderful things like the Internet and social media; most of them didn't even have access to the printing press. Learning about occultism wasn't as simple as making up a good reading list, ordering the books and buckling down to study, or even searching out a good forum of like-minded people with whom to discuss magick. Instead, it was necessary to quest and search and even connive to get your hands on any occult texts you could find. When you were fortunate enough to run across the rare grimoire, you copied down as much of it as you could as quickly as you could. Hence, the spirit catalogs do not necessarily reflect the direct experiences of a grimoire's author, but are more often simply collections of spirit descriptions copied from other sources. For example, the list of demons in the *Goetia* can be traced to earlier texts such as *Liber Officiorum Spirituum* (*"Book of the Offices of Spirits"*) and Johann Weyer's *Pseudomonarchia Daemonum* (*"False Monarchy of Demons"*).

Secondly—and this is of vital importance to our current discussion—most spirits are generally useful for most purposes. That idea is certainly counter-intuitive to modern occultists, who all too often desire to pigeonhole spirits into rigid classifications. Thus, for example, we view a spirit of Venus as only a spirit of Venus, and call upon it only for Venusian things like beauty, lust, passion or inspiration. Yet, to the ancient mind, a spirit may be mostly associated with Venus, but it could be called upon for many other purposes as well: divination, protection, healing, prosperity, creating or destroying friendships, etc. Its association with Venus told you more about how to properly approach and work with the spirit rather than restricting what tasks the spirit could perform.

It is true that the grimoires do record different functions for the spirits, and they stress that you should not call a spirit to perform a task outside of its office. For example, you wouldn't summon a Fire Elemental and demand he should make it rain. However, outside of that simple bit of common sense, the offices attributed to the spirits were often much less rigid in the minds of the grimoires' authors than they are to us. This is why their functions and classifications tend to change from one grimoire to the next.

This is also why so many of the functions given to spiritual entities seem to repeat. A look at the *Goetia* will show you that nearly all of the 72 spirits can perform divination: revealing the past, present or future, finding lost or stolen items, etc. A number of them teach languages or sciences, create or destroy love or friendships, grant familiar spirits, build up or destroy dignities, and more. While a few of them have highly specialized skills (such as one who causes arrow wounds, specifically, to fester), most of them can pretty much do what any of the others can do. These lengthy lists of largely similar spirits are not the result of a mage actually summoning dozens of individual entities for the same purpose. Instead, he was merely collecting descriptions of as many spirits as possible, in the hopes one or two of them would prove faithful and reliable. In practice, he would have stuck with the two or three who did the jobs he needed done every time.

A good example is found in the goety portion of the *Book of Abramelin*. There, we are given a long list of spirits, followed by talismans that (mostly) bear their names, divided into chapters by their functions. Whenever you have a need, you simply employ a talisman in an evocation of its spirit and it will do as the talisman indicates. And, yes, we are told to avoid attempting to force a spirit to perform a function outside of its office. However, at the same time, the book describes four further spirits—your familiars—who will always be at your side, and who can accomplish most of what the other spirits can:

> If the operations can be performed by the familiar spirits, it is not necessary to employ others therein.
>
> [...]
>
> The operations of the following chapters can also (to a great extent) be administered by the familiar spirits, namely:
> Chapter II. (Scientific information.)
> Chapter IV. (Visions.)
> Chapter XII. (Secrets of other persons.)
> Chapter XVIII. (Healing of maladies.)
> Chapter XIX. (Affection and love.)
> Chapter XXIII. (Demolishing buildings.)
> Chapter XXIV. (Discovery of theft.)
> Chapter XXVII. (Causing visions to appear.)
> Chapter XXVIII. (Obtaining money.)
> Chapter XXX. (Visions of operas, comedies, etc.)[2]

In other words, the four familiars can and should do nearly anything you need done for most day-to-day circumstances. It would only be necessary to call one of the other spirits if we need something very specific which the familiars can't accomplish. Even in the case of those other spirits, the grimoire doesn't expect you to

---

2. Abraham ben Simeon of Worms and S.L. MacGregor Mathers, *The Book of the Sacred Magic of Abra-Melin the Mage* (London: J.M. Watkins, 1898), Book II, Chapter 20: "How the Operations Should be Performed."

summon each and every one it has listed. Instead, it instructs one to choose a few of the spirits who appear the most useful, and allows for contacting more spirits in the future as it becomes necessary.

If we read between the lines in the *Book of Abramelin*, and in many other grimoires, a picture very different from "summon-demand-banish" begins to emerge. We were never intended to summon each and every spirit in a given catalog, nor to pick and choose among them at need. Instead, we are supposed to establish contact with just a few of the spirits—those who would be our familiars, patrons and house gods—and build lifelong relationships with them.

Patrons and House Gods

Besides its lengthy spirit lists, the *Book of Abramelin* is also a wonderful example, maybe the best in the genre, of a patron entity with whom you are expected to engage in a lifetime of devotion: in this case, the Holy Guardian Angel. While there are still many students today who mistake Abramelin for an over-long summoning ritual, it is in fact something much deeper. Once contact has been established with the HGA, and a permanent bond formed, you are expected to continue working with it for the rest of your life. It becomes your guide, your teacher, your protector, and your primary means of contact with the spirit world. It doesn't matter if your magick falls under the heading of Jupiter or Sol or Mars or Saturn, you will first and foremost invoke your Guardian Angel, who will tell you if the magick is permissible and open the gates between the worlds to make it possible.

But this is not just an Abramelin thing; other grimoires either describe or hint at the same concept. In the *Pauline Art* section of the *Lemegeton*, we are told to choose just one angel (in a list categorized by zodiacal rising signs) from whom we can learn innumerable mysteries. The *Sworn Book of Honorius* (aka *Liber Juratus*) is supposed to have been revealed in its entirety by a single angel named Hocroel. Likewise, in the *Key of Solomon*, the king names the angel Homadiel[3] as the revealer of his grimoire. Even John Dee, with all of the angels he interrogated, first and foremost established contact with Uriel, who then superintended the entire revelation of the Enochian material. There are further examples I could give, but they all illustrate the same point. We aren't intended to isolate and cold-contact strange spirits in order to work our spells. Magick works best when you know someone on the other side of the veil, and that takes a lot of time and devotion to a single entity.

This is, after all, how things were done in ancient times. One of the most primordial of human religious practices is ancestor worship, which began with the rather simple idea of caring for your loved ones even after they had passed away. Relics of

---

3. In some versions, Raziel.

their lives or from their bodies (and in some cultures even entire corpses) were set aside as sacred, along with gift offerings and flowers and eventually lamps, giving birth to primitive altars and shrines where we could consult with their spirits. Places were still set for them at dinner, or food would be placed on the altars. In this way the ancestral spirits were still included in the daily life of the family.

In return, the spirits of the deceased were expected to protect the home, ensure good hunts and harvests, bring fertility, predict the future, heal the sick, etc., etc. In time the practice grew into a very complex religion, with established traditions and protocols to follow. Eventually the larger and stronger families rose to dominate the others, giving rise to what we know as royal families and kingdoms. The ancestral spirits of these families were given elaborate temples and became the tutelary deities of the nation, to whom everyone had to pay devotion (and taxes).

Most of what we know about ancient temple religions comes from records left by the temple priests. This is why we readily recognize names like Marduk, Inanna, Osiris, Isis, Mithras, Zeus, Apollo, etc., because those are the gods for whom records were left. Yet these few deities are only a scratch on the surface of a culture's true pantheon. The common people still had their own ancestral spirits, not to mention local spirits (like the Roman Lares, or northern European Kobolds) and popular house gods (such as the Greek Hestia or the Celtic Brighid). Given all of these, each pagan household had its own pantheon, complete with its own traditions, protocols and taboos.

Meanwhile, as the cities and temples were being established, the tribal shamans were still living in the outlying areas, doing what they had done since pre-history. I have previously written at some length (see *Secrets of the Magickal Grimoires*), about the similarities between primitive shamanism and what we find in the later Solomonic tradition. The shaman typically bonded with—or even outright married—a patron deity. (The later religion of Santeria would refer to this as one's "head spirit.") This deity would be the teacher and protector of the shaman, and his principle liaison with the spirit world. Second to this patron would be a team of familiar spirits acquired/inherited by the shaman via his initiatory ordeal. In Santeria, by way of example, some of these spirits simply come as part of the religion, such as the Warriors (who are household protectors). Others are specific to the individual, such as the Nganga spirit (what we would call a familiar) through whom most practical magick—witchcraft—is accomplished.

We can see much of this dynamic in the grimoires, the best example again being the Book of Abramelin. There one is crowned with the Holy Guardian Angel as your personal patron and head spirit.[4] Then, once this celestial connection has

---

4. The "knowledge" half of the oft-repeated phrase "knowledge and conversation of the HGA" indicates an intimate connection—a marriage.

been established, one receives the four principle familiar spirits along with a few extra spirits who might specialize in specific areas. As we have already seen, the text never implies we should attempt to summon every last spirit in the book. Quite to the contrary, it suggests we stick to just a few.

Though less obvious, we can find this same dynamic in other grimoires. Note, for instance, that several spirits in the *Goetia* are said to "give good familiars," such as Paimon, Buer, Purson, Morax, Malphas, Sabnach, Shax, Alloces, Amy, Amduscius, and Belial. From the modern (summon-demand-banish) standpoint, this makes little sense. Aren't the 72 spirits themselves familiars? Why call a spirit to simply acquire another spirit?

The answer is because the 72 demons of the *Goetia* are not familiar spirits themselves. They are high ranking chthonic beings, deities in their own right, and it was never intended for us to conjure them up and pester them for our every little whim. Instead, we are to summon one of the above-mentioned spirits in order to obtain a personal familiar, a spirit who can then do just about anything we need done on a day-to-day basis. Even if you were to summon (say) Belial, put him in a brass vessel, give him an altar and work with him every day, you will not have technically captured Belial himself so that no other mage can call upon him. One can argue that you have simply captured a spirit of Belial, a familiar given to you by Belial who simply answers to the name "Belial."[5]

All of this goes to illustrate the point that, no matter how large your culture's pantheon or how many spirits you have to choose from in a given list, it was always intended for you to choose (or inherit or otherwise acquire) only those few who work best with and on your behalf:

> ...each man will procure for himself those (spirits) which be of his nature
> and genius and fit for that wherein thou wouldest employ them.[6]

Patron Deities and Archangels

I began my occult practices via the modern Western methods, learning much from books like Donald Kraig's *Modern Magick* and the works of Israel Regardie, the Ciceros, Don Tyson and a few others. Plus, of course, I collected a heap of Wiccan and neopagan books of varying degrees of worth. (It was the 1990s, after all.) This meant that I was heavily influenced by the psychological model of magick (Crowley's "Initiated Interpretation" was one of my favorites), and I certainly bought into

---

5. This, in fact, is exactly how the Nganga spirit works. One never reveals the true name of the spirit in the Nganga, instead referring to it in public by the name of the deity set over it.

6. *Book of the Sacred Magic of Abramelin the Mage*, Book III, "Essential Remarks Upon the Foregoing Symbols."

the summon-demand-banish method. That is, at least, until I began actually summoning the angels.

There is a tumultuous window of time in my life, during the very late 1990s and into the new century, where everything about my spiritual path radically changed. It was during this time I summoned my first couple of angels, began my talks with the Santo Ochani Lele, started to finally understand the grimoires, performed Abramelin, and then went on to join the Hermetic Order of the Golden Dawn and progress from the grade of Neophyte to Adeptus Minor. It was also during this time I began to delve deeper and deeper into historical, anthropological and archeological texts to learn magickal secrets (rather than modern pop occult books). As such, it is not always easy for me to remember exactly which of my ideas changed at which time during this period. Everything was in flux at once.

Therefore it isn't likely I'll recall the very point where I left behind the so-called "initiated interpretation" of magick and adopted the older "spirit model." I do know that my first evocations were done via modern methods, mostly taken from Kraig and Regardie, hence GD-style, and I know at that time I was operating under the assumption of the psychological model. Yet, I recall that my encounters with the angels I summoned were very real, meaning that I remember encountering objective persons, with no feeling whatsoever that I was just talking to some part of my own psyche. While I don't recall a sudden "aha!" moment because of this, perhaps those experiences planted a seed in my mind that wouldn't fully blossom until my later talks with Ochani.

The first successful evocation I ever performed was for the archangel Michael, a being I had encountered in my previous work and whom I considered something of a patron already. The circumstances were the furthest from ideal you could imagine: I had to do the work in a small trailer on an isolated construction site in the middle of the night, so having a purified area was out of the question.[7] I didn't even have a robe or incense. But I did have a talisman, and I opened with Golden Dawn rituals like the Opening by Watchtower and the Hexagram Ritual of Sol. He appeared to me visibly and spoke to me clearly; I suppose for little other reason than that he likes me. I was astounded and honored that he would appear so strongly for my first inept attempt at evocation.

The next angel I would summon—and with whom I would work more over the years than any other angel (save only for my Holy Guardian Angel, of course)—was the Intelligence of Jupiter: Iophiel. In case you are unfamiliar with this archangel, here is a short bio about him, as posted to my *Ananael* blog:

---

7. It is true that some grimoires suggest finding such out of the way areas for evocations, but they are usually talking about chthonic and earth-bound spirits. Celestial spirits want temples!

Iophiel is the Intelligence of the planet Jupiter and the Archangel who tends the Garden of Eden. In some traditions he is one of the Seven Spirits that Stand before the Face of God. He presides over vegetation and produce, fertile fields and livestock, feasting and friendship, prosperity and happiness. Think of Dickens' Ghost of Christmas Present, and that spirit's connections to Jovial gods such as Odin and Zeus. He is also an angelic Prince of the Torah, and as such is one of the companion angels of Metatron. Of course, Jupiter has his stern side as well. He is the grizzled warrior, quick to draw his weapon and strike when moved by Honour. It was Iophiel's duty to drive the fallen Adam and Eve from the Garden—and it is implied that he guards the Gates of Eden with the Sword of Ever-Turning Flame to this day. If you're looking for blessings from Paradise, you have to go through this Archangel. Fortunately, he likes humans and wants you to have those blessings—so long as you are willing to work or fight for the right to have them.

Where it comes to getting along in the real world, I find that Jupiter has just about everything you could need. Friends and family, abundance and productivity are pretty much the basis of a happy life.[8] Thus I have approached Jupiter beings in times of necessity more than any others.

I would perhaps even go so far as to say that I have developed, via no specific intention, into a Jupiter wizard. Not only have I called upon Iophiel as a matter of course for the bulk of my occult career, but I have also worked regularly with Sachiel, another Jupiterian archangel. Plus, in my course on ritual magick, my students spend one class creating and charging talismans with raw Jupiter energy. Overall, I work with Jupiter a lot.

And it all began with Iophiel. My first evocation of this angel was, like Michael's, done via Golden Dawn-style ritual. My methods were still inexperienced, but at least this time I was at home in a consecrated sacred space, with ritual garb and tools, incense and altar. And once again the evocation was successful; he deigned to answer my call and allowed me to see a vision of his form—both of which came as something of a shock to me at the time.

I recall his visual appearance as if I had seen it only yesterday; though I don't recall him doing much talking at all. He stood tall and rigid, his arms crossed upon his chest and his short wings spread outward from his shoulders. He was extremely thin at the waist, but became more thick and muscular in his chest, shoulders and arms—his overall shape gave me the distinct impression of a tree. His face, as is quite usual for me, was just a blinding flare of light.

His appearance was quite stern, yet his energy was entirely friendly and approachable. This is less usual than you might think where angels are concerned; they are quite often aloof and irritable, with no particular love for us ridiculous talk-

---

8. I find I call upon the other planets—such as Sol, Mars or Luna—in more extreme or specialized situations.

ing apes. But Iophiel didn't come across that way. He was, indeed, jovial and even reassuring; and he came through with what I needed in no time at all.

However, I was still operating by the summon-demand-banish method, which meant I didn't begin with any intention of calling him again. At the time, he was merely an angel of Jupiter whom I thought could help me with a problem. I could have chosen any Jupiter spirit, and I do not recall why I settled upon Iophiel in particular.

I have likewise forgotten exactly what emergency I was dealing with at the time, though I do remember Iophiel came through for me in spectacular fashion. My path was set in that moment, because I knew without a doubt I would be calling upon Iophiel again and again in the future.[9] While there was yet no inkling in my mind to establish a permanent altar to him, even at this early date I was set to build a lifelong relationship with him.

Later I would begin my game-changing talks with Ochani Lele and undertake the Abramelin operation—and these would be the final nails in the coffin of "summon-demand-banish" for me.

Keeping House Gods

It was during this period that I began to entertain the idea of keeping some house gods. I dabbled with simple altars for two deities (Yahweh and Asherah) whom I considered my patrons at the time, and though the experiments were largely successful, I found I didn't continue with them for very long. My performance of Abramelin overshadowed everything I had been doing before, and those early altars soon gave way to my Guardian Angel's altar instead. This became my first true "house god," whose altar I would maintain and work with on a regular basis.

My next house deity was Bast. Though I did not consider her a personal patron, our house is pretty much overrun with cats who clearly believe they own the place. (Don't they?) Plus, on more than a few occasions I or my family have been called upon to rescue cats from various situations. In time, we realized our house was basically a "Bast House," and so we erected an altar to the cat goddess accordingly. She gets offerings of cat food and water every day, as her altar is where we feed the house cats. She gets candles, incense and other food offerings less frequently. Whenever we have problems associated with our cats, it is her altar we work with.

Michael finally became a permanent resident, not through an altar, but through an Orthodox-style Icon of the archangel that serves as his "portal" into our home. He has not had his own altar thus far; instead I make offerings to him on the altar where I do most of my work. I decorate the altar to him for the occasion, and hang

---

9. I suspect even modern magicians, if they practice long enough, will find themselves returning to the same spirits again and again.

his icon above it. At all other times, his icon hangs directly by the front door where he can keep a protective eye on everyone.[10]

Iophiel, too, was destined to become an established house god. Like Michael, he has a place that he (that is, a statue of him) lives when not involved in rituals, though I wouldn't call it an actual altar. When I want to work with him, I decorate my main working altar for him and bring his statue down from its dedicated shelf, which also holds other talismans and objects sacred to Jupiter. When the offerings have been completed and the work is done, the statue goes back to the shelf.

I have also worked with the archangel Samael in a similar fashion; he has a dedicated shelf directly beneath Iophiel's, and I also work with him on my main working altar. I never set out to have Samael as a true house god; to this day I have not, yet, consecrated an icon or statue to him. Yet, over the years I found myself calling upon him—and only him—in times of great need to protect my home and family. He too is someone I have gotten to know in the spirit world, and who has come to know and respect me in return. I have no need or desire to call upon other Martial spirits whom I don't know.

Finally, the newest member of our spiritual household is Ganesha, a very Jupiterian Hindu deity. This is really my wife's project more than mine, so I know few details of how she is maintaining his altar. I do know he is a welcome addition to our clan, along with his spiritual Rat companion who should be wonderful for my much-loved pet rats.

Most of the house gods, including Samael, receive offerings either yearly (preferably on a day sacred to them) or whenever we have need of their aid. My Guardian Angel, of course, receives weekly offerings of flame and incense when I work with her each Sabbath, plus larger offerings on my spiritual birthday.[11]

Making the offerings, maintaining the deities' altars, invoking them when needed—all of this has made these gods and angels active members of our family. We care about them, and they care about us. We give them a home, we feed and care for them, we show them respect and a willingness to give as much as we would take. Therefore, when we have need of them, they respond without us having to conjure or compel them. We enjoy a direct and continuous connection with these entities, and we have developed a mutually beneficial friendship.

We simply have no need to refer to a list of unknown angels or spirits when we need something in the real world.

---

10. As I write this, we actually do have plans to erect a permanent altar for him to go with the Icon.

11. The day I completed the Rite of Abramelin.

Taking Your Relationship to the Next Level

Your relationship with your house gods will extend beyond merely making offerings and asking them for help. Once an entity becomes your patron, you effectively become a priest of that entity. You become responsible for maintaining and caring for the entity, and it will become involved in your overall spiritual path. Perhaps that goes without saying for something like your Holy Guardian Angel, but it goes for absolutely any entity with whom you establish a devotional connection. They will take part in your magick, your initiations, and even assert influence over your mundane life. To illustrate this somewhat, I would like to share with you some of my experiences with Iophiel outside of my personal home temple.

I already considered Iophiel a longtime friend by the time I joined the Golden Dawn, and there I found entirely new opportunities to work with him. As I said previously, Jupiter is a pretty good "go-to" planet for nearly anything you need, and my Temple is no stranger to working with its energies. Sometimes we invoke pure Jupiter energy, but more often we choose to work with a specific entity. It was from one of these operations that I obtained a small square of tin, charged with Jupiter and inscribed with Iophiel's signature (sigil), that I carried on my person for many years. I, of course, made use of that talisman in all my work with Iophiel, but it is currently missing. Either he got tired of the talisman and wants me to make a new one, or it is simply hidden from me for the time being and will reappear later—something that has happened to me with talismans before.

However, the creation of that talisman was not my most memorable working with Iophiel in the GD Temple. The prize for that must go to the day we summoned Iophiel directly into the Temple. I was fortunately allowed to take the role of medium for this work and allow him to "mount" me, where he could speak and act through my physical form.

Granted, I am not a natural seer; there were and are others in the Temple better suited as mediums than myself. However, because Iophiel is one of my primary patron angels, it was decided I was likely the best choice for this one. I spent seven days beforehand in ritual preparation—seclusion, fasting, daily prayer, ritual cleansing, etc.—and was thus in a good state to succeed despite my being more used to the role of conjurer in such rituals.

We, of course, used Golden Dawn methods to evoke the archangel. I sat on the dais in the east of the Hall and received the spirit, most of my physical form covered with a long veil. The experience was incredible; not only was Iophiel the first angel to mount me other than my Guardian Angel, but it was the first time it had happened in a group ritual. I sat there for some time, fading in and out of awareness, as each member of the Temple approached one by one to speak with the angel. In each case he listened to the person, offered whatever blessing they had come to request, and then delivered a personalized message. I had little clue what any of those messages meant, and could in fact only remember a small few of them at all. In what I do remember, the messages rarely had anything at all to do with what the people thought they had come to speak with Iophiel about. Yet nearly everyone walked away from that dais with tears in their eyes, as he told each of them something deeply important in their hearts.

But I don't believe anyone was as fundamentally affected by that ritual as my wife and me. She had just recently had gall-bladder surgery and was still healing from the procedure. Thus I wasn't surprised when, after she had spoken with him and he had delivered his message to her, he reached out and touched her abdomen. He directed a strong rush of energy into her through my hands, giving no explanation, though I assumed he had acted to heal her surgery wound. Afterward, however, she was a bit unnerved because, as she told me, he had touched her much lower than her gall-bladder scar...

Now, without giving too much unnecessary detail, my wife and I had always assumed children were not a physical possibility. Yet, by our calculations, she became pregnant sometime within a month of the Iophiel evocation at the Temple. Not only did she suffer no physical ailments from the pregnancy, we were in fact entirely unaware that there *was* a pregnancy until the day she was rushed to the hospital for delivery. (I thought I was taking her in for appendicitis!) A beautiful baby girl was dropped into our arms that day, seemingly from nowhere. Once the shock and trauma wore off a bit, we did the math and realized that Iophiel had given us a wholly unexpected and life-changing gift.

Ever the natural skryer, my wife was told in the delivery room that the baby's name was Annaliese. From that very day, we have considered Iophiel to be her spiritual father and protector. Oh, and I even clearly remember the message he gave to my wife before he touched her that day: "There is still joy and laughter in the world." Amen to that!

Conclusion

The above is one of my favorite tales of the involvement of the angels in my life, though it is hardly the only one. However, I feel it serves to illustrate the profound impact your patrons should have on your personal life. We can set aside our magickal tools and rituals as sacred (meaning "apart from the mundane"), but the spirits should be an active influence on every part of your life. You need them at your side whenever you leave the house—even if it's just to the store to pick up mouthwash and tube-socks. The world is full of unexpected obstacles and dangers (there are countless ways to die or get injured between your house and that store!), and you want your guardians to have your back twenty-four hours a day. Having "friends on the other side" is what sets you apart from the masses as a wizard (or witch, conjurer, sorcerer, etc.).

Because I have befriended and built long-term relationships with the angels, they have acted on many occasions (both within and outside the context of magick or ritual) on my behalf. They have directly saved my life on several occasions. They have provided things I need, helped me with my human relationships, supported (and directed) my spiritual work, and much more.

But all of these boons have come not from treating the angels as "tools" or "symbols" to be manipulated at my desire. Nor have they come from cold-contacting one spirit after another with whom I have no established relationship. They have come, instead, from a place of mutual respect and friendship born of many years of living and working with a relatively small family of patrons and familiars. Our relationships are symbiotic: I help them by feeding and caring for them as much as they help me with my mundane concerns.

Plus, I write essays like this, encouraging others to treat the spirits in the same respectful manner. They love it when I do that.

Zorge,
Aaron Leitch
March 2015

The Evocation of Metatron: A Golden Dawn Z-2 Ritual

CHARLES CHIC CICERO & SANDRA TABATHA CICERO

CHARLES CHIC CICERO & SANDRA TABATHA CICERO are, along with Adam Forrest, Chief Adepts of the Hermetic Order of the Golden Dawn. They are members of several Rosicrucian and Martinist organizations. Chic is a Past Grand Commander of the Grand Commandery of Knights Templar in Florida. Tabatha is the Supreme Magus of the Societas Rosicruciana in America. They are the authors of many books, including Self-Initiation in the Golden Dawn Tradition *(Llewellyn, 1995),* Secrets of a Golden Dawn Temple *(1992),* The Essential Golden Dawn: An Introduction to High Magic *(2003),* The Golden Dawn Magical Tarot *(2000),* The Babylonian Tarot *(2006), and* Tarot Talismans: Invoking the Angels of the Tarot *(2006). They have also edited the* Golden Dawn Journals, *and edited and provided commentary for new editions of several of the classic works of their friend and mentor Israel Regardie.*

The Evocation of Metatron: A Golden Dawn Z-2 Ritual

And an angel of the Lord appeared to him, standing to the right of the altar of incense.

—*Luke* 1:11[1]

 VOCATION, DERIVED FROM the Latin term *evocatio* meaning "calling forth," refers to the act of summoning a spiritual entity into physical or visible manifestation external to the magician. The magician performing the evocation would request something from the summoned entity: knowledge of various matters, health, material wealth, protection, etc. Tools utilized by the magician to effect a successful evocation include the Triangle of Manifestation, into which the evoked spirit would appear, and the Magic Circle of Protection that surrounded the magician.

The Magic Circle is an area that has been purified and consecrated by the magician to be a sacred space. It is a sanctified area of protection in which the magician can perform his or her art. The magic circle as depicted in the grimoires was often drawn on the floor with chalk, or paint, or sometimes salt. Around the circumference were written various divine and angelic names as well as pentagrams and sigils of power.

There has been much discussion as to whether a physical circle, drawn on the floor, is needed for protection within the context of the Golden Dawn evocation. Although the old grimoires insisted on having a physical circle for this type of work, it must be remembered that the medieval worldview in which the grimoires originated is far different from the worldview of many practicing Golden Dawn Magicians.

Most of the grimoires were written and used by medieval Christian clerics and others who were ordained to the minor orders, which included the position of

---

1. *Gospel According to Luke* (New American Standard Bible [NASB] Version). —APF

exorcist. University students would be ordained to the minor orders as part of their core curriculum. According to author Richard Kieckhefer, "many were ordained to lower orders and continued to claim the privileges of clergy although they had no clerical employment."[2] There was a glut of unemployed and semi-employed clerics who would have access to books of exorcism and be expected to command demons if need be. As a result, it was primarily among these exorcist-clerics that medieval ceremonial magic as set forth in the grimoires flourished. It is no surprise then that the grimoires reflect a dualistic worldview in which humans and spirits have an adversarial relationship. Many of the texts which recommend commanding spirits often deal with Goetic spirits (or are derived from such texts), who are assumed to be hostile witnesses and unwilling participants—present only because they are ordered to be so through the commandment of God.

Take for example the following description of how to deal with a Goetic spirit from the *Goetia*:

> The Thirteenth Spirit is called Beleth (or Bileth, or Bilet). He is a mighty King and terrible. He rideth on a pale horse with trumpets and other kinds of musical instruments playing before him. He is very furious at his first appearance, that is, while the Exorcist layeth his courage; for to do this he must hold a Hazel Wand in his hand, striking it out towards the South and East Quarters, make a triangle, without the Circle, and then command him into it by the Bonds and Charges of Spirits as hereafter followeth. And if he doth not enter into the triangle at your threats, rehearse the Bonds and Charms before him, and then he will yield Obedience and come into it, and do what he is commanded by the Exorcist.[3]

This reflects a medieval worldview which holds that part of the punishment for fallen spirits is that they are bound to serve human magicians who know the right rituals and the proper divine names. In other words, they are being commanded as prisoners, indentured servants, or slaves.

> The magicians of the Middle Ages clearly recognized that the practice of evocation had risks as well as benefits, and they set out to deal with dangers efficiently from the start. The method they used, typical for the time, was sheer brute force...the magician readied his arsenal of words of power and consecrated weapons, and then launched his conjurations like assaults, battering the spirit into submission with threats and rhetoric fortified with the Names of God.
>
> A spirit who did not show up quickly enough might have its name and sigil, written on a piece of parchment, scorched over hot coals in the hope that this might torture it into obedience! It's little wonder that spirits, faced

---

2. Richard Kieckhefer, *Magic in the Middle Ages* (Cambridge: Cambridge University Press, 2000), p. 154.

3. ['Solomon,' S.L. MacGregor Mathers, and] Aleister Crowley, *The Book of the Goetia of Solomon the King* (Boleskine, Foyers, Inverness: Society for the Propagation of Religious Truth, 1904).

with this kind of treatment, were seen as dangerous and treacherous, apt to wriggle out of agreements through any loophole they could find. Most human beings put in the same situation would behave similarly.[4]

One problem with Goetic spirits and similar entities that are historically and magically known as evil spirits, is that they are often originally based on pagan gods and goddesses, but seen and developed through the biased lens of the medieval Christian exorcist-cleric, who thought that all pagan gods were fallen spirits. The result is the corruption of sacred pagan deities into a class of evil spirits who could be enslaved by the magician. The best known of these corrupted forms is the Phoenician goddess Astarte, who in the *Goetia* has degenerated into the spirit Ashtoreth:

> a Mighty, Strong Duke, and appeareth in the Form of an hurtful Angel riding on an Infernal Beast like a Dragon, and carrying in his right hand a Viper. Thou must in no wise let him approach too near unto thee, lest he do thee damage by his Noisome Breath.[5]

Another example is the proud Egyptian war-god Horus who has deteriorated into:

> Haures, or Hauras, or Havres, or Flauros. He is a Great Duke, and appeareth at first like a Leopard, Mighty, Terrible, and Strong, but after a while, at the Command of the Exorcist, he putteth on Human Shape with Eyes Flaming and Fiery, and a most Terrible Countenance. He giveth True Answers of all things, Present, Past, and to Come. But if he be not commanded into a Triangle, he will Lie in all these Things, and deceive and beguile the Exorcist in these things, or in such and such business.[6]

Since Golden Dawn magicians do not believe that pagan gods and goddesses are fallen spirits, we have no need to call upon these corrupted forms and their associated and often harmful baggage. We are used to working with deities from various pantheons, angels, archangels, planetary intelligences, spirits, etc. in their pure and original forms, with respect, and without the need to force, threaten, or torture a hostile or unwilling entity to do our bidding. The antagonistic medieval worldview of human/spirit interaction is not one we share.

For the final word on Goetic spirits, we can do no better than quote John Michael Greer:

> Finally, many of the older grimoires, and a few more recent books, discuss the evocation of demons.[7] Here the best advice is a single word: don't.

---

4. John Michael Greer, *Circles of Power: Ritual Magic in the Western Tradition* (St. Paul, MN: Llewellyn Publications, 1997), p. 244.

5. Solomon, Mathers, and Crowley, *op. cit.*

6. *Ibid.*

7. Take note of the difference between the terms *dæmon* and *demon*. The Greek word *daimōn* (Latinized to *dæmon*) simply means "spirit," and was originally the name for benign nature spirits as well as intermediate or guardian spirits between gods and humans (a guardian angel) without regard to whether the spirit was

> There's nothing of value to be gained by summoning what the Cabala calls the inhabitants of Gehenna, the Kingdom of Shells, and whatever is done with their aid will turn against the doer, sooner or later. They have a place in the universe and a right to exist, but they are as alien and destructive to the fabric of human life as a black hole or the heart of a Star. The only time a magician should have any dealings with them is when, as sometimes happens, they intrude on the human world and must be sent back to their own realm through ritual exorcism.[8]

There are a plethora of beneficial spiritual entities that can be evoked to visible appearance by Golden Dawn adepts. These include Qabalistic Archangels and angels, Enochian angels, zodiacal spirits, planetary intelligences and spirits, and elemental rulers and spirits.

The higher forms, Archangels and Angels, are "of God," and therefore the human magician cannot command them to do anything. Instead, the adept must approach these beings with humility, with prayer and invocation, respectfully requesting their presence and aid. These powerful beings can be petitioned to send those angels and spirits under their command to render assistance to the magician in whatever capacity is sought. *If the magician's will and intent is in harmony with that of the divine*, the goal of the ritual will be fulfilled.

There may be circumstances where commanding a being may be the appropriate form of communication, such as when the military command model fits into the spiritual hierarchy of the entity to be summoned. For example, if Kamael, archangel of Gevurah, has sanctioned a Gevuric working, the magician, after successfully taking on the form of Kamael, may command angels under his authority.

Why were the circle and triangle selected as the primary figures of evocation in the first place? The circle is a symbol of unity, of eternity, of deity without beginning or end. Infinite divinity. To stand at the center of a circle is an expression of one's unity with the Highest, and all the protection and security that such a position affords. The Triangle on the other hand is a symbol of containment. By the number three, the triangle is aligned with the third Sephirah of Binah on the Tree of Life, the sphere of restriction, limitation, and location of form, just as the third connecting line of the triangle limits and contains the space previously unlimited by two lines, and as three points are needed in triangulation to determine an object's physical position. The circle and the triangle are therefore the figures of the limitless and the limited, respectively.

The heavy emphasis on physical circles and triangles for protection developed out of the old grimoiric traditions that dealt with adversarial, hostile spirits. Today,

---

good or evil. In the Christian era, the word *demon* was used to mean an evil spirit. Modern magicians tend to use the term *demon* to refer to an evil spirit and the term *dæmon* to refer to a beneficial guardian spirit.

8. Greer, *op. cit.*, p. 251.

it is presumed that the Golden Dawn adept who wishes to evoke an entity is already skilled in invoking, banishing, consecrating, visualization, etc. Therefore, there is really no need to construct a physical magical circle on the floor. Instead, the magic circle is created on the astral by the performance of the appropriate Banishing Rituals and consecrations, with great effect. A skilled magician who is working only with archangels, angels, and similar holy beings may view the Triangle of Art not as a prison for an unruly spirit, but more like a landing pad or a portal between the worlds—an area that helps to facilitate manifestation.

Some spirits utilized in the Golden Dawn such as planetary spirits, though not considered evil or hostile, are seen as blind, potent, raw forces that must be controlled by their immediate angelic superiors in their respective spiritual hierarchies. Such was the case in one of the few evocation rituals to survive in writing from the original Golden Dawn, the Evocation of the Great Spirit Taphthartharath (the Spirit of Mercury) by Allan Bennett, V.H. Fra. Iehi Aour. In a case such as this, having a physical circle can be protective and insulating. There is certainly no harm in constructing a full-blown magical circle, which is a useful magical tool like any other. It can add focus to the magician's visualization, mental poise, and concentration. But such tools are not meant to be crutches for magicians who are unsure of themselves. A fearful magician is one who should stay away from evocations of any kind.

In *The Golden Dawn*, Regardie included a Z-2 Ritual of Evoking the Enochian Angel AXIR, a Servient Angel of the Earth Quadrant of the Earth Tablet. In his Foreword to the Z-2 documents, Regardie presented his ideas on how to create a physical circle, which he felt was necessary only for evocations:

> It is preferable to paint the circle and divine names on the floor or on canvas, or on a neutral coloured sheet of linoleum so that the circle and names appear brilliant and clear cut. But for convenience' [*sic*] sake, and for quicker working, it is useful to lay out a circle in coloured tapes. The colour naturally will depend on the nature of the ceremony. At the appropriate angles of quarters of this taped circle, pentacles or flashing Tablets of the requisite Divine Names or symbols may be placed.[9]

Today it is far more common for Golden Dawn magicians to perform Spirit Vision Work, sometimes called Skrying and Travelling in the Spirit Vision, or simply Skrying, rather than evocations. The theory is that in Spirit Vision work, the magician is ascending in consciousness to the spiritual realm where the entity dwells, rather than bringing the entity down to the magician's level on the physical plane. (As one of our esteemed companions put it, evocation is like hiring a tutor to come to your

---

9. Israel Regardie, *The Golden Dawn: An Account of the Teachings, Rites, and Ceremonies of the Order of the Golden Dawn* (St. Paul, MN: Llewellyn, 1971 [First ed. Chicago: Aries Press, 1937–1940]), vol. 3, p. 154.

home and teach you French, while Spirit Vision Work is like going to Paris to study French.) Nevertheless, performance of a ceremonial evocation is an excellent method for exploring nearly every tool in the magician's toolkit, calling as it does upon the diverse magical skills of banishing, purification, consecration, invocation, god-form assumption, talisman consecration, vibration, projection, and visualization.

It is a misconception that in evocation a spirit will take on a physical form every bit as solid as you or me. In *Aspects of Occultism*, author Dion Fortune helped put this misunderstanding to rest:

> In the great majority of cases of evocative magic, the form is built up on astral and can only actually be seen by the clairvoyant, though any sensitive person can feel its influence.
>
> The initiated magician is usually, unless engaged in some special experiment or research, content to evoke to visible appearance on the astral, depending upon his psychic powers for communication with the entity evoked. He does not go to the trouble to evoke to visible appearance on the physical because, if he is an adequate psychic, astral appearance serves his purpose just as well; in fact, better, because it is more congenial to the nature of the beings ...and places less limitation upon their activities.[10]

The Z Documents

The practice of Evocation lies within a particular set of teachings within the Golden Dawn system of magic collectively known as the "Z Documents," the "Z Docs," or simply the "Zeds." These manuscripts explained how the various sections and aspects of the order's Neophyte Ritual could be used as practical ritual formulæ for endless varieties of theurgic procedures. Of particular interest to our discussion is the manuscript known as *Z-2: The Formulæ of the Magic of Light.* "The Magic of Light" is the name given to the practical magic of the Golden Dawn's Inner Order as classified under the five letters of the *Pentagrammaton*—YHShVH (יהשוה), or *Yesheshuah*, the Hebrew name of Jesus, which is the *Tetragrammaton*, YHVH (יהוה), with the letter Shin (ש) placed in the center of the Four-Lettered Name. Evocations and invocations are classified under the Hebrew letter Yod (י) and the element of Fire. Consecrations of talismans and the production of natural phenomena are classified under the second letter Heh (ה) and the element of Water. All works of spiritual development and transformations are attributed to the letter Shin (ש) and the element of Spirit. All works of divination are assigned to the letter Vav (ו) and the element of Air. All works of alchemy are classified under the final letter Heh (ה) and the element of Earth.

---

10. Dion Fortune, *Aspects of Occultism* (London: Aquarian Press, 1962), pp. 6–7.

Golden Dawn adepts were expected to study the brief outlines of magical rites provided in the Z-2 document, and create their own unique versions of the same in fully expanded rituals. Regardie supplied readers with Z-2-style rituals that he had created based on the Z-2 outlines, but he also admonished students not to slavishly copy his versions. Skilled students were fully expected to draft their own rituals using their own creativity and inspiration.

The Order's initial teachings on evocation as presented in Z-2 are given below, along with our comments.

Z-2 Instructions for a Ritual of Evocation Falling Under the Letter Yod

A—The Magic Circle.

Comment: The choice of creating an astral magic circle via Banishing Rituals as opposed to drawing a physical circle on the floor has already been discussed earlier in this article.

B—The Magician, wearing the Great Lamen of the Hierophant; and his scarlet Robe. A Pentacle, whereon is engraved the Sigil of the Spirit to be invoked, has painted on the back of it the circle and cross as shown on the Hierophant's Lamen.

Comment: This section alludes to the important idea that the magician undertaking this Working has attained the level of Z.A.M. and is qualified to hold the position of Hierophant. In other words, the magician must be skilled and knowledgeable. The Lamen to be worn is exactly the same as the Lamen of the Hierophant, but inscribed on the back with the sigil of the entity to be invoked, in the appropriate colors.

C—The Names and Formulæ to be employed.

Comment: The Divine names, Archangelic names, Angelic names, and powers that are attributed to and facilitate the manifestation of the particular entity in accordance with its specific spiritual hierarchy, in accordance with the Third Law of Magic (the Law of Correspondence).

D—The Symbol of the whole evocation.

Comment: This is the sigil of the spiritual entity to be evoked. This was crafted into a Pentacle inscribed with three concentric circles between which are written the hierarchical names of the appropriate powers, to be used as the Material Basis for the evoked being.

E—The Construction of the Circle and the placing of all the symbols, etc., employed, in the places properly allotted to them; so as to represent the interior of a G.D. Temple in the Enterer, and the purification and consecration of the actual piece of ground or place selected for the performance of the Evocation.

Comment: The temple is laid out in accordance with the Neophyte Hall. If Zodiacal forces are to be evoked, the magician would plan the working in accordance with planetary hours, astrological configuration at the time of the working, etc. The astral circle is raised via preliminary banishing and invoking rituals of the pentagram and/or hexagram. The circle is purified and consecrated using the Stolistes/Dadouchos formula of the Neophyte Grade.

F—The Invocation of the Higher Powers. Pentacle formed of three concentric bands, name and sigil therein, in proper colours, is to be bound thrice with a cord and shrouded in black, thus bringing into action a Blind Force to be further directed or differentiated in the Process of the Ceremony. Announcement aloud of the Object of the working; naming the Spirit or Spirits which it is desired to evoke. This is pronounced standing in the Centre of the Circle and turning towards the quarter from which the Spirit will come.

Comment: (See the commentary to Step D.) An invocation to the Highest Divine Powers as well as the Higher powers within the hierarchy of the entity to be evoked. The magician also proclaims his or her specific intent and objective for performing the evocation.

G—The Name and Sigil of the Spirit, wrapped in a black cloth or covering, is now placed within the circle, at the point corresponding to the West, representing the Candidate. The consecration of Baptism by water and fire of the Sigil then takes place, and the proclamation in a loud and firm voice of the Spirit (or Spirits) to be evoked.

Comment: Movement and speeches here mirror the Neophyte Ceremony, when the blindfolded Candidate is barred in the South, to be purified and consecrated before entering the Gateway of the West. The Pentacle is purified and consecrated using the Stolistes/Dadouchos formula. The Material Basis, like the blindfolded candidate, is primed to be molded and directed toward the goal of the ceremony.

H—The veiled Sigil is now to be placed at the foot of the Altar. The Magician then calls aloud the Name of the Spirit, summoning him to appear, stating for what purpose the Spirit is evoked: what is desired in the operation; why the evocation is performed at this time, and finally solemnly affirming that the Spirit shall be evoked by the Ceremony.

Comment: This portion of the ritual recalls the point during the Neophyte Ceremony, when the blindfolded Candidate is brought to the foot of the altar to give the obligation, promising to observe every clause.

I—Announcement aloud that all is prepared for the commencement of the actual Evocation. If it be a good Spirit, the Sigil is now to be placed within the White Triangle on the Altar, the Magician places his left hand upon it, raises in his right hand the magical Implement employed (usually the Sword) erect; and commences the Evocation of the Spirit N. to visible appearance. The Magician stands in the Place of the Hierophant during the Obligation, irrespective of the particular quarter of the Spirit.

But if the nature of that Spirit be evil, then the Sigil must be placed without and to the West of the White Triangle and the Magician shall be careful to keep the point of the Magical Sword upon the centre of the Sigil.

Comment: The Magician stands east of the altar facing west in the position of the Hierophant in the Neophyte Ceremony.

J—Now let the Magician imagine himself as clothed outwardly with the semblance of the form of the Spirit to be evoked, and in this let him be careful not to identify himself with the Spirit, which would be dangerous; but only to formulate a species of mask, worn for the time being. And if he knows not the symbolic form of the Spirit, then let him assume the form of an Angel belonging unto the same class of operation, this form being assumed. Then let him pronounce aloud, with a firm and solemn voice, a convenient and potent oration and exorcism of the Spirit unto visible appearance.

Comment: The Magician engages in god-form assumption, or in Archangel-form assumption. The word "exorcism" is derived from the Greek *exorkizein*, which means to summon or direct by the power of Divine Names, especially with regard to a sworn oath or obligation on the part of the one who is being summoned.

At the conclusion of this exorcism, taking the covered sigil in his left hand, let him smite it thrice with the flat blade of the Magic Sword. Then let him raise on high his arms to their utmost stretch, holding in his left hand the veiled sigil, and in his right the Sword of Art erect. At the same time stamping thrice upon the ground with his right foot.

Comment: Smiting (or rather tapping) the veiled Pentacle thrice with the sword is not so much a barring of the Pentacle as is an awakening into manifestation. Stomping on the ground thrice symbolizes the tamping down of those unbalanced forces which may be attached by the ceremony, in the same way as the Hierophant stomps on the invisible station of the Evil Triad in the Neophyte ceremony. The "exorcism" referred to here is the expulsion of any remaining mundaneness attached to the physical Pentacle.

K—The veiled and corded sigil is then to be placed in the Northern part of the Hall at the edge of the Circle, and the Magician employs the oration of the Hierophant, from the Throne of the East, modifying it slightly, as follows: "The voice of the Exorcism said unto me, 'Let me shroud myself in darkness, peradventure thus may I manifest myself in Light, etc.'" The Magician then proclaims aloud that the Mystic Circumambulation will take place.

Comment: The magician moves clockwise to the North, again mirroring the Neophyte Ceremony, when the blindfolded candidate is barred in the North, to be purified and consecrated before entering the Gateway of the East in the Mystic Circumambulation.

L—The Magician takes up the Sigil in his left hand and circumambulates the Magic Circle once, then passes to the South and halts. He stands (having placed the sigil on the ground) between it and the West, and repeats the oration of the Kerux. And again consecrates it with Water and Fire. Then takes it in his hand, facing westward, saying, "Creature of. . . . . . ., twice consecrate, thou mayest approach the Gate of the West."

Comment: The oration of the Keryx is "Unpurified and Unconsecrated, Thou cans't not enter the Path of the West." The Pentacle is purified and consecrated again. Great pillars of fire and cloud are visualized on either side of the magician which helps to strengthen the telesma of the Pentacle. The answering speech is based on the Hegemon's statement of guidance to the Candidate.

M—The Magician now moves to the West of the Magical Circle, holds the Sigil in his left hand and the Sword in his right, faces South West, and again astrally masks himself with the form of the Spirit, and for the first time partially opens the covering of the Sigil, without however entirely removing it. He then smites it once with the flat blade of the sword, saying, in a loud, clear, and firm voice: "Thou canst not pass from conceal-ment unto Manifestation, save by the virtue of the Name Elohim. Before all things are the Chaos and the Darkness, and the Gates of the Land of Night. I am He Whose Name is Darkness. I am the Great One of the Path of the Shades. I am the Exorcist in the midst of the Exorcism. Appear thou therefore without fear before me, so pass thou on." He then reveils the Sigil.

Comment: The magician again takes on or strengthens the form of his or her own Higher Genius followed by that of the Archangel. The speech here is based upon the Hiereus' barring of the Candidate in the Neophyte Ceremony. The importance of knowing the name of "Darkness," is stressed here, which alludes to the ancient technique of naming forces in magic, "for by Names and Images all Powers are awakened and re-awakened." For if the knowledge of Darkness is not within the magician, that of Light cannot be grasped. The tap of the sword is another call to manifestation. The Hebrew Divine name of Elohim recalls the godnames of Geburah (Elohim Gibbor) and Binah (YHVH Elohim) on the Black Pillar of Severity. The "Exorcist in the midst of the Exorcism" works to expel all that is impure and unbalanced from the physical basis of the Pentacle.

N—Take the Sigil to the North, circumambulating first, halt, place Sigil on the ground, stand between it and the East, repeat the oration of the Kerux, again consecrate with Fire and Water. Then take it up, face North, and say "Creature of . . . . . , thrice consecrate, thou mayest approach the Gate of the East."

Comment: This mirrors Step L above, but here the oration of the Keryx is "Unpurified and Unconsecrated, Thou canst not enter the Path of the East," when the blindfolded candidate is barred in the North, to be purified and consecrated before entering the Eastern Gateway. Great pillars of fire and cloud are visualized on either side of the magician, which again helps to strengthen the telesma of the Pentacle.

O—Repeat Section M in North East. Magician then passes to East, takes up Sigil in left and Sword in right hand. Assumes the Mask of the Spirit form, smites the Sigil with the Lotus Wand or Sword, and says, "Thou canst not pass from concealment unto manifestation save by virtue of the name YHVH. After the Formless and the Void and the Darkness, then cometh the knowledge of the Light. I am that Light which riseth in the Darkness. I am the Exorcist in the midst of the Exorcism. Appear thou therefore in visible form before me, for I am the Wielder of the Forces of the Balance. Thou hast known me now, so pass thou on to the Cubical Altar of the Universe!"

Comment: This mirrors Step M above. The Hebrew Divine name of YHVH recalls the godnames of Binah (YHVH Elohim) for "the Light that shineth in the Darkness." YHVH also recalls the Light in the godnames of Chokmah (Yah or Yod Heh) as well as Netzach (YHVH Tzabaoth) on the White Pillar of Mercy. It also alludes to the balancing force of Tiphareth (YHVH Eloah va-Daath), the Sephirah that brings "Knowledge of the Light" on the Middle Pillar.

P—He then recovers Sigil and passes to Altar, laying it thereon as before shown. He then passes to the East of the Altar, holding the Sigil and Sword as already explained. Then doth he rehearse a most potent Conjuration and Invocation of the Spirit unto visible appearance, using and reiterating all the Divine, Angelic, and Magical Names appropriate to this end, neither omitting the signs, seals, sigils, lineal figures, signatures and the like from that Conjuration.

Q—The Magician now elevates the covered Sigil towards heaven, removes the veil entirely, leaving it yet corded, crying with a loud voice, "Creature of . . . . . , long hast thou dwelt in darkness. Quit the Night and seek the Day." He then replaces it upon the Altar, holds the Magical Sword erect above it, the pommel immediately above the centre thereof, and says, "By all the Names, Powers, and Rites already rehearsed, I conjure thee thus unto visible appearance." Then the Mystic Words.

Comment: This mirrors an important and cathartic point in Neophyte Ceremony, when the hoodwink is removed from the candidate's eyes and full potency of the ceremony is revealed to him or her for the first time. The Pentacle is addressed as if the magician is speaking directly to the candidate. The Mystic Words "Khabs Am Pekht, Konx om Pax, Light in Extension" should signal the beginning of the archangel's manifestation within the Triangle of Art.

R—Saith the Magician, "As Light hidden in the Darkness can manifest therefrom, so shalt thou become manifest from concealment unto manifestation."

He then takes up the Sigil, stands to East of Altar, and faces West. He shall then rehearse a long conjuration to the Powers and Spirits immediately superior unto that one which he seeks to invoke, that they shall force him to manifest himself unto visible appearance.

He then places the Sigil between the Pillars, himself at the East facing West, then in the Sign of the Enterer doth he direct the whole current of his Will upon the Sigil. Thus he continueth until such time as he shall perceive his Will power to be weakening, when he protects himself from the reflex of the current by the Sign of Silence, and drops his hands. He now looks towards the Quarter that the Spirit is to appear in, and he should now see the first signs of his visible manifestation. If he be not thus faintly visible, let the Magician repeat the conjuration of the Superiors of the Spirit, from the place of the Throne in the East. And this conjuration may be repeated thrice, each time ending with a new Projection of Will in the Sign of the Enterer, etc. But if at the third time of repetition he appeareth not, then be it known that there is an error in the working.

> **Comment:** The sentence "He shall then rehearse a long conjuration to the powers and spirits immediately superior unto that one which he seeks to invoke, *that they shall force him to manifest himself unto visible appearance*" reinforces the fact that all commands to the Spirit are made by that entity's Archangelic Superiors.
>
> Utilizing the Projection Sign, the magician focuses his or her Will and that of the energies present on the Material Basis in the Triangle of Art.

So let the Master of Evocations replace the Sigil upon the Altar, holding the Sword as usual: and thus doing, let him address a humble prayer unto the Great Gods of Heaven to grant unto him the force necessary to correctly complete that evocation. He is then to take back the Sigil to between the Pillars, and repeat the former processes, when assuredly that Spirit will begin to manifest, but in a misty and ill-defined form.

> **Comment:** If the entity has not attained complete manifestation in the Triangle of Art at this point, the magician should repeat the Invocation of the Highest Powers up to three times if necessary.

(But if, as is probable, the Operator be naturally inclined unto evocation, then might that Spirit perchance manifest earlier in the Ceremony than this. Still, the Ceremony is to be performed up to this point, whether he be there or no.)

Now as soon as the Magician shall see the visible manifestation of that Spirit's presence, he shall quit the station of the Hierophant, and consecrate afresh with Water and with Fire, the Sigil of the evoked Spirit.

Comment: It has been our experience that manifestation will usually have been achieved by this point, and Step S below may be skipped.

Rather than break the flow of the manifestation with another physical purification and consecration at this point, we suggest testing the entity with appropriate gestures such as the LVX Signs. If the manifestation is truly that of the desired entity, he will return this salute. If not, the entity will vanish or change forms. If this happens, banish and start over. "No balanced force, no power of good, will object or resent legitimate forms of testing its integrity."[11]

S—Now doth the Master of Evocations remove from the Sigil the restricting cord, and holding the freed Sigil in his left hand, he smites it with the flat blade of his Sword, exclaiming, "By and in the Names of.. . . . . I do invoke upon thee the power of perfect manifestation unto visible appearance." He then circumambulates the Circle thrice holding the Sigil in his right hand.

T—The Magician, standing in the place of the Hierophant, but turning towards the place of the Spirit, and fixing his attention thereon, now reads a potent Invocation of the Spirit unto visible appearance, having previously placed the Sigil on the ground, within the Circle, at the quarter where the Spirit appears.

This Invocation should be of some length; and should rehearse and reiterate the Divine and other Names consonant with the working.

Comment: The magician recites a potent, personalized invocation toward the Material Basis in the Triangle of Art.

That Spirit should now become fully and clearly visible, and should be able to speak with a direct voice, if consonant with his nature. The Magician then proclaims aloud that the Spirit N. hath been duly and properly evoked in accordance with the sacred Rites.

Comment: This mirrors the Keryx in the ⓪=◻ Ritual, proclaiming that the new Neophyte has been duly initiated. (Within the context of an evocation, this step feels redundant and breaks the flow of the energy.)

U—The Magician now addresses an Invocation unto the Lords of the Plane of the Spirit to compel him to perform that which the Magician shall demand of him.

V—The Magician carefully formulates his demands, questions, etc., and writes down any of the answers that may be advisable. The Master of Evocations now addresses a

---

11. Regardie, *op. cit.*, vol. 4, p. 26.

Conjuration unto the Spirit evoked, binding him to hurt or injure naught connected with him, or his assistants, or the place. And that he deceive in nothing, and that he fail not to perform that which he hath been commanded.

Comment: The magician should not converse with any evoked being until the entity has pledged to uphold an oath. The magician should have created an oath ahead of time, especially designed for the entity.

W—He then dismisses that Spirit by any suitable form, such as those used in the higher grades of the Outer. And if he will not go, then shall the Magician compel him by forces contrary to his nature. But he must allow a few minutes for the Spirit to dematerialise the body in which he hath manifested, for he will become less and less material by degrees. And note well that the Magician (or his companions if he have any) shall never quit the Circle during the process of evocation, or afterwards, till the Spirit hath quite vanished.

Comment: Rather than issuing demands, the magician should thank the entity before giving it the License to Depart. Then appropriate Banishing Rituals may be performed. The Pentacle may be wrapped and the temple ritually closed down.

Seeing that in some cases, and with some constitutions, there may be danger arising from the Astral conditions and currents established, and without the actual intention of the Spirit to harm, although if of a low nature, he would probably endeavour to do so. Therefore, before the commencement of the Evocation, let the operator assure himself that everything which may be necessary, be properly arranged within the Circle.

But if it be actually necessary to interrupt the Process, then let him stop at that point, veil and re-cord the Sigil if it have been unbound or uncovered, recite a License to Depart or a Banishing Formula, and perform the Lesser Banishing Rituals both of the Pentagram and Hexagram. Thus only may he in comparative safety quit the Circle.

Comment: Leaving the circle before the evocation is completed would only be done in the case of an emergency. The magician should endeavor not to leave the circle for any reason until the ritual is ended.

Any Pentacles must be wrapped in cloth and put away until they are needed again. If they are not needed and have fulfilled their purpose, they must be discharged and completely banished using the appropriate figures. They may then be purified and their elements released though burning.

Note— Get the Spirit into a White Triangle outside the midheaven, then shall he speak the truth of necessity.

The Evocation of Metatron: An Explanation

The ritual presented here is an example of a Golden Dawn evocation ritual for the manifestation of Metatron, the Archangel of Kether, the first Sephirah on the Qabalisitc Tree of Life. The ceremony utilizes the Golden Dawn's Banners of the East and West in Z-2 Working of Evocation. These Banners take the place of the Magic Circle and the Triangle of Manifestation. The Banner of the East becomes the ground cloth of Divine protection. Its symbolism is explained in the Portal Ritual and later in the Z-1 document:

> The field of the Banner of the East is White, the color of light and purity. As in the previous case, the Calvary Cross of six squares is the number of Tiphareth, the yellow Cross of Solar Gold, and the cubical stone, bearing in its center the sacred Tau of Life, and having bound together upon it the form of the macrocosmic Hexagram, the red Triangle of Fire and the blue Triangle of Water—the Ruach Elohim and the Waters of Creation.
>
> In addition to this explanation, it affirms the Mode of Action employed by the Divine Light in its operation by the Forces of Nature. Upon it is the symbol of the Macrocosm so coloured as to affirm the action of the Fire of the Spirit through the Waters of Creation under the harmony of the Golden Cross of the Reconciler. Within the centre of the Hexagram is a Tau cross in White, to represent its action as a Triad; and the whole is placed on a white field representing the Ocean of the Ain Soph Aour . . . the Banner itself, the Perfect Law of the Universe, the red cords and tassels the Divine Self-renunciation, Whose trials and sufferings form, as it were, the Ornament of the Completed Work. The whole represents the ascent of the Initiate into Perfect Knowledge of the Light.[12]

The Banner of the West is partly explained in the Zelator Initiation and also in the Z-1 document:

> "The White Triangle refers to the three Paths connecting Malkuth with the other Sephiroth; while the red cross is the Hidden Knowledge of the Divine Nature which is to be obtained through their aid. The Cross and Triangle together represent Life and Light." In addition to this explanation from the Zelator Grade, it represents eternally the possibility of Rescuing the Evil; but in it the Tiphareth cross is placed within the White Triangle of the Supernals as thereby representing that Sacrifice as made only unto the Higher. The red Cross may be bordered with gold in this instance, to represent the Perfect Metal obtained in and through the Darkness of Putrefaction. Black is its field which thus represents the Darkness and Ignorance of the Outer, while the White Triangle is again the Light which shineth in the Darkness but which is not comprehended thereby. Therefore is the Banner of the West the symbol of Twilight—as it were the equation of Light and darkness.

---

12. Regardie, *op. cit.*, vol. 3, p. 91.

> The Banner of the West, when it changes its position in the Temple, represents that which bars and threatens, and demands fresh sacrifice ere the Path leading to the Higher be attained.[13]

The Banner of the West is used as a barrier preventing all that is evil and unbalanced from entering sacred space. Both Banners are fitting symbols for the protective space of Divinity and the containing symbol of the Triangle of Manifestation. Both are also used as symbols of protection on the Astral Plane as indicated in the Order's manuscripts on "Clairvoyance":

> It may assist to formulate this Banner *(the Banner of the East)* about his own being. The Central Cross of the Banner will suggest his own form with outstretched arms—a true calvary cross. About him, the Seer will visualise vividly the interlaced red and blue triangles of the Tiphareth hexagram, at the same time imagining that the white triangle of the Supernals has descended into his heart. The alternate and occasionally simultaneous use of these Banners is a powerful means of banishing the evil, and invoking balanced power to one's aid. In the rubrics of certain rituals, the injunction occurs to formulate this Banner about talismans or Flashing Tablets that are being consecrated, as this process assists the descent or the incarnation of the Light, or the invoked force, into the symbol.[14]

Keep in mind, however, that although the Ritual of the Evocation of Metatron given at the end of this article is based upon the Z-2 instructions, it does not copy them obsequiously to the letter.

The Evocation of Metatron

It should go without saying that the Zelator Adeptus Minor should be skilled in the arts of Talisman Consecration, Invocation and Banishing, Spirit Vision work, and the Assumption of Godforms before attempting any work of Evocation.

Required Items: The following items will be needed for the Ritual of Evocation:

- ✦ Double Cubical Altar (draped white)
- ✦ Banners of East and West
- ✦ Black and White Pillars
- ✦ Enochian Tablets in the four quarters
- ✦ Tablet of Union
- ✦ Cross and Triangle
- ✦ Hierophant Regalia

---

13. *Ibid.*, vol. 3, pp. 93–94. The sacrifice referred to in this passage pertains to the Candidate, who must sacrifice lower and imbalanced aspects along his or her quest for the light.

14. *Ibid.*, vol. 4, p. 27.

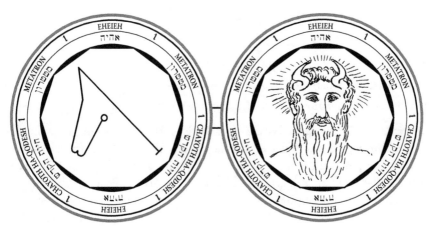

Fig. 1. Pentacle of Metatron

- ✦ Hierophant's Throne
- ✦ Four Elemental Tools of the Z.A.M.
- ✦ Magic Sword
- ✦ Lotus Wand
- ✦ Cup of Consecrated Water
- ✦ Censer with frankincense
- ✦ Charcoal and lighter
- ✦ Ten white Lamps or pillar candles (in glass)
- ✦ Five Flashing Tablets of the Pentagramaton (יהשוה)
- ✦ Masking tape or duct tape in the following colors: white, red, blue, yellow, gold, black
- ✦ 4" Hierophant's Lamen with sigil of Metatron on reverse side[15]
- ✦ Two 4" Pentacles identical in design but with different color schemes[16]

---

15. The Lamen to be worn is exactly the same as the Lamen of the Hierophant, but inscribed on the back with the sigil of Metatron, in the appropriate Briatic (Queen Scale) colors. Metatron is the Archangel of Kether, therefore the Briatic Color of Kether (white, ornamented in flashing black) will be used on the reverse side of the Lamen.

16. Two separate Flashing Pentacle disks, respectively known as the Yetziratic and Assiatic Pentacles, identical in design but different in color, are needed. The obverse side of both Pentacles should be inscribed with the same design as the reverse of the Lamen—with the sigil of Metatron within three concentric circles, between which are written the hierarchical names of the Ketheric powers. The reverse side of both Pentacles should be inscribed with a second symbol of Metatron devised by the magician. The Yetziratic Pentacle is to be painted in the Prince Scale color of Kether (brilliant white ornamented with black),

✦ White modeling clay mixed with gold glitter, formed into a 4" circle[17]

✦ Two white cloths, at least 10 inches square

✦ One black cloth, at least 10 inches square

✦ 36 inches of white ribbon or cord, cut into two sections

✦ 36 inches of black ribbon or cord, cut into two sections

The Pentacles: On the day before the evocation is to take place, the magician should take the Lamen, the two Pentacles, and the Material Basis, and bind them together with a white cord. (The Material Basis is on the bottom, with the Assiatic Pentacle above it. The Yetziratic Pentacle is placed above the Assiatic Pentacle, and the Lamen is placed on top of the whole.) These items should then be consecrated as talismans in accordance with the Z-2 formulæ of the Magic of Light.[18] After the consecration, the Lamen may be wrapped in white cloth and kept with the regalia of the Hierophant, to be worn during the evocation. The Pentacles and the Material Basis should be wrapped in white cloth.

The Floor Plan: The Banners of the floor plan are situated in such a way that, if standing upright, they would face each other. The larger Banner of the East on the floor is known as the Banner of Invocation, while the Banner of the West situated on the floor between the Pillars is known as the Banner of Evocation as well as the Triangle of Art. Using the colored tapes, mark off the ritual space as shown in the diagram. For the Banner of Invocation, use the following colors: field of the Banner—white; triangle pointing west—red; triangle pointing east—blue; Calvary Cross—yellow or gold; Tau Cross—white. For the Banner of Evocation use the following colors: field of the Banner—black; Triangle of Manifestation—white; Calvary Cross—red outlined with gold. The Altar is located on the shaft of the Tau Cross, and the Hierophant's Throne is situated on the crossbar of the Tau Cross. The Flashing Tablets of the Pentagrammaton should be placed at the five points of

---

while the Assiatic Pentacle is to be painted in the Princess Scale color of Kether (white flecked with gold, ornamented with black flecked with silver).

17. The clay serves as the Material Basis for the evocation. This could be a suitable gemstone, sculpture, or other artistic rendering appropriate to the nature of the spiritual entity evoked. For the Metatron evocation, use white modeling clay in the shape of a 4-inch circle, about 2 inches in thickness, sprinkled with gold glitter to represent Kether in the Princess Scale. (This should be placed upon a plate or plain wooden disk of similar size for support.)

18. Charging the Lamen, the Pentacles, and the Material Basis as talismans a day ahead of time will mean that it will not be necessary to treat these items as inert matter (or as a blindfolded Neophyte) subject to a series of barrings, purifications, and consecrations during the evocation, as these steps will have already have been performed in the preliminary Talisman Consecration ritual.

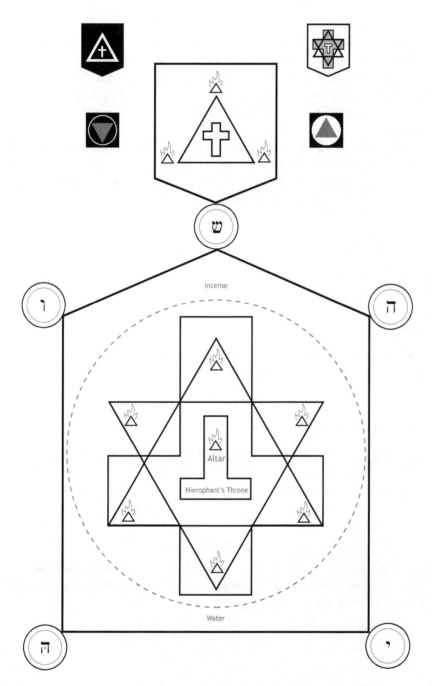

Fig. 2. Floor Plan for the Z-2 Evocation of Metatron

the Banner of Invocation. The ten white pillar candles are placed at the points of the three triangles with the tenth candle on the altar at the center of the Tau Cross.

The Elemental Tablets should be uncovered in their respective quarters around the Hall. Upon the Altar should be the Cross and Triangle (center), the Tablet of Union (above the cross and triangle), and the four Elemental Tools of the Z.A.M.[19]

The Censer of Incense should be in the east, and the Chalice of Water should be in the west.

Prior to the ritual, the magician should place the Material Basis in the center of the Calvary Cross of the Banner of Evocation Triangle. The Assiatic Pentacle should be imbedded into the clay so that it can be easily seen from the Circle of the Banner of Invocation. The Yetziratic Pentacle is placed on the central altar, west of the white triangle.

1. THE OPENING

After a period of relaxation and meditation, give five knocks and then proclaim:

Hekas! Hekas! Este Bebeloi!

Banishings

With the sword, perform the Lesser Banishing Ritual of the Pentagram. Perform the Lesser Banishing Ritual of the Hexagram.

Put the Sword aside.

Purification and Consecration

Take up the Chalice of Water. Starting in the east and moving clockwise, purify the Temple in all four quarters by tracing a Cross and the Invoking Water Triangle ▽. Say:

So therefore first the Priest who governeth the Works of Fire must sprinkle with the Lustral Waters of the Loud, Resounding Sea. Hear Thou the Voice of Water!

(Upon returning to east): **I purify with Water!**

Replace the cup. Take up the Incense. Starting in the east and moving clockwise, consecrate the Temple with Fire in all four quarters by tracing a cross and Invoking Fire Triangle △. Then say:

---

19. The four elements of the Mystic Repast may also be placed on the Altar, but they should not take the place of the Elemental tools of the Z.A.M.

And after all the Phantoms have been Banished, thou shalt see that Holy and Formless Fire, that Fire which darts and flashes through the Hidden Depths of the Universe. Hear thou the Voice of Fire!

(Upon returning to east:) I consecrate with Fire!

Replace the incense.

Preliminary Invocations

Take up the Lotus Wand. Go to the east and perform the Supreme Invoking Ritual of the Pentagram. As you do this, hold the white portion of the wand when performing the Qabalistic Cross. When invoking the elements, grasp the white band of the Lotus Wand when tracing the Spirit Pentagrams pointing with the wand-head. Grasp the Kerubic bands of the Lotus Wand when tracing the elemental Pentagrams with the wand-head:

- ✦ *Fire: the yellow band of Leo*
- ✦ *Water: the blue-green band of Scorpio*
- ✦ *Air: the violet band of Aquarius*
- ✦ *Earth: the red-orange band of Taurus*

Finish with the Qabalistic Cross, holding the white portion of the wand. Remain west of the Altar facing east. Make the Sign of the Rending of the Veil. Visualize the Veil opening as you step through it. Say the following Enochian oration:

OL SONUF VAORSA GI, GOHO IAD BALATA. ELEXARPEH. CO-MANANU. TABITOM. ZODACARE, CA, OD ZODAMERANU. ODO CICLE QAA PIAPE PIAMOEL OD VAOAN. (Oh-ell son-oof vay-oh-air-sah jee, go-ho ee-ah-dah bah-lah-tah. El-ex-ar-pay-hay. Co-mah-nah-noo. Tah-bee-toh-em. Zohd-ah-kah-ray, kah, oh-dah zohd-ah-mehr-ah-noo. Oh-doh kee-klay kah-ah pee-ah-pay pee- ah-moh-el oh-dah vay-oh-ah-noo.)

I invoke ye, ye Angels of the celestial spheres, whose dwelling is in the Invisible. Ye are the guardians of the gates of the Universe, be ye also the guardians of this mystic sphere. Keep far removed the evil and the unbalanced. Strengthen and inspire me so that I may preserve unsullied this abode of the Mysteries of the eternal Gods. Let my sphere be pure and holy so that I may enter in and become a partaker of the secrets of the Light Divine.

The Rise of Light and Invocations to the Highest

Go deosil (clockwise) to the northeast and say:

The visible Sun is the dispenser of Light to the Earth. Let me therefore form a vortex in this chamber that the Invisible Sun of the Spirit may shine therein from above.

Take the Lotus Wand by the white portion and circumambulate the temple three times deosil, saluting with the Neophyte Signs when passing the east. Then stand west of the altar facing east and perform the Adoration to the Lord of the Universe. Give the Projection Sign of a Neophyte (the Sign of Horus) while reciting the first three stanzas. Give the Sign of Silence (the Sign of Harpocrates) after the last verse:

Holy art Thou, Lord of the Universe! *(Projection Sign)* Holy art Thou, Whom Nature hath not formed! *(Projection Sign)* Holy art Thou, the Vast and the Mighty One! *(Projection Sign)* Lord of the Light and of the Darkness. *(Sign of Silence)*

Invoke the Highest as follows:

Unto Thee, sole wise, sole eternal, and sole merciful One, be the praise and the glory forever, Who hath permitted me, who now standeth humbly before Thee, to enter thus far into the sanctuary of Thy Mysteries. Not unto me, but unto Thy name be the glory. Let the influence of Thy Divine Ones descend upon my head, and teach me the value of self-sacrifice, so that I shrink not in the hour of trial, but that thus my name may be written on high, and my Genius may stand in the presence of the Holy Ones—in that hour when the Son of Man is invoked before the Lord of Spirits and His name in the presence of the Ancient of Days.

Pause. Then say:

In the name of the Lord of the Universe, who works in Silence and whom naught but Silence can express, I declare this Temple duly opened in the Magic of Light!

Knock ꜛꜛꜛꜛ – ꜛ.

2. THE WORK

Knock once and say the following:

In the Holy name of *EHEIEH*, may my own Higher Genius be under the authority of the Source Eternal and Divine and in command of this ceremony. I charge all ye Archangels, Angels, Rulers, Kings, and Elementals called to this place to witness and aid in this Rite. I call upon the Crown, *EHEIEH*, the One Source Most High, to look with favor upon me as I perform this ceremony of evocation. Grant me success in this, my working of the Magic of Light. My purpose in performing this ceremony is threefold.

(Knock) First, that I might form a more perfect link between my human soul and the Infinite Light Divine as represented in Kether.

(Knock) Second, that I may be strengthened in the High Arts of Angelic Communication, be it in my realm or in theirs,[20] and my knowledge thereby increase.

(Knock) Third, that I might establish true and ongoing communication with the mighty Archangel Metatron: that he guide me and teach me the true knowledge of Sacred things.

Thus may I glorify the Ineffable Name of the Holy One in my words and actions. So mote it be.

*Perform the Invoking Hexagram Ritual of Kether. Still grasping the wand by the white portion, perform the Qabalistic Cross west of the Altar. Then go clockwise to the east and draw an Invoking Hexagram of Kether and visualize it in a pure white light while intoning **ARARITA**.*

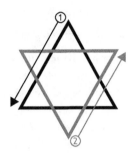

*In the center of the figure place the sigil of Saturn ♄ in brilliant white. Vibrate **EHEIEH**. Then draw the letter Aleph א in brilliant white and intone the name of the letter **ALEPH**. Trace the same figures and intone the same names in the south, west, and north respectively.*

*Fig. 3. **Invoking Hexagram of Kether***

Upon returning to the east, give the Analysis of the Keyword.

Then invoke the powers of Kether as follows:

The Heaven is above and the Earth is beneath. And betwixt the Light and Empyrean dwells the many-faced jewel of the Divine in diverse form, the many and the One! In the Divine name of the Highest, **EHEIEH ASHER EHEIEH**, "I Am That I Am," and by the majesty of the Holy titles **ARIKH ANPIN**, The Vast Countenance, **OR MUPHLA**, the Hidden Light, **ATIQ YOMIN**, the Ancient of Days, and **ATIQA QADISHA**, the Most Holy Ancient One! I supplicate the Powers and Forces governing the Nature, Place, and Authority of **KETHER**, to which is allotted the First Sephirah of the Crown on the Tree of Life, and the Chiefest Archangel **METATRON**, who ruleth over the choir of Angels known as the **CHAYOTH HA-QODESH**, the Holy Living Creatures, and the First House of Assiah known as **RESHITH HA-GALGALIM**, the Primum Mobile, the First Whirlings, to bestow this present day and hour and confirm their mystic and potent influence upon this rite of summoning.

---

20. A reference to evocation, which takes place in the physical realm of humanity, and to Spirit Vision, which takes place in the astral planes.

Supernal Brilliance which dwellest in the Hidden Light to which no man can approach, wherein is Unity and Holiness unimaginable. I beseech Thee, who art the Macrocosmic *YECHIDAH* and the Primal Glory! Thou who art revered as the Ancient of Ancients, Existence of the Existences, Concealed of the Concealed, and the Ancient of Days! Lux Occulta! Lux Æterna! Look upon me in this Ceremony which I perform to Thine Honor. Grant Thine aid unto the highest aspirations of my Soul, in Thy Divine Name *EHEIEH*, by which Thou dost reveal Thyself as the perfection of creation, and the Light of the World to come.

Assume the Sign of Osiris Slain and say:

In the Divine name *IAO*, I invoke Thee, O great Ketheric Angel *HU*,[21] that Thou mayest lay thy hands upon my head, to aid me in my Work. O messenger of the beloved One, let thy shadow be over me. Confirm and strengthen me, and keep me steadfast in the Path of the Light. Confer upon me the Power of discernment, that I may choose rightly between the evil and the good, and challenge all things of doubtful or fictitious seeming with sure knowledge and sound judgment.

Grant that I may successfully evoke the sublime Prince of Angels, the great archangel *METATRON* into the Material Basis provided for him within this sacred space. May all the Holy Powers of the Light Divine find this ceremony pleasing, and may they grant their aid to my Work.

Circumambulate the Temple thrice, giving the Neophyte Signs when passing east. Then stop west of the altar facing east, raise your hands toward the heavens and vibrate **HU** *three times, giving the Projection Sign after each vibration. At the end of this give the Sign of Silence.*

Assume the Sign of Osiris Risen and say:

I invoke Thee the great angel *HRU* who art set over the Operations of this Secret Wisdom. Strengthen and establish me in my search for the Mysteries of the Divine Light. Increase my spiritual perception and assist me to rise beyond that lower selfhood which is nothing unto the highest selfhood which is in God the Vast One.

Circumambulate the Temple thrice, giving the Neophyte Signs when passing east. Then stop west of the altar facing east, raise your hands toward the heavens and vibrate **HRU** *three times, giving the projection Sign after each vibration. At the end of this give the Sign of Silence.*

---

21. Hebrew הוא, transliterated HUA or HVA, pronounced *Hu.*

O God, the Vast One, Thou art in all things. O Nature, Thou Self from nothing, for what else can I call Thee. In myself, I am nothing, in Thee I am Self, and exist in Thy Selfhood from Nothing. Live Thou in me and bring me unto that Self which is in Thee, Amen.

Be my mind open unto the Higher. Be my heart a center of the Light. Be my body a Temple of the Rosy Cross!

Perform the Qabalistic Cross. Then maintain the Sign of Osiris Slain while contemplating the Divine Light of Kether and invoke your Higher Genius:

O thou great and blessed Augoeides, thou mighty and secret Soul that is my link with the infinite Spirit, I beseech thee in the name of *EHEIEH*, that thou manifest in me mine own Higher Self. Manifest thou unto me, I beseech thee, mine Angel, for my assistance in the Great Work so that I, even I, may go forward from that lower selfhood which is in me, unto that highest selfhood which is in God the Vast One. That thou mayest be able to manifest thyself unto me, in me, and by a material manifestation I do here offer unto thee the elements of Foundation. For the Light of my Genius is upon me, and I have made *EHEIEH* my hope. So help me, the Lord of the Universe and my Higher Soul.

Perform the Exercise of the Middle Pillar.

Assume an appropriate godform—either that of your own Higher Genius (if already skilled with the assumption of it), or the general form of a mighty angel in white. Stretch your arms toward the east and say:

I have passed through the Gates of the Firmament. Give me your hands, for I am made as ye, Ye Lords of Truth!

Assume the Sign of Osiris Risen. Say:

I am the First and I am the Last. I am He that liveth and was dead, and behold, I am alive for evermore, and hold the Keys of Hell and Death. I am the Purified. I have passed through the Gates of Darkness unto the Light. I know the first ones and those after them know me. But I am the Mind of Mind.

I am the knowledge of my inquiry; and the finding of those who seek after me; and the command of those who ask of me; and the power of the powers in my knowledge of the angels, who have been sent at my word; and of gods in their seasons by my counsel; and of spirits of every man who exists with me; and of women who dwell within me. I am the one who is honored, and who is praised. Give heed then, you hearers and you also, the angels and those who have been sent.

I am the substance and the one who has no substance. I am a mute who does not speak, and great is my multitude of words. I am the knowledge of my name. Hear me, you hearers and learn of my words, you who know me. I am the hearing that is attainable to everything; I am the speech that cannot be grasped. I am the name of the sound and the sound of the name.

I am the Sun in its rising, I have passed though the hour of cloud and night. I am *AMOUN*, the Concealed One, the Opener of the Day. I am *OSIRIS ONNOPHRIS*, the Justified One, Lord of Life triumphant over death. There is no part of me that is not of the gods. I am the Preparer of the Pathway, the Rescuer unto the Light. Out of the Darkness, let that Light arise.

Circumambulate the Temple thrice vibrating: **IAO! IAO IAO!** *Upon returning to the west, give the LVX Signs in silence. Then, still grasping the white band of the Lotus Wand, say:*

> Let the names and sigils of the powers of Kether be proclaimed, that they may be re-awakened in the Spheres of those present, and in the sphere of this Temple—for by Names and Images are all Powers awakened and re-awakened.

Fig. 4. Sigil of Eheieh

Trace the Invoking Hexagram of Kether toward the east, visualizing it in a pure white light while intoning **ARARITA**. *In the center of the figure place the sigil of Saturn* ♄ *in brilliant white. Vibrate* **EHEIEH**. *Then draw the letter Aleph* א *in brilliant white and intone the name of the letter. Then say:*

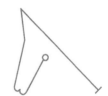

> **EHEIEH! EHEIEH! EHEIEH! EHEIEH!** *(Trace the sigil of Eheieh toward the east.)* The Vast and the Mighty One! Ruler of the Light and the Darkness! I adore Thee and I invoke Thee!
>
> **METATRON!** *(Trace the sigil of Metatron toward the east.)* Great Prince of Countenances! **METATRON KETHERIEL!** Blessed be Thy Name unto the countless ages.
>
> **CHAYOTH HA-QODESH!** *(Trace the sigil of the angelic host toward the east.)* Thou

Fig. 5. Sigil of Metatron

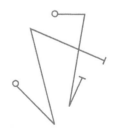

Fig. 6. Sigil of Chayoth ha-Qodesh

Most Holy Living Creatures who work to increase the Ketheric Light into the Yechidah of the magician!

State the following Invocation to Eheieh.

EHEIEH. EHEIEH. EHEIEH. EHEIEH. Thou who dwellest in the Boundless Light of Kether, in whom only is Being, who alone can say I Am, beginner of movement, bestower of the gift of life in all things, Thou who fillest the limitless universe with Thy essence, grant unto me the presence of the Prince of Countenances, the great Angel Metatron, He who bringeth others before the face of God. Let him lead me in my aspirations after that divine and only selfhood which is in Thee, that I may be enabled so to live that by the absolute control and purification of my natural body and soul, I having no other desire, may become a fit dwelling for my higher Genius For the desire of Thy house, O Adonai, hath eaten me up, and I desire to be dissolved and be with Thee. May my human nature, becoming as the perfect Malkuth, the resplendent intelligence, be thus exalted above every head and sit on the throne of Binah, and being clothed with the Sun, illuminate the darkness of my mortal body. Cause the Divine influx to descend from that great Archangel Metatron, to rend away the veils of darkness from my mortal vision, that I may know Thee, Adonai, the only true Self, and Yeheshuah Yehovashah, Thy perfect Messenger, the Guardian Angel in me, my only hope of attainment to the eternal Glory.

Circumambulate thrice while invoking:

All ye Gods, Archangels, angels, and spirits, draw nigh. Hear what the Spirit saith unto the Assemblies. Hail unto ye, Lords of the Land of Life, hear ye these my words for I am made as ye are, who are the formers of the soul. I invoke ye, Ye Powers and Forces of Kether, in the Most Holy name of *EHEIEH*, and *EHEIEH ASHER EHEIEH*, to lend your aid to the servant of *EL ELYON*, the Most High God in this evocation of the Mighty Archangel *METATRON* to visible appearance.

Return to the west, facing east and give the Sign of Osiris Slain while giving the following oath:

I (magical name) being a member of the Red Rose and the Cross of Gold, do this day spiritually bind myself with this Oath, that I prove myself to be a worthy Frater (Soror) in the Work of the Magic of Light! I promise and swear that this Work of Evocation is not undertaken for the purposes of mundane amusement, earthly pleasure, low material gain, or evil magic but rather as a joyful task in the Completion of the Great Work. I swear and affirm that I shall evoke the Archangel *METATRON* for the purpose of forming a more perfect link between human soul and the Infinite Light Divine as represented in Kether, strengthening my abilities in the High Arts of Angelic communication, and for establishing a true and ongoing communication with the mighty Archangel *METATRON*, that he guide me and teach me the true knowledge of Sacred things. I swear by the Firmament of Heaven. Let the Powers of the Empyrean bear witness to my pledge.

If needed, add incense to the censer in the east. Take up the Yetziratic Pentacle of Metatron in your left hand (holding in your right hand the white band of the Lotus Wand) and go to the east of the circle, facing the Banner of Evocation between the pillars. Vibrate the name and then address the Archangel with the following Invocation of Metatron.

METATRON! METATRON! METATRON! I call Thee, Great *META-TRON* who is charged by God with sustaining humankind. Thou who art first among the ten Archangels of the Briatic World! King and Princes among all Angels! Thee, Thee I invoke!

Thou who art identified with the Patriarch *ENOCH* and the God Hermes-Thoth! Thee, Thee I invoke!

Thou who art The Chancellor of Heaven and the Angel of the Covenant! Thee, Thee I invoke!

Thou who art reverently called the Lesser *YHVH*! Thee, Thee I invoke! Liberating Angel and Heavenly Scribe! Thee, Thee I invoke!

Of Thou it was written: "Behold, I send an angel before thee, to keep thee in the way." Thee, Thee I invoke!

Thou who with thy sister Kerub Sandalphon protecteth the Mercy Seat of the Shekinah under the shadow of Thy Wings. Thee, Thee I invoke!

Thou who art called the *SAR HA-PANIM*, the Holy Prince of the Divine Presence, sustain and grace this Temple with your Presence.

In the Name of *EHEIEH*, I invoke Thee!
In the Name of *YHVH*, I invoke Thee!
In the Name of *ELOHIM*, I invoke Thee!
In the Name of *ADONAI*, I invoke Thee!
In the Name of *YESHESHUAH* the Reconciler, I invoke Thee! *META-TRON KETHERIEL*!

METATRON SAR HA-PANIM! Holy Prince of the Divine Presence, sustain and grace this Temple with your Presence.

Trace a circle, imaged in brilliant white towards the east between the Pillars.

I call Thee in and by the name of *ARARITA*, for One is his beginning, One is his Individuality, his Permutation is One!

Trace the Hexagram of Kether in brilliant white.

I call Thee in and by the Most Holy Name that crowns the Tree of Life, *EHEIEH*, "I AM."

Trace the sigil of Saturn in brilliant white.

I call Thee in and by your own mighty Name of *METATRON*, and I beseech Thee to descend from Thine abode in the Briatic realm, and from Thine abode in the Yetziratic Realm as leader of the *CHAYOTH HA-QODESH*!

Trace the sigil of the Archangel in brilliant white.

At this point, visualize the area between the Pillars (the Threshold) darkly swirling with mist and cloud. Focus your will on the Purpose of the evocation. Silently charge your Middle Pillar centers again with Divine Light.

Place the Lotus Wand aside and hold the Yetziratic Pentacle with both hands.

I call upon Thee, O *METATRON*, by virtue of this consecrated Pentacle and by virtue of this Thy sigil.

Using the Pentacle, trace the sigil of the Archangel toward the East. The mist may lighten as you do so.

And by virtue of Thine own true Name which I vibrate through the Threshold in the Briatic and Yetziratic Realms. I call unto Thee and beseech Thee, O *METATRON*, Come forth and appear!

METATRON! (Projection Sign.) METATRON! (Projection Sign.) META-TRON! (Projection Sign.)

Sign of Silence. Assume the Sign of Osiris Risen.

O Lord of the Universe, thou art in all things, and thy name is in all things. Before thee the shadows of the Night roll back and the darkness hasteth away.

Through the Threshold between the pillars, a landscape should now be clearly seen. It may appear as an expanse of the heavens drenched with light with no hint of shadow, or as a tall, shining cathedral, or as an endless fractal pattern. As all adepts are taught, test the vision with Hebrew Double letters. Once you are sure that the vision is true, go to the west of the altar and wrap the Yetziratic Pentacle in black cloth and bind it thrice with a white cord. Place the Pentacle on the white Triangle on top of the central altar. Say:

O Thou Archangel *METATRON*, in the Divine Name of *EHEIEH ASHER EHEIEH*, I wrap Thine Yetziratic Pentacle in the Darkness and bind it with bonds of pure Light. Dwelling within this Pentacle, Thine eyes are blind but to the Threshold in the East, and Thine ears are deaf but to my Call; Thy tongue is silent but to answer this Evocation, Thy feet are motionless but to carry Thee to the Triangle of Art prepared to receive Thee with a pleasing Material Basis. Therefore, in and by all the Names of all the Holy Powers already invoked, I evoke Thee, Thou Mighty Archangel *METATRON*, to grace this Temple with Thy Presence. Manifest in a visible form within the Triangle of Art Threshold the Threshold upon the Banner of Evocation without this Magic Circle! *EHEIEH! EHEIEH! EHEIEH! EHEIEH ASHER EHEIEH!*

From Thine hands, O Lord, cometh all good. From Thine hands flow down all grace and blessing. The characters of Nature with Thy finger Thou hast traced, but none can read them unless he hath been in thy school. Therefore, even as servants look unto the hands of their masters and handmaidens unto their mistresses, even so do our eyes look up unto Thee, for Thou alone art our help, O Lord of the Universe. All is from Thee, all belongeth unto Thee. Either Thy love or Thine Anger all must again re-enter. Nothing canst thou lose, for all must tend to Thine honor and majesty. Thou art Lord alone, and there is none beside Thee. Thou doest what Thou wilt with Thy Mighty Arm and none can escape from Thee. Thou alone helpest in their necessity the humble and meek-hearted and poor who submit themselves unto Thee; and whosoever humbleth himself in dust and ashes before Thee, unto such a one art Thou propitious. Who should not praise Thee, O Lord of the Universe, unto whom there is none like, whose dwelling is in the Heavens and in every virtuous and god-fearing heart.

O God, the Vast One, Thou art in all things. O Nature, Thou Self from nothing, for what else can I call Thee. In myself, I am nothing, in Thee I am Self, and exist in Thy Selfhood from Nothing. Live Thou in me and bring me unto that Self which is in Thee, Amen.

Circumambulate thrice while saying:

In the Most Holy Name of *EHEIEH*, I invoke and beseech Thee to look with favor upon this ceremony. *EL ELYON*, the Most High, grant me success in this. In the Name of the Holy Tetragrammaton *YHVH*, the Name of Manifestation, and in the Name of the Holy Pentagrammaton, *YEHESH-UAH*, the Name of Manifested Spirit, grant that with the Divine aid, I will truly evoke Thine Archangel *METATRON* to visible manifestation.

Perform the Qabalistic Cross. Take up the Sword and strike the Pentacle once with the flat of the blade. Speak toward the Threshold:

The great Angel Metatron spake and said. I am the Angel of the Presence Divine. The wise gaze upon the created world and behold therein the dazzling image of the Creator. O Thou sublime and mighty Archangel

METATRON, I evoke Thee in the Divine Name *EHEIEH*, "I AM." Move, appear, and manifest in the Triangle that awaits Thee!

At this point Metatron may begin to manifest within the Threshold, but the magician should continue until the Archangel passes through the Threshold and manifests physically in the Material Basis on the Triangle of Art. Vibrate:

METATRON! METATRON! METATRON!

Circumambulate once around the circle while saying:

O *METATRON*! I evoke Thee in and by the most Sacred Name of *EHEI-EH*! Move, appear, and show Thyself!

Stand west of the altar, strike the Pentacle for the second time with the sword and speak toward the Threshold.

O *METATRON*! I evoke Thee in and by the exalted Name *EHEIEH ASHER EHEIEH*, "I AM THAT I AM," the Existence of Existences Move, appear, and manifest in the Triangle that awaits Thee!

Vibrate:

METATRON! METATRON! METATRON!

Circumambulate once around the circle while saying:

O *METATRON*! I evoke Thee in and by the Most Exalted Title of *ARIKH AN-PIN*, the Vast Countenance. Move, appear, and show Thyself!

Stand west of the altar, strike the Pentacle for the third time with the sword and speak toward the Threshold.

O *METATRON*! I evoke Thee in and by the exalted Name *EHEIEH ASHER EHEIEH*, "I AM THAT I AM," the Existence of Existences Move, appear, and manifest in the Triangle that awaits Thee!

Vibrate:

METATRON! METATRON! METATRON!

Circumambulate once around the circle while saying:

O *METATRON*! I evoke Thee in and by the Most Exalted Title of *OR MUPHLA*, the Hidden Light. Move, appear, and show Thyself!

Stand west of the altar, strike the Pentacle for the fourth time with the sword and speak toward the Threshold.

O *METATRON*! I evoke Thee in and by the name of the Most Holy Ancient One, *ATIQA QADISHA*.

Carry the wrapped Yetziratic Pentacle clockwise to the four quarters in this order: west, south, north, east, where it is successively barred, purified and consecrated as if it were the blindfolded Candidate in the Hall of the Neophytes. The Archangel should become visible through the Threshold at his point (and possibly at an earlier point).

Replace the Pentacle on the white triangle of the central altar and remove the black cloth, saying:

> Too long hast Thou dwelt in the Darkness—Quit the Night and Seek the Day.

Physical manifestation may well begin to occur at this point. Take up the Lotus Wand by the white band.

> O *METATRON*, Thou mighty Archangel, I call Thee! I summon Thee! Come forth from Thy Briatic abode. Come forth and assume physical form! A Material Basis has been prepared and consecrated for Thee in the Triangle of Art without this Magic Circle. I evoke Thee unto visible appearance in the Triangle that has been prepared for Thee. I evoke Thee in and by all the Blessed Ketheric Names of Power already proclaimed!
>
> In the name of the Lord of the Universe, and by the power of my Augoeides, and by the aspiration of my own Higher Soul, and by the white brilliance of the Genius within me, O *METATRON* I evoke Thee. For the Crown of my Father is upon me, and in *YHVH* is my trust. Move, appear, and manifest in the Triangle that awaits Thee!

Employing the focus of will and the energies built up within the circle, give the Projection Sign at the Material Basis and the Assiatic Pentacle in the Triangle of Evocation, then make the Sign of Silence. Say:

> O *METATRON*! I evoke Thee in and by the most Sacred Name of *EHEI-EH*!

Give the Projection Sign, then the Sign of Silence.

> O *METATRON*! I evoke Thee in and by the exalted Name *EHEIEH ASHER EHEIEH*!

Give the Projection Sign, then the Sign of Silence.

> O *METATRON*! I evoke Thee in and by the name of the Vast Countenance, *ARIKH ANPIN*!

Give the Projection Sign, then the Sign of Silence.

> O *METATRON*! I evoke Thee in and by the name of the Hidden Light, *OR MUPHLA*!

Give the Projection Sign, then the Sign of Silence.

O *METATRON*! I evoke Thee in and by the name of the Most High God, *EL ELYON*!

Give the Projection Sign, then the Sign of Silence.

O *METATRON*! I evoke Thee in and by the name of the *ATIQA QADI-SHA*, Most Holy Ancient One Move, appear, and manifest in the Triangle that awaits Thee!

(To a clairvoyant, the area of the Triangle of Evocation should be pulsing with Light.)

O *METATRON*! I evoke Thee in and by the virtue of this Pentacle conse-crated in Thy Name in accordance with the Hermetic Art. And I evoke Thee with the knowledge of Thine own true Name whose number is 964. Come forth and appear!

Strike the Pentacle with the sword blade.

METATRON! (Projection Sign.) METATRON! (Projection Sign.) META-TRON! (Projection Sign. Sign of Silence.)

In and by the name of *EHEIEH*! In the name of *YHVH*!

Give the Projection Sign, then the Sign of Silence.

In and by the name of *ADONAI*! In the name of *ELOHIM*!

Give the Projection Sign, then the Sign of Silence.

In and by the name of the Reconciler YEHESHUAH! In the name of YE-HOVASHAH!

Give the Projection Sign, then the Sign of Silence.

In the Name of *METATRON KETHERIEL* and of *METATRON SAR HA-PANIM.*

Give the Projection Sign, then the Sign of Silence.

ZODACARE OD ZODAMERANU! ZODAMERANU![22]

Give the Projection Sign, then the Sign of Silence.

(If at this point the Archangel has still not appeared, repeat the Invocation of Eheieh and the Invocation of Metatron up to three times if necessary. Once the Archangel has fully manifested, test him with the Double Hebrew Letters assigned to the planets[23]

---

22. Enochian for "Move therefore and show yourself! Show yourself!"

23. The Hebrew letters of the seven planets can be used as important test symbols:
   ✦ If you suspect that some image from your memory is influencing your vision, trace the symbol of the Letter Tav ת in white Light. (Tav is the Letter of Saturn, the Planet which governs memory.)
   ✦ If you think that you have constructed the scene in your imagination, rather than receiving a true astral

and with the LVX Signs. If it is Metatron, he will return the LVX Signs. If it is not Metatron, the entity will flee, vanish, or change forms. In this event, banish and start over.)

After Metatron returns the LVX Signs, greet him as follows:

In the Grand Word *YESHESHUAH*, by the Keyword INRI, and through the concealed Word LVX, I greet Thee and salute Thee, O *METATRON*; as a Companion in the Order as well as a Brother in the Great Chain of Being; and in and by those same words of Power I required Thee to bind Thyself by this Oath:[24]

"I, Metatron, the Archangel, in the Presence of the Lord of the Universe Who Works in Silence and Whom naught but Silence can express, do solemnly promise to cause no harm to (magician's motto) nor any other human being, nor to this Temple of the Magic of Light. I undertake to answer all questions put to Me truthfully. I pledge to do everything in my power to aid the Magician that the virtues of Kether may be enhanced within him (her), that he (she) be better enabled to carry out the Great Work. I vow to form a more perfect link between the Magician's human soul and the Infinite Light Divine as represented in Kether.

"I vow to strengthen the Magician in the High Arts of Angelic Communication, and increase his (her) knowledge thereby.

"I promise to establish true and ongoing communication between the Magician from this day forward; and I will guide and teach him (her) the true knowledge of Sacred things. I shall always come promptly to his (her) call when summoned. I swear to uphold all these things without evasion, reservation, or equivocation. Such are the words of this, my Oath, whereunto I pledge myself in the Presence of the Most Ancient *EHEIEH*, and the Most High *YHVH*; in the Presence of the Mighty *ELOHIM* and the Lord *ADONAI*. So Mote it Be!"

Answer:

So Mote it Be!

---

image, trace the letter Kaph כ. (Kaph is Letter of Jupiter, the Planet of construction.)

✢ To vanquish feelings of revenge or hatred, use Peh פ, the letter of Mars.

✢ To rid yourself of delusions of arrogance and inflated ego, use Resh ר, the letter of the Sun.

✢ If your vision lapses into a fantasy or intellectual vanity, use Daleth ד, the letter of Venus.

✢ If you suspect that what you are looking at is a deception, use Beth ב, the letter of Mercury.

✢ For wandering thoughts, use Gimel ג, the letter of the Moon.

24. The magician should never converse with any evoked entity prior to having the entity promise to the uphold the Oath prepared for him ahead of time.

At this point, conversation with the Archangel may commence and continue for as long as necessary. When the conversation is finished, address Metatron as follows:

> O Thou true and faithful Archangel *METATRON*, Thou hast fulfilled the charge set before Thee. I thank Thee for thy Presence in this Temple, and I pray that Thou mayest be nourished and elevated by that ray of the Divine Light which Thou hast borne as Holy Messenger to me this day.

Grasping the white band of the Lotus Wand, trace a Cross in front of Metatron and draw a ray of White Brilliance down on the Archangel in the Triangle. After letting the Archangel bathe in this Sacred Light for a brief period, give him license to Depart.

> O *METATRON*, I bid Thee to depart in Peace unto Thine Adobe, and may the Blessings of *EHEIEH ASHER EHEIEH* be upon Thee. Let there always be peace between us, and be Thou ready to come when I call upon Thee.

Trace the Banishing Hexagram of Kether in pure white toward the East and visualize it in a pure white light while intoning **ARARITA**, **EHEIEH**, *and* **ALEPH**. *Trace the sigil of Metatron in the center of the figure while vibrating* **METATRON**.

After the Archangel departs completely, return to west of the Altar, knock once and say:

> So mote it Be!

Purify and consecrate the temple with Water and Fire as in the beginning of the ritual.

Perform the Reverse Circumambulation three times widdershins. Feel the energy that you have carefully built up throughout the ceremony begin to dissipate.

Give the Adoration to the Lord of the Universe:

> Holy art Thou, Lord of the Universe! *(Projection Sign)* Holy art Thou, Whom Nature hath not formed! *(Projection Sign)* Holy art Thou, the Vast and the Mighty One! *(Projection Sign)* Lord of the Light and of the Darkness. *(Sign of Silence)*

Pause. Then say:

> I now release any Spirits that may have been imprisoned by this ceremony. Depart in peace to your abodes and habitations. Go with the sanction of *EHEIEH* and the blessings of *YEHESHUAH YEHOVASHAH*.

Perform the Supreme Banishing Ritual of the Pentagram. Hold the white band of the wand when giving the Qabalistic Cross and the Archangelic names. Trace the Banishing Pentagrams while grasping the appropriate colored bands (as in the Supreme Invoking Ritual of the Pentagram at the beginning of the ceremony.) Be sure to point with the black end of the wand for banishing.

Perform the Lesser Banishing Ritual of the Hexagram. Perform the Lesser Banishing Ritual of the Pentagram.

Then say:

Unto Thee, sole wise, sole eternal, and sole merciful One, be the praise and the glory forever, Who hath permitted me, who now standeth humbly before Thee, to enter thus far into the sanctuary of Thy mysteries. Not unto my name, O Adonai, but to Thine be ascribed the Kingdom, the Power, and the Glory, now and forevermore! Amen!

Perform the Qabalistic Cross.

Knock five times as in the beginning. Then say:

I now declare this temple duly closed. So mote it be!

References

E Cinere Phœnix, V.H. Frater. "Evocation of the Angel Chassan to Visible Appearance," in Israel Regardie. *The Complete Golden Dawn System of Magic.* Phoenix, AZ: Falcon Press, 1984.

Fortune, Dion. *Aspects of Occultism.* London: Aquarian Press, 1962.

Greer, John Michael. *Circles of Power: Ritual Magic in the Western Tradition.* St. Paul, MN: Llewellyn Publications, 1997.

Kieckhefer, Richard. *Magic in the Middle Ages.* Cambridge: Cambridge University Press, 2000.

Regardie, Israel. *The Golden Dawn: An Account of the Teachings, Rites, and Ceremonies of the Order of the Golden Dawn.* Rev. and enl. [4th ed.]. St. Paul, Minn.: Llewellyn Publications, 1971.

Robinson, James M. *The Nag Hammadi Library.* San Francisco: Harper & Row, 1977.

['Solomon,' S.L. MacGregor Mathers, and] Aleister Crowley. *The Book of the Goetia of Solomon the King: Translated into the English Tongue by a Dead Hand and Adorned with Divers Other Matters Germane, Delightful to the Wise: the Whole Edited, Verified, Introd. and Commented by A. Crowley.* Boleskine, Foyers, Inverness: Society for the Propagation of Religious Truth, 1904.

YSHY, Frater. *Adept Magic in the Golden Dawn Tradition.* Dublin: Kerubim Press, 2014.

✛

The Prayer for Success

JAKE STRATTON-KENT

Jake Stratton-Kent has been a practicing goetic magician for more than 40 years. He is the author of several books, including The Serpent Tongue: Liber 187 *(Hadean Press, 2011);* Goetic Liturgy *(Hadean Press, 2015); and his* Encyclopædia Goetica *in three volumes:* The True Grimoire *(Scarlet Imprint, 2010),* Geosophia: The Argo of Magic *(Scarlet Imprint, 2010), and* The Testament of Cyprian the Mage *(Scarlet Imprint, 2014). He has also contributed to anthologies, including* Diabolical *(Scarlet Imprint, 2009), and has been an editor and contributor for* Conjure Codex I *(Hadean Press, 2011) and* II *(Hadean Press, 2013).*

The Prayer for Success

...invocation which you recite towards Phre[1] in the morning three times or seven times. Formula: 'Iotabao, Sokh-ommoa, Okh-okh-Khan, Bouzanau, Aniesi, Ekomphtho, Ketho, Sethori, Thmilaalouapokhri may everything succeed that I shall do to-day,' and they will succeed.

—*Papyrus Demotica Magica* xiv *(The London–Leiden Magical Papyrus)*[2]

HE SUBJECT OF THIS ESSAY is a particular practice, characterised by examples in the magical papyri as well as the grimoires. The practice involves prayers at set times related to the solar cycle, often with several repetitions. A simplified form of the same practice appears in fairly late Solomonic rites as daily prayers specific to the planets. The earlier forms took the same form each day, relating specifically to the solar cycle rather than correspondences for the day.

The instructions and the prayer itself are fairly brief, and easily overlooked. In reality they are foundational practices in these traditions. As such, I have referred to them in passing myself numerous times, as well as being similarly guilty of taking them for granted. Some readers may be familiar with them, and I hope this article is useful to them. Others may not, and for them, too, it may provide some useful insight.

First, then, I introduce the key example in Solomonic works, including the *True Grimoire*. In the second book of the *Key of Solomon*, as given in the Mathers version, chapter II is entitled "In What Manner the Master of the Art Should Keep, Rule, and Govern Himself." This, clearly, is a guide to the regular conduct of the

---

1. *Phre*: Late Egyptian (Demotic and Coptic) for *Ra* or *Rē*. *Ph-* or *p-* is the masculine article "the"; so in Coptic Ⲫⲣⲏ *(ph-Rē)* or ⲠⲣⲎ *(p-Rē)* is the Name of both the God and the celestial luminary ⲣⲎ *(Rē,* "Sun") as "**the** Sun." —APF

2. *Papyrus Demotica Magica* xiv.512–515, translated in F. Ll. Griffith and Herbert Thompson, *The Demotic Magical Papyrus of London and Leiden* (London: H. Grevel & Co.), p.117. Alternative translations by Janet H. Johnson for this and the other excerpts from *PDM* xiv may be found in Hans Dieter Betz, *The Greek Magical Papyri in Translation, Including the Demotic Spells. Volume One: Texts* (Chicago, Ill.: University of Chicago Press, 1986), pp. 195 ff. —APF

magician, regardless of whether they have an operation in hand. The chapter gives various instructions, including preparations for the purifying bath and other forms of mental and physical purification. Rather than being appropriate to a specific operation, these matters are fundamental to works of Solomonic magic in general, as the chapter title suggests. In the Mathers version, the instructions conclude thus:

> Hereafter, for three days at least, thou shalt abstain from all idle, vain, and impure reasonings, and from every kind of impurity and sin, as will be shown in the Chapter of fast and of vigil.[3]

It is important in this respect that the Egyptian ritual heading this article bears the postscript: "If it be that you do not apply purity to it, it does not succeed; its chief matter is purity."[4] This is one of many indications that we are dealing with the same tradition, expressed via differing theologies. Resuming with its Solomonic relative:

> Each day shalt thou recite the following prayer, at least once in the morning, twice about noon, thrice in the afternoon, four times in the evening, and five times before lying down to sleep; this shalt thou do on the three ensuing days:—

> THE PRAYER.

> HERACHIO [*sic*], ASAC, ASACRO, BEDRIMULAEL, TILATH, ARABONAS, IERAHLEM, IDEODOC, ARCHARZEL, ZOPHIEL, BLAUTEL, BARACATA, EDONIEL, ELOHIM, EMAGRO, ABRAGATEH, SAMOEL, GEBURAHEL, CA-DATO, ERA, ELOHI, ACHSAH, EBMISHA, IMACHEDEL, DANIEL, DAMA, ELAMOS, IZACHEL, BAEL, SEGON, GEMON, DEMAS.

> O Lord God, Who art seated upon the Heavens, and Who regardest the Abysses beneath, grant unto me Thy Grace I beseech Thee, so that what I conceive in my mind I may accomplish in my work, through Thee, O God, the Sovereign Ruler of all, Who livest and reignest unto the Ages of the Ages. Amen.

> These three days having passed, thou must have all things in readiness, as hath been said, and after this a day appointed and set apart. It will be necessary for thee to wait for the hour in which thou shouldst commence the Operation; but when once it shall be commenced at this hour, thou shalt be able to continue it unto the end, seeing that it deriveth its force and virtue from its beginning, which extendeth to and spreadeth over the succeeding hours, so that the Master of the Art will be enabled to complete his work so as to arrive at the desired result.[5]

Clearly, in the original conception, active Solomonic magicians—employing any of the materials from such a grimoire—will be using this prayer on a regular basis.

---

3. 'Solomon' and S. Liddell MacGregor Mathers, *The Key of Solomon the King: Clavicula Salomonis* (London: George Redway, 1889), Book Two, Ch. II.

4. *PDM* xiv.515, Griffith and Thompson, *loc. cit.* —APF

5. Solomon and Mathers, *loc. cit.*

Indeed, if magic is truly their 'lifestyle' or vocation, making it part of their regular devotions would be a practical expedient. This has been the basis for my frequent recommendations of this prayer on various occasions. The manner of performing it may vary depending on context and circumstances. Some examples will arise in the course of this discussion.

This prayer appears—with various spellings, number of names, and other departures from the above—in a great many manuscripts of the *Key*. Also, usually much abbreviated, in such works as the *Grimorium Verum*, &c. These texts include the *Book of Saint Cyprian*, where the form is much adapted but still very recognisable. This important example will be considered again later on.

Meanwhile, a more complete and accurate form of names, drawing from various manuscripts of the *Key*, is given here:

> ASTRACHIOS, ASAC, ASACRA BEDRIMULAEL, SILAT, ARABONAS, IERAHLEM, IDEODOC, ARCHARZEL, ZOPHIEL, BLAUTEL, BARACATA, ADONAI, ELOHIM, EMAGRO, ABRAGATEH, SAMOEL, GEBURAHEL, CA-DATO, ERA, ELOHI, ACHSAH, EBMISHA, IMACHADEL, DANIEL, DAMA, ELAMOS, IZACHEL, BAEL. SCIRLIN; GENIUM DOMOS![6]

Such prayers have their prototype in the papyri, where, as in the Solomonic grimoires, they are performed at the solar stations.[7] Those of the papyri are essentially prayers for success—success, that is, in whatever magical operations follow. They are performed at sunrise and other points of the sun's cycle through the sky.

In the Christian period, these times form part of the prayer cycle observed by monks and rung on church bells. There are Islamic equivalents also, in the calls to prayer during the day. Originally they likely derive from cults with a solar theology, both Egyptian and Middle Eastern. The sun god is invoked in the roles of witness and fortuitous power. From these origins, they became part of the great synthesis of Western magic.

In this context, I have recommended the solar prayers of *Liber Resh vel Helios*[8] as adjuncts to this practice. This recommendation concerns more than the solar timing elements coinciding with one another. This is one of many ways in which specific parts of the Thelemic 'liturgy' can complement certain approaches to the grimoires and papyri. To elaborate, the quotation from the London–Leiden Magical Papyrus commencing this article is paralleled and enlarged upon by another in the same collection:

---

6. My restoration, also employed in *The True Grimoire*, p. 105.

7. For instance, *PDM* xiv.475–480, 486.

8. Alesiter Crowley, *Liber Resh vel Helios sub figurā CC*, in *The Equinox*, vol. 1, no. 6, September 1911 (London: Weiland & Co.). —APF

You rise in the morning from your bed early in the day on which you will do it, or any day, in order that every thing which you will do shall prosper in your hand, you being pure from every abomination. You pronounce this invocation before Phre three times or seven times. 'Io, Tabao, Sokhom-moa, Okh-okh-khan-bouzanau, An-iesi, Ekomphtho, Ketho, Sethouri, Thmila, Alouapokhri, let everything that I shall apply my hand to here to-day, let it happen.'[9]

The use of solar timing is frequent in the Demotic papyri, in some cases advocating dawn for rituals of various kinds, other times specifying the solar adorations—or prayers to Phre, that is, Ra—be performed first. In the former case, the usual prayers may well be simply taken for granted.

In any case it is more than obvious that the Thelemic liturgy contains elements proper to such processes, and their 'Crowleyan' context need not concern the operator. We are simply following the advice of the papyri, to "recite the spells of praising Ra at dawn in his rising." It should be obvious that the Dawn adoration from *Liber Resh vel Helios* fits this prescription:

Hail unto Thee who art Ra in Thy rising, even unto Thee who art Ra in Thy strength...

So, judiciously applied, these and other Thelemic rites may legitimately substitute for some liturgical elements of antiquity and of the grimoires; and also facilitate the incorporation of some of them into our repertoire. The particular parts of Thelemic liturgy which I mean emphasise the Egyptian rather than the Masonic components, and can thus dovetail with elements drawn from the papyri.

The Later Solomonic Form

In the course of preparing this essay, I had the opportunity to personally examine the Hunter Manuscript.[10] This is a member of the Rabbi Solomon Text-Group [RS] in the typology proposed by Mathiesen,[11] now known from other texts recent-

---

9. *PDM* xiv.476–480., Griffith and Thompson, *op. cit.*, pp. 111–113.

10. The Hunter MS is in a private collection, dates from around the beginning of the 19th century, and was at one time in the possession of Idries Shah, author of *The Secret Lore of Magic: Books of the Sorcerers* (London: Frederic Muller, 1957). It bears the very typical title *The Keys of Rabbi Solomon. Translated accurately from the Hebrew into English by Edward Hunter. The whole embellished by a vast number of mysterious Figures, Talismans, Pentacles.* —APF

11. Robert Mathiesen, "The Key of Solomon: Toward a Typology of the Manuscripts," in *Societas Magica Newsletter*, Issue 17 (Spring 2007). —APF

ly published by Peterson (the Sibley *Clavis*[12]) and by Skinner and Rankine (the Morissoneau *Clavicules de R. Salomon*[13]). Therein I chanced upon the ninth chapter:

> [The magician] ought not to be satisfied with the reciting of the oraisons during the time of particular operations, but they must exactly tell [*i.e.*, recite] every day whether they work or not the operations that has been the plan of all those who have advantageous success in the art; upon which you must observe, that these oraisons must be recited, with the face turned towards the east, and with great attention. You will find them [given herein] in the days of the week.

Regardless of the introduction of planetary considerations, the intent and purpose here are sufficiently close to those of the Prayer for Success type to bear closer comparison. As I proceeded upon that task—examining the prayers, invocations and conjurations of the days—I came across numerous names close or identical to those in the Prayer for Success. As I proceeded updating the following account, I examined both *The Clavis or Key to the Magic of Solomon* and *The Veritable Key of Solomon* more closely. In the *Clavis*, the editor has noted the same correspondence, and as a scholar of note, attributed the historical influence the same way I am inclined. That is, the Prayer for Success precedes and is the source of the names in the planetary rites, showing their relation to be more than merely of type.

The Personalisation of Godnames

Returning to the appearance of the Solomonic prayer in the *Book of Saint Cyprian*, there it appears as follows:

> Once one has dealt with the vestments, say:
> "In this solemn hour I invoke with my whole will and desire those excellent spirits who accompany me in my works: Astroschio, Asath, Bedrimubal, Felut, Anabatos, Sergem, Gemen, Domos, and Arbatel, so that you are propitious to me, illuminate me in all that my human intelligence cannot

---

12. *The Clavis or Key To Unlock the Mysteries of Magic of Solomon. Translated from the Hebrew into French and from French rendered into English with additions by Ebenezer Sibley M.D.* . . . *The whole enriched with Coloured Figures, Talismans, Pentacles, Circles, Characters, &c.* in the Weiser private collection, published in Ebenezer Sibley, Frederick Hockley, and Joseph H. Peterson, *The Clavis or Key to the Magic of Solomon* (Lake Worth, FL: Ibis Press, 2009). —APF

13. Wellcome MS 4670, *Les Clavicules de R. Salomon. Traduites exactement du texte Hebreu en Francais par Mr Pierre Morissoneau, Professeur des Langues Orientales, et Sectateur des Sages Cabalistes. Le tout enrichi d'un grand nombre de Figures mysterieuses, de Talismans, Pentacules, Cercles, Canderies et Caracteres* ("*The Clavicles of R. Solomon. Translated accurately from the Hebrew text into French by Mr Pierre Morissoneau, Professor of Oriental Languages, and Disciple of the Cabbalistic Sages. The whole enriched by a great number of mysterious Figures, of Talismans, Pentacles, Circles, Canderies, and Characters*"), translated by Paul Harry Barron in Stephen Skinner & David Rankine, *The Veritable Key of Solomon* (Singapore: Golden Hoard Press, 2010). —APF

apprehend clearly, repair defects so that there is in attention the good desire and will in my works. So be it.”[14]

Aside from Arbatel, whom our author has added to a traditional series, the spirits invoked here are identical with those of the *True Grimoire* prayer in one of its shorter forms. What is remarkable in Cyprian's text is the way Solomonic 'names of power' are so clearly identified as persons, rather than simply a battery of potent words. There is no doubt about the authenticity of this; but in the grimoires it is more often implied than overt, to the point where modern eyes do not notice it. The spirits invoked in the Prayer for Success are personalities, guards, and friends, a fact Cyprian refers to more than once. As this prayer has considerable bearing on work with the *True Grimoire*, and on Solomonic magic generally, an important question arises: who are they? This is an act of conjuration, repeated on a regular basis. Just who is it invoking?

In order to go about answering this, a series of introductions is required. Most forms of this incantation in the *Key* and elsewhere are shortened and corrupt; referring to the restored form from my *True Grimoire*, given above, an outline of considerable interest emerges, which will hopefully spur further research. Some of the names require fairly detailed treatment, hence a few subheadings in this section. Enough is clear from this outline to show the magician's 'helpers' to be an extremely interesting and revealing group.

The Spirit Names—Astrachios to Adonai

Astrachios: Possibly related to *Esther* (or *Ishtar*) plus *chiah* (“life”). It is reasonable to assume that the first name is important, and this beginning remains consistent despite some garbling; Mathers' form, *Herachio*, is inscrutable, having no basis in the manuscripts. Astrachios is also one of Cyprian's superiors, the sixth. “Life of Astarte” would be a reasonable 'interpretation.'

Asac: precedes *Asacra*, the duplication has resonance.

Asacra Bedrimulael: Perhaps “and sacred (holy) Bedrimulael.” This appears to be an angelic or archangelic name, but not a familiar one. The staccato repetition of *Asac Asacra* is probably intentional. Groups of names form naturally with regular recitation, and there are traces of rhythm and metre.

Silat is the name of a female demon, according to Davidson,[15] hence my selection here. The form is not consistent in the variant texts. The name *Bilet* or *Bileth*

---

14. My translation, in Jake Stratton-Kent, *The Testament of Cyprian the Mage* ([Dover, Kent]: Scarlet Imprint/Bibliothèque Rouge, 2014).

15. Gustav Davidson, *A Dictionary of Angels: Including the Fallen Angels* (New York: Free Press, 1967), s.v. Silat. —APF

should be seriously considered for various reasons. Among these is that it appears in the *Key of Rabbi Solomon*, Invocation for Monday. As the name of a powerful ruling spirit, it is distinctly appropriate to this practice.

Arabonas is close to *Anabona*, a major name of the Art Almadel system, to which it is likely related. It is extremely tempting to further link this name to *Anobath*, an intermediary spirit in the *Book of the Offices of Spirits*, &c. Anobath is the name of a 'demon,' more specifically a fallen angel, but there are ample reasons why this should not be a disqualification. Arabonas appears in the Prayer for Sunday in the *Key of Rabbi Solomon*; therein magical prayers are specifically prescribed for daily use like the Prayer for Success. In his *Clavis*, Joseph Peterson has also noticed the crossover between these daily rites and the Prayer for Success; clearly the latter influenced the former. *Anabona* also appears in two conjurations of Mathers' *Key of Solomon* (Book One, ch. VI). In the second of these conjurations, Anabona is the second name invoked, the first being Tetragrammaton; this points to an exalted status for this name.

Ierahlem: appears as *Jerablem* in the *Key of Rabbi Solomon*, Prayer for Sunday.

Ideodoc: appears as *Jodadae* in the *Key of Rabbi Solomon*, Prayer for Sunday.

Archarzel may suggest "Archangel," preceding the name of Zophiel, the angel of Saturn, below. However, *Archasiel* appears in the *Key of Rabbi Solomon*, Conjuration for Saturday. See also Hebrew *Acharchel*, "behind the entrenchment," thus "safe, protected" (*Strong's* H316).

Zophiel: He is an important figure in accounts of the 'War in Heaven,' being a lieutenant of Michael. This name, too, appears in the *Key of Rabbi Solomon*, Prayer for Sunday. The Saturnine connection is possibly more explicatory of his role here.

Blautel: To date, no information has come to light regarding this name.

Baracata is likely *Baraqijal*, a Rebel Angel in the apocryphal *Enoch* and the *Book of Jubilees* who teaches astrology; also *Barakiel*, one of the seven archangels, who wields lightning; Jupiter; and *Barachiel*, an angel of the Art Almadel.

Adonai or *Adonay* is by far the premier name of the French blue grimoires, and likely designedly so. It may well represent Lucifer–Michael in that context. It is the first name also among Cyprian's superior powers, and conspicuous in the rites and paraphernalia of the Art Almadel.

Elohim The next word, *Elohim*, "gods," is a common Hebrew name in the grimoires. In this context, the explanation of Éliphas Lévi is hard to improve on:

> In the belief of the ancients, the world is governed by seven secondary causes—*secundii*, as Trithemius calls them—which are the universal forces designated by Moses under the plural name of Eloïm, gods. These forces, analogous and contrary to one another, produce equilibrium

by their contrasts and rule the movement of the spheres. The Hebrews termed them the seven great archangels, giving them the names of Michaël, Gabriel, Raphaël, Anaël, Samaël, Zadkiel and Oriphiel. The Christian Gnostics named the last four Uriel, Barachiel, Sealtiel and Jehudiel. Other nations attributed to these spirits the government of the seven chief planets, and assigned to them the names of their chief divinities. All believed in their relative influence; astronomy divided the antique heaven between them and allotted the seven days of the week to their successive rule. Such is the reason of the various Ceremonies of the magical week and the septenary cultus of the planets.[16]

In other words, the term Elohim represents the gods of the planets and the seven-day week, whether in the form of appropriate angels or otherwise. This understanding—as Syrian in origin as it is Jewish—underpins the Paracelsian usage of 'Olympians' and 'Olympic spirits.' It is the basis and origin of the planetary magic of the grimoires. In incantations, Elohim can reasonably be interpreted as "O ye gods!" It is also the name of the second power in Cyprian's list of superiors.

The Spirit Names—Emagro to Izachel

Emagro: Meaning unknown at this time.

Abragateh: Probably *Abraxas*, as this appears in the *Key of Rabbi Solomon*, Prayer for Sunday.

Samoel, the next 'god' addressed, is *Samael*, a Mars angel, often indicating a devil, and interchanged with both Belzebuth and Asmodeus in related legends.

Geburahel indicates an angel of Geburah, martial in nature; possibly a title of Samael.

Cadato is likely from *qadosh*, "holy."

Era: Possibly derived from the Hebrew *ara*, *ari*, a lion, from whence Ariel.

Elohi is *Elohe*, another common Solomonic godname. In contexts such as these, however, such names are divorced from the qabalistic and even Jewish context. They have become personified as angels, and addressed as separate personalities.

Achsah: Unknown at this time.

Ebmisha: Unknown at this time.

Imachadel: Plainly constructed like an angel name, currently unidentified.

---

16. Éliphas Lévi, *Dogme et Rituel de la Haute Magie* (Paris: Germer Baillière, 1854–1856). Translated by A.E. Waite as *Transcendental Magic: Its Doctrine and Ritual* (London: George Redway, 1896), Book II, ch. VII, "The Septenary of Talismans." —APF

Daniel is a Rebel Angel in *I Enoch*; also the name of the prophet and hero of the *Book of Daniel*.

Dama: Unknown, possibly from Hebrew *dumah*, "silence, death."

Elamos may relate to *elam*, another Hebrew word for "silence"; *alam*, "silent justice"; and *alm*, "bound" (Strong's numbers H481 and H482).

Izachel is *Ezeqeel*, another Rebel Angel in *I Enoch*; also *Yechezqel* or *Ezekiel*, the name of a major prophet.

Bael—also given as *Boel*—in the grimoires is a chief power of the East, similar or identical to Oriens. Under either name, he is a tremendously important figure in the history of Western magic, the grimoires being a latter stage. As mentioned in my *The Headless One*,[17] the name Boel is known from the *PDM*, and the context is far from arbitrary. His name is associated with a family of related rituals involving lamp divination; other themes arise too in this context which are highly illuminating. In the papyri, it is obvious that Boel is a high-ranking angel. Interestingly enough, another important angel of this grimoire cycle is mentioned alongside him on a few occasions, namely Aniel (Anael of the *Grimorium Verum* mirror divination process). Other aspects of the rituals in the papyri concern the Headless One, another of the Kings.

In these rituals there are many phrases relating to fire. This surpasses what may be expected in a process involving divination by the lamp; there is no corresponding emphasis on water in the incantations of bowl divination texts.

> Boel, Boel (*bis*) . . . he that giveth light exceedingly, the companion of the flame, he in whose mouth is the fire that is not quenched, the great god that sitteth in the fire, he that is in the midst of the fire . . . . come into the midst of this fire that is here before thee, he of Boel, Aniel.[18]

These words may connect with the fire theology of the *Chaldean Oracles*, and thus to Theurgic ritual, which emphasised light and flame, in a visionary context of divine manifestations no less. Griffith and Thompson's text of another such lamp divination ritual further underlines this possibility:

> Grow, O light, come forth O light, rise O light, lift thyself up O light, come forth O light of the god, reveal thyself to me, O servant of the god, in whose hand is the command of to-day, who will ask for me.[19]

Other expressions, concerning the staff of a deity, a lake of heaven, and so forth, also plainly represent a defined mythological context, involving several

---

17. Jake Stratton-Kent, *The Headless One* ([n.p.]: Hadean Press, 2012), p. 10.

18. *PDM* XIV. 194–195, 200. Griffith and Thompson, *op. cit.*, pp. 59–61. —APF

19. *PDM* XIV. 502–504. Griffith and Thompson, *op. cit.*, p. 115. —APF

'characters.' There are further details which outline an angelology in which Sabaoth—the "God of eternal time"—is the superior deity, to whom the angels answer. The invocation for another Demotic lamp divination, however, identifies the deity of whom Boel is "first servant":

> Thou art the great god Sabaoth; come down with Boel . . .[20]

The majority of names and themes contained in these texts are Egyptian. A key phrase, more constant than the mention of Sabaōth (a Chaldean name) but evidently identical, is Tagrtat, "he of eternity." To keep a complex matter as simple as possible, this explains several things about Bael and Boel:

✦ In the *Zohar*, Boel (בואל) is a name of Raphael.[21] Raphael aka Arlaph is of course a defender against demons in early amulets.[22] The *Zohar* also speaks of Raphael as "empowered to heal the earth, thanks to whom earth is restored to health along with all her forces and the human being endures thereon."[23] This likely connects with healing spirits such as we encounter with the decans. His role in the earlier Enoch literature identifies him as one of the Watchers,[24] a guide in the Underworld (Sheol, essentially Hades),[25] and one of the four faces or presences who serve the Lord of Spirits, in which role Raphael is "set over all disease and and every wound of the children of the people."[26] All of which is reminiscent of our Four Kings as leaders of the aerial spirits.

✦ In the grimoires, Bael, Boel, or Baal is a chief of demons,[27] after Oriens the first of the powers of the East.[28] The two converge a good deal also.[29]

---

20. *PDM* XIV.524.

21. *Sepher ha-Zohar* 2:147a, *Parashath Terumah.* —APF

22. See Obizuth in my *Testament of Cyprian the Mage* and in the *Testament of Solomon*, translated by F.C. Conybeare, "The Testament of Solomon," in *The Jewish Quarterly Review*, Vol. 11, No. 1 (Oct., 1898), pp. 1–45.

23. *Sepher ha-Zohar* 1:47a, *Parashath Bereshith.* Translated by Daniel Matt, *The Zohar: Pritzker Edition*, vol. 1 (Stanford, California: Stanford University Press, 2004). —APF

24. *I Enoch (Ethiopic Book of Hēnok)* 20.3. Raphael—alongside Suru'el (or Uriel), Raguel, Michael, Saraqa'el, and Gabriel—is one of "the Holy Angels who watch (or stand guard)" over Sheol. —APF

25. *Ibid.*, 22.3–14. —APF

26. *I Enoch* 40.9. Translated by E. Isaac, *(Ethiopic Apocalypse of) ENOCH*, in James H. Charlesworth, *The Old Testament Pseudepigrapha, vol. 1: Apocalyptic Literature and Testaments* (Garden City, New York: Doubleday & Co., 1983). —APF

27. E.g., in the *Goetia* of the *Lemegeton* and in the *Pseudomonarchia Dæmonum* of Weyer. —APF

28. E.g., in *Officium de Spiritibus ("The Offices of the Spirits")* in Folger Shakespeare Library MS V.b.26. —APF

29. E.g., in Agrippa, *De Occulta Philosophia*; and in J.B. Großschedel, *Calendarium Naturale Magicum Perpetuum.* —APF

✦ Boel or Boall appears as the only 'Prelate' listed in the spirit catalog of *The Offices of Spirits* via *The Book of Oberon*.[30]

✦ Boel holds the keys to the gates of the four quarters of the earth in the *Zohar*.[31]

✦ Boel is one of seven throne angels, and the angel of Saturn.[32] The connection with Saturn is particularly striking given his role of "first servant" to Sabaoth. In the mythic structures concerned, Saturnus or Kronos represented the god more typically identified with the Sun, who with the Moon is a measurer of time. This is likely why the theurgists possessed an invocation of Kronos while the chief deities named in the *Oracles* are Apollōn and Hekatē.

Boel is plainly a demiurgic figure, akin to Mikael and Metatron in other angelologies. He fits readily into the strata of Jewish and pagan magic alike wherein Sabaoth (aka Zurvan or Aiōn) is conceived of as supreme deity.

In the papyri concerned, the appearance of Boel and his relation to a chief deity is extremely emphatic; in the lamp divination genre, he plays as conspicuous a role as Anubis does in that of vessel divination.[33] Nevertheless, unless tongue in cheek, I find inexplicable the words of Morton Smith regarding these rites in his essay, "The Demons of Magic":

> Lord Bouel (Bouel is [a] good, old Egyptian god who plays a large role in the Demotic papyrus) . . .[34]

The large role is indisputable, but the god Baal of earlier Egyptian texts is thoroughly Semitic; he is also strongly identified with the Egyptian deity Set. Boel's presence in the *PDM* rituals is actually extraordinary and important. It is important also to note the frequent allusions of these rites to the Sun's authority in the underworld, and his passage therein. Some of the phrases refer to the god residing in impenetrable darkness but bearing the Sun's rays; rituals imitate this by using a windowless chamber and so on. There is mention of the setting of the Sun in the incantations, and also timing of the final rite at sunset, as well

---

30. "Boab vel Boall," the 58th spirit in *Officium de Spiritibus* in Folger MS V.b.26; published in Daniel Harms, James R. Clark, and Joseph H. Peterson, *The Book of Oberon: A Sourcebook of Elizabethan Magic* (Woodbury, Minnesota: Llewellyn Publications, 2015). —APF

31. *Sepher ha-Zohar* 2:133b, *Parashath Terumah*. —APF

32. Pietro d'Abano, *Heptameron seu Elementa Magica*, and in many texts deriving in part from the *Heptameron*, ranging from Folger MS V.b.26 to Barrett's *The Magus*. —APF

33. See "The Art Armadel" in my *True Grimoire*, and "Nebiros and Hermes Chthonios" in *Geosophia*, vol. II.

34. Morton Smith, "The Demons of Magic," paper presented at the 25th Philadelphia Seminar on Christian Origins, May 5, 1988 (http://ccat.sas.upenn.edu/psco/year25/8805.shtml). —APF

as employment of dawn and noon preliminaries. The relation of the Prayer for Success to these has been mentioned already.

Most of the context of the rites in the *PDM*, and it is important to underline it, is utterly Egyptian. This reinforces several central themes of my historical writings, centering on the early significance of decans and solar theology and their later influence. These particular papyri are Egyptian Demotic rather than Greek, and show comparatively little sign of foreign influence. The appearance of Sabaoth and Boel in them in relation to both fiery and solar themes is thus highly significant. Here are potent Egyptian solar themes at the early stages of the Great Synthesis. There is an internal coherence to these themes as the Egyptian material begins its mingling with Semitic astrological lore. These themes moreover—as syncretism developed—grew within Hermeticism and Theurgy, and remained strong afterwards throughout the grimoire period.

The Finale

It need not surprise us that the rituals referenced above are frequently associated with the Prayer for Success we are here considering in its grimoire form. The last three words of the grimoire Prayer for Success I personally interpret as a phrase: *Scirlin* (the intermediary spirit of the grimoire) and *Genium Domos*, "house spirit."[35] This is of course due to practical considerations first and foremost. Various factors support the interpretation however, including the placing immediately after Bael. Bael, it would be fair to assume, is instrumental, and after the god he serves the main focus of the invocation. Scirlin as intermediary spirit acting on Bael's authority—or even equivalent to him—makes sense following such an otherwise climactic name.

Conclusion

Concluding our consideration of the prayer as it appears in the *Book of Saint Cyprian*, our author closes this section with the advice that the operator is now prepared to make a start. The only difference in practice, he says, between the neophyte, the initiate, and the master is that the novice pleads, the adept persuades, and the true teacher commands. This may vary, he says, according to the character, worthiness, and energy of the practitioner.

However, the prayer contains the names of numerous spirits, and even the names of God are not necessarily understood as such. The implication of course is that the advice concerns our dealings with them, rather than Him.

---

35. Which would derive from *Genius Domūs*, "Spirit of the House" in uncorrupted Latin. —APF

References

Betz, Hans Dieter. *The Greek Magical Papyri in Translation, Including the Demotic Spells. Volume One: Texts.* Chicago, Ill.: University of Chicago Press, 1986.

Conybeare, F.C. "The Testament of Solomon," in *The Jewish Quarterly Review*, Vol. 11, No. 1 (Oct., 1898), pp. 1–45.

Davidson, Gustav. *A Dictionary of Angels: Including the Fallen Angels.* New York: Free Press, 1967.

Griffith, F. Llewellyn, and Herbert Thompson. *The Demotic Magical Papyrus of London and Leiden.* London: H. Grevel & Co., 1904. Republished as *The Leyden Papyrus: An Egyptian Magical Book.* New York: Dover Publications, 1974.

Harms, Daniel, James R. Clark, Joseph H. Peterson. The *Book of Oberon: A Sourcebook of Elizabethan Magic.* Woodbury, Minnesota: Llewellyn Publications, 2015.

Isaac, E. *(Ethiopic Apocalypse of) ENOCH,* in James H. Charlesworth, *The Old Testament Pseudepigrapha, vol. 1: Apocalyptic Literature and Testaments.* Garden City, New York: Doubleday & Co., 1983.

Matt, Daniel. *The Zohar: Pritzker Edition, vol. 1.* Stanford, California: Stanford University Press, 2004.

Sibley, Ebenezer, Frederick Hockley, and Joseph H. Peterson. *The Clavis or Key to the Magic of Solomon.* Lake Worth, FL: Ibis Press, 2009.

Skinner, Stephen, and David Rankine. *The Veritable Key of Solomon.* Singapore: Golden Hoard Press, 2010.

Smith, Morton. "The Demons of Magic," paper presented at the 25th Philadelphia Seminar on Christian Origins, May 5, 1988 (http://ccat.sas.upenn.edu/psco/year25/8805.shtml). Last accessed 2015.

Solomon, and S. Liddell MacGregor Mathers. *The Key of Solomon the King: Clavicula Salomonis.* London: George Redway, 1889.

Stratton-Kent, Jake. *Geosophia: The Argo of Magic. Encyclopædia Goetica, Volume 2.* [Dover, Kent]: Scarlet Imprint/Bibliothèque Rouge, 2010.

—. *The Headless One.* [n.p.]: Hadean Press, 2012.

—. *The True Grimoire. Encyclopædia Goetica, Volume 1.* [Dover, Kent]: Scarlet Imprint/Bibliothèque Rouge, 2010.

—. *The Testament of Cyprian the Mage: Comprehending the Book of Saint Cyprian & His Magical Elements and an Elucidation of the Testament of Solomon. Encyclopædia Goetica, Volume 3.* [Dover, Kent]: Scarlet Imprint/Bibliothèque Rouge, 2014.

Strong, James. *The Exhaustive Concordance of the Bible.* Nashville: Abingdon Press, 1890.

✤

Lay Thy Tongue Upon My Heart

*Forty Days of Ritual Communion
Between a Pagan Adept
and the Archangel
Raphael Tipherethel*

M. Isidora Forrest

M. Isidora Forrest is a senior Adept of the Hermetic Order of the Golden Dawn; a priestess of the international Fellowship of Isis; a Mænad for Dionysos; and a founder of the Hermetic Fellowship, a non-profit devoted to spiritual practice and education in the Western Esoteric Tradition. She has been devoted to Isis ever since the Goddess told her, in no uncertain terms, that she was not yet ready to be Her priestess. (Isidora respects a Goddess Who doesn't coddle.) More than twenty years—and a lot of research, ritual, agony, and ecstasy— later, Isidora has earned the title of Prophetess in the House of Isis. She is the author of Isis Magic: Cultivating a Relationship with the Goddess of 10,000 Names *(Abiegnus House, 2013; first ed. Llewellyn, 2001), and* Offering to Isis: Knowing the Goddess through Her Sacred Symbols *(Llewellyn, 2005), and a contributor of articles and rituals to the* Golden Dawn Journal *series of books edited by Chic and Tabatha Cicero. Isidora lives and works in the not-at-all-Egypt-like climate of the Pacific Northwest with her husband Adam Forrest, a fierce black cat named Korē, and both a Temple of Isis and a grape arbor sacred to Dionysos in the backyard. You may stay in touch with Isidora and her ongoing exploration of Isis through her blog at* Isiopolis *(isiopolis.com).*

✢

Lay Thy Tongue Upon My Heart

Forty Days of Ritual Communion
Between a Pagan Adept
and the Archangel
Raphael Tipherethel

Raphael Tipherethel,
Archangel of Beauty, I invoke Thee.

Open Thine ears.
Open Thy wings.
Open Thy mind.
Open Thy heart
to me.

Let the Sun arise in the Heart of the Tree.
Let the Moon arise below.
Let the Stars illumine above.
Let the Master of my Work come.
Let the Archangel Whose heart Tiphereth is, come!

Open my ears.
Open my wings.
Open my mind
to Thee...

And lay Thy tongue upon my heart.

AN OFT-REPEATED APHORISM in our College is "Do the Work." It's a reminder to not get distracted, to continually return to the Great Work of personal spiritual discovery and transformation that we come together to support each other in doing.

This article is about what some of that Work can look like.

But first, the caveats. The Work is always highly subjective. It is, in part, a kind of self-psychoanalysis under Divine guidance. That's why Adepts don't often write about it. It's extremely personal stuff. The subjective nature of the Work also means that much of what Raphael communicates to me, for the most part, relates to me and to my Work. Your mileage not only may, but will, vary.

This means that you'll need to know a little something about me, especially my religious and magical background, in order to put what you're about to read into context. Some of you may know me from my work with the Goddess Isis, so you'll already know that I am Pagan. In fact, I've been Pagan for many more years than I ever spent in the Unitarian Universalism my parents introduced me to. Specifically, I'm a priestess of Isis and a maenad for Dionysos.

At this point, perhaps you're wondering what ever-so-Pagan me is doing spending 40 days with an Archangel. Well, I'm also a Hermetic Adept, in the tradition of the Golden Dawn and R∴R∴ & A∴C∴, where we are quite used to Working with Angels and Archangels (among other Spirits and Deities). Yet the reason I spent 40 days invoking and communing with this particular Archangel is that, many years ago, Raphael invited me to be His priestess. I know. And I did not take Him up on it at the time. But recently, I decided to take this opportunity to not only focus on my Adept Work for a period of time, but also to explore that long-ago invitation and discover what, if anything, I wanted to do about it.

Why do this Work?

In pursuit of her or his own Great Work, invocation of and conversation with non-corporeal Beings is one of a number of key techniques available to the Adept. In some traditions, attaining "knowledge and conversation of the Holy Guardian Angel" is the primary task. In addition to being a kind of Divinely guided self-psychoanalysis that aids in the Adept's spiritual growth and personal human growth, the Work has other benefits.

Communion like this also helps the Adept develop a personal philosophy, discovering her or his own answers to the great questions posed by philosophy—from the nature of reality to ethics. It can also assist us in developing a personal theology. Who and what is Divinity? Deities or Deity? What is holy? We may explore what worship is and what it does or does not mean to us.

For me, it is also a way to taste Mystery, a sacred flavor I happen to like very much, as well as a way to expand what I understand about love, both human and Divine; for indeed, love is at the core of the Work. There is an important, and for some, troubling, clause in the Oath of the Minor Adept in which the prospective Adept swears to do the Work that she may, with the Divine aid, "at length attain to be more than human." This type of communion with higher Divine Beings can help us figure out what that clause really means.

On the more practical side, it can help us understand, on a deep level, just how much more is available to human consciousness than our day-to-day consciousness would ever guess. It can make us more effective magicians, increasing our magical power and helping us understand—if we are doing our Work sincerely—how to use that power with wisdom. And finally, I pass on to you a little something Raphael mentioned to me as an additional benefit: it helps us develop our relationship with the incorporeal, which prefigures our future.

The Conditions & the Rite of Contact

You should also know that I did not have the luxury of doing this Work as an Abramelin-like retreat. I did it while putting in my usual eleven-hour workday and commute at a fairly demanding job. Such is the lot of the modern Adept with a mortgage. The point is, while it isn't easy to carve an extra hour and a half out of your day, it can be done—at least for a limited period of time.

My official start date was the winter solstice; it seemed like good symbolism to start on the darkest day of the year and grow toward the light. But even before the official start, I did some preliminary invocations of Raphael Tipherethel (Raphael as the Archangel of Tiphereth) to ask whether He was willing to participate with me in this Work and if He had any conditions. There were no conditions and He was indeed willing. As I always do when preparing to Work with a Deity or Spirit with Whom I am only passing familiar, I stuffed my head with all the Raphael research I could find, from biblical references to appearances in the Greek Magical Papyri to gematria.

The Rite of Contact for the Work had to be not only effective, but also relatively short and simple so that I could spend most of my allotted time in ritual communion with the Archangel. My first attempt was an adaptation of a Working I'd previously put together for our Adept College. Raphael immediately made it known that the invocation I'd used was much too formal for Him and He instead inspired the brief and significantly more simple and intimate invocation that begins this article. Once established, we did not change the rite throughout our 40-day Working.

I did have one luxury that you may not have should you choose to try your own 40 days with Raphael. Our temple space is dedicated temple space and so I was able to leave the temple set up throughout the 40 days. This meant that, rather than having to do Banishing Hexagrams at day's end, I could instead simply seal the temple with the sigil of Raphael until the invocation of the following day. This not only saved time, but also helped build the energy of the Archangel in the temple.

What follows is the Rite of Contact used throughout the 40-day period. The ritual script assumes knowledge of common G∴D∴ and R∴R∴ & A∴C∴ formulæ.

Invocation of Raphael Tipherethel

Breathe the Four-Fold Breath.

 Perform the Qabbalistic Cross.

 Perform the Middle Pillar exercise vibrating YHVH Eloah va-Daath in all centers. Following this, vibrate Tiphereth and Raphael in Tiphereth center.

 Circulate the Light throughout the Sphere of Sensation (aura).

ADEPT. **Hail, Holy Light! In Thy Divine Name of Beauty, YHVH Eloah va-Daath, I ask Thee to assist me in opening all my senses that I may perceive the presence of Thy Mighty Archangel, Raphael Tipherethel, for the continuance of our Work. This I ask in Thy Divine Name of Beauty. Amen.**

Creating the Temple of Raphael Tipherethel

RITUAL NOTE: Burn Tipheretic incense and play recorded music as desired throughout the Rite.

 Stand in center of temple, facing east.

 Perform Qabbalistic Cross.

 Perform Analysis of the Key Word.

 Trace the Lesser Invoking Hexagrams of Tiphereth in the quarters and Tipheretic Hexagrams above and below. Trace all six forms in each case, visualizing the hexagrams in glowing yellow Light.

ADEPT *(vibrating)*. ***YOD HEH VAV HEH ELOAH VA-DAATH!***

 *(Tracing Lesser Invoking Hexagrams of Tiphereth toward the east and vibrating:) **ARARITA!** (Speaking:)* **Let the Ways be opened unto Raphael Tipherethel!**

 *(Tracing Lesser Invoking Hexagrams of Tiphereth toward the south and vibrating:) **ARARITA!** (Speaking:)* **Let the Ways be opened unto Raphael Tipherethel!**

 *(Tracing Lesser Invoking Hexagrams of Tiphereth toward the west and vibrating:) **ARARITA!** (Speaking:)* **Let the Ways be opened unto Raphael Tipherethel!**

 *(Tracing Lesser Invoking Hexagrams of Tiphereth toward the north and vibrating:) **ARARITA!** (Speaking:)* **Let the Ways be opened unto Raphael Tipherethel!**

 *(Tracing Lesser Invoking Hexagrams of Tiphereth toward the ceiling and vibrating:) **ARARITA!** (Speaking:)* **Let the Ways be opened unto Raphael Tipherethel!**

(Tracing Lesser Invoking Hexagrams of Tiphereth toward the floor and vibrating:) **ARARITA!** *(Speaking:)* **Let the Ways be opened unto Raphael Tipherethel!**

Once all hexagrams are traced:

ADEPT *(tracing Hebrew letter Tav in the center of the ceiling hexagram and vibrating).* **TAV!**

(Tracing Hebrew letter Tav in the center of the floor hexagram and vibrating:) **TAV!**

(Tracing Hebrew letter Resh in the center of the east hexagram and vibrating:) **RESH!**

(Tracing Hebrew letter Peh in the center of the southern hexagram and vibating:) **PEH!**

(Tracing Hebrew letter Aleph in the center of the western hexagram and vibrating:) **ALEPH!**

(Tracing Hebrew letter Lamed in the center of the northern hexagram and vibrating:) **LAMED!**

(Standing in Orant posture, facing east, and vibrating:) **TIPHERETH! RAPHAEL!**

The Archangelic Calling

Take some time to do a freeform singing or chanting invocation and vibration of His Name.

ADEPT *(Singing, vibrating, chanting).* **Raphael! Tiphereth! Raphael Tipherethel** *(and so on...)*

When ready, take a seat (I had several cushions placed in the center of the temple for this purpose) and invoke.

ADEPT. **Raphael Tipherethel, Archangel of Beauty, I invoke Thee.**
  Open Thine ears.
  Open Thy wings.
  Open Thy mind.
  Open Thy heart
  to me.

  Let the Sun arise in the Heart of the Tree.
  Let the Moon arise below.
  Let the Stars illumine above.
  Let the Master of my Work come.
  Let the Archangel Whose heart Tiphereth is, come!

Open my ears.
Open my wings.
Open my mind
to Thee...

And lay Thy tongue upon my heart.

(Vibrating:) **RAPHAEL TIPHERETHEL!**

The Vision

This is the time for the ritual communion with the Archangel. When Vision is complete, thank the Archangel in your own words.

Sealing the Ways with the Sigil of Raphael

If your temple may be undisturbed for the 40-day period, put the temple into stasis and protect it until the next day by tracing the sigil of Raphael from the Rose of the Rose Cross Lamen in the center of each of the Tipheretic hexagrams.

Fig. 1. The Rose Sigil of Raphael

Daily Closing

Stand in center of temple, facing east.

ADEPT. Not unto my name, not unto my name, but unto Thine, O YHVH Eloah va-Daath, be the glory, Who hath allowed me to enter thus far into the Sanctuary of Thy Mysteries.

Perform Qabbalistic Cross.

Perform Analysis of the Key Word.

ADEPT. Amen.

Closing at the End of 40 Days

Stand in center of temple, facing east. Visualize the hexagrams in the temple in glowing yellow Light.

ADEPT *(in thanks and gratitude, vibrating).* **YOD HEH VAV HEH ELOAH VA-DAATH!**

(Tracing Lesser Banishing Hexagrams of Tiphereth and Hebrew letter Resh toward the east and vibrating:) **ARARITA! RESH!**

(Tracing Lesser Banishing Hexagrams of Tiphereth and Hebrew letter Peh toward the south and vibrating:) **ARARITA! PEH!**

(Tracing Lesser Banishing Hexagrams of Tiphereth and Hebrew letter Aleph toward the west and vibrating:) **ARARITA! ALEPH!**

(Tracing Lesser Banishing Hexagrams of Tiphereth and Hebrew letter Lamed toward the north and vibrating:) **ARARITA! LAMED!**

(Tracing Banishing Hexagrams of Tiphereth and Hebrew letter Tav toward the ceiling and vibrating:) **ARARITA! TAV!**

(Tracing Banishing Hexagrams of Tiphereth and Hebrew letter Tav toward the floor and vibrating:) **ARARITA! TAV!**

ADEPT. Not unto my name, not unto my name, but unto Thine, O YHVH Eloah va-Daath, be the glory, Who hath allowed me to enter thus far into the Sanctuary of Thy Mysteries.

Perform Qabbalistic Cross.

Perform Analysis of the Key Word.

ADEPT. Amen.

Day One

The Archangel enters the temple heavily. He descends from above, landing with an earthquake thud. The temple, and I, shudder. Colors fill my vision: gold, white, amethyst purple, with flashes of summer green. This time, His wings are classic, avian wings of white, tipped in molten, living gold. Deep purple tattoos illuminate and enliven His skin—serpents and sigils. Brilliant Light shines forth from His eyes and His mouth. Upon His forehead are the Hebrew letters Resh and Tav, a sort of shorthand or nickname: "Reth."

We greet each other and I test the vision with the LVX Signs, which the Archangel returns easily. Once the exchange is complete, His attitude becomes instantly casual and He sits on the floor across from me, one golden arm draped informally across a golden, upraised knee. His wings, living things with minds of their own, are in a constant state of abstract motion; movement that contrasts with Raphael's own still and focused presence. Almost immediately, He tells me what our Work together will be: new techniques for using my Higher and Divine Genius in Sacred Magic, various aspects of my Adept Work, and the overcoming of certain fears that are currently holding me back.

Immediately upon this declaration of the Work, my Genius, Beluel, manifests, seeming to flow out from me with a distinctly physical sensation and standing to my left. In my previous Work with Beluel, He has always been masculine. This time, Beluel is feminine, perhaps as a balance to the masculine Archangel, or perhaps, as my Genius, to serve as a more obvious iteration of me.

Since I have been preparing for this for a while, I have a couple of questions burning a hole in my metaphorical pocket: What are Angels, and are there differences between Angels and the Goddesses and Gods?

It has always seemed to me that at least Archangels could be considered to be about the same as Goddesses and Gods. For instance, it would be perfectly reasonable to translate Raphael's name as "The Healing God." In the Greek Magical Papyri, the magician conjures "by the God Raphael."[1] Yet Raphael's name is usually translated—reading the "El" ending separately—as "Healer of God" or "Healing Power of God," presumably to discourage a polytheistic approach in which the Angelic Powers would be perceived in any way as separate from God. As a Pagan, I'm perfectly comfortable with a polytheistic approach, yet my question is mainly intended so that I can understand Angels in relation to the Deities to Whom I am devoted.

Raphael explains that Angels are coalescences of Divine energy. Angels can come into being when the human mind "agrees," and the human heart "agrees" (for example, by invoking), and when the Divine mind and heart also "agree." With that agreement between human and Divine, the Angel coalesces, comes into Being as His or Her own mind and heart also "agree" to mediate. This ability to coalesce whenever human-Divine agreement occurs is one of the mechanisms that makes it possible for specific Angels to be present in multiple locations throughout the world; *"Such is the power of the human being,"* says Raphael. Such is the nature of the Archangel, I think.

The Archangel says that, while Deities and Angels are similar in Being and Power, due to the way Angels come into being—in a way, coalescing anew each time—They are less specific and more flexible. The Goddesses and Gods have more distinct personalities, more established imaginal Forms, and more self-contained energy. The Deities are their own direct channels to the Undifferentiated, while Angels mediate and are mediated. Nevertheless, on a Yetziratic level, both function similarly and are human-comprehensible parts of the greater Divine Whole.

---

1. *PGM* III.1–164, line 149.

How We'll Proceed

During my time with Raphael, there were many sessions I initiated by asking questions of the Archangel. There were many others in which we followed Raphael's immediately apparent agenda. But rather than simply give you what amounts to diary entries of those sessions—for I fear you'd be bored—let's instead look at the Work by theme. Raphael's variety of visionary appearances taught things about His nature as well as the nature of Tiphereth. There were a number of techniques of sacred magic He showed me. The Archangel and my Genius together helped me learn new things about the Genius Itself. There were metaphysical aspects of our Work as well. And, though I did not know it until about a quarter of the way through our 40 days, the culmination of our Work was to be the reenactment, in vision, of the sacrifice at the heart of the R∴R∴ et A∴C∴ 5=6 Adepta Minor Ritual. In preparation for this, Raphael taught me more about the nature and meaning of sacrifice and quite a lot about purification as well. As it turns out, that's a concern of His.

I won't be sharing everything about this Work with you. As I said earlier, some of it is too personal and I prefer to keep it private; and some probably only applies to me. I will, however, share things that I think may have a wider application, things that seem strange, interesting, or worth meditating on, and things that may serve as examples of what some of the Work of an Adept can look like.

The Forms of Raphael

If you are experienced with visionary Work, you will not be surprised to hear that Raphael Tipherethel presented Himself in a variety of different forms during our time together. Nor will you be surprised to learn that none of those forms were of the "Christmas-card angel" type. (In fact, I had specifically requested Him to come in an interesting and impressive form; I was not disappointed.)

In addition to a humanoid form, Raphael had a number of bird-like or bird-related forms. On several occasions, He first showed up as an egg and then unfurled Himself until He filled the temple as the Tattooed-and-Serpent-Bearing One. At least twice, He was the Serpent encircling the Orphic Egg, cracking it open (*"That's how the Light gets in,"* He joked, alluding to one of my favorite Leonard Cohen songs). On another occasion, He emerged from the egg as a serpent-headed human. Often, He would arrive as a bird—an enormous, amethyst-eyed, golden eagle or a small gold-and-white bird. This was what He called His *"Journeyform"* and it meant we were going to leave the Tiphereth Temple and travel somewhere else in Yetzirah. At these times, I would take on the form of the kite hawk, the sacred raptor of my Goddess Isis.

As noted above, Raphael could appear as a serpent or be accompanied by them. Usually, they encircled His wrists and ankles like living jewelry, as well as entwined

His caduceus. Surely, this form is due to the snake's ancient association with healing. From the snake-wrapped staff of the Healer God Asklepios to the brazen serpent with which Moses healed the seraphim-bit Israelites, the snake—with its ability to shed its skin, emerging new and healed from the experience and bearing its ambiguous poison/medicine venom—is an eternal symbol of the often mysterious power of healing. According to the early Christian writer Origen, the Pagan philosopher Celsus, writing against Christianity, mixed up a Gnostic Christian sect called the Ophites (from Greek *ophis*, "snake") and whom Origen considered heretics, with 'true' Christians. On an Ophite diagram that Origen claims to have seen, the third of the Ophities' seven world-ruling "archontic dæmons" was "Raphael, the serpent-like."[2]

My favorite of His forms is described in my notebook: "Reth's beauty today is like this: hair of burning wheat, eyes almond-shaped and black with just enough eyeshine so that you know they're alive; wings like solar flares..." In this form, He is human-like and masculine, accompanied by jewel-scaled serpents, and with purple tattoos that come and go upon His glowing, golden skin. When I ask Him about the changing tattoos, He says they are the changing Forms of His Name. I ask their purpose and He says that they help stabilize His energy so that He can be here with me and that it is the *"same principle as a talisman."* To which I reply something brilliant like, "Oh, that is so very cool."

Raphael also appeared in non-human and non-animal forms. Several times, particularly as we got closer to the 5=6 sacrifice redux, He was a red rose or a rose vine, alluding to the rose at the center of the Rose Cross Lamen, the beautiful rose that is also the emblem of the Sacrificial One. Infrequently, He was simply a golden glow and a voice—a median-toned, agreeable voice, by the way. One time, He came in all these forms at once.

Although I was specifically Working with Raphael Tipherethel, it was inevitable that His other associations, as Archangel of Air and of the planet Mercury would sometimes bleed over into the Tipheretic Work. For instance, the many bird-forms of the Archangel may be due to His connection with Air as much as with Tiphereth's situation on the Middle, or Airy, Pillar of the Tree of Life. In tenth-century-CE Northumbria, Raphael was associated with birds in a different way. In a set of very magical-papyri-sounding ritual prayers, Raphael is invoked to keep birds away from this agricultural community's crops—just as He drove out the demon Asmodeus in the *Book of Tobit*.[3] Raphael's mercurial concern with knowledge is harmonious with Tiphereth's association with knowledge not only of head, but also

---

2. Origen, *Contra Celsum*, book VI, chapter 30.

3. Karen Louise Jolly, "Prayers from the Field: Practical Protection and Demonic Defense in Anglo-Saxon England," *Traditio*, vol. 61, 2006, pp. 95–147.

of heart, as well as with the Deity Name assigned to Tiphereth: YHVH Eloah va-Daath ("Yahweh, God and Knowledge").

Talking with Angels

Many of my interactions with the Archangel included discussions about the nature of the Divine, of reality, of humanity, how it all began, and what we humans are supposed to be doing here. In this section, I'll share some of these questions and answers to give you an idea of what it was like. I'm still thinking about many of these issues, deciding whether to adopt them into my personal philosophical or theological understanding. I should note, however, that something I have long found useful in thinking about the spiritual realms is the Hermetic Qabbalistic model of reality. Since Qabbalah would, presumably, be part of Raphael Tipherethel's vocabulary, too, you can understand Hermetic Qabbalah as background for our discussions.

One of the first questions I ask is, "What is the Divine nature?"

"The First Comprehensible [by which I think He means the Divine at Kether] *is Pure Peace. It cares nothing but that all things achieve peace. Beyond that is the In-comprehensible* [by which I believe He means the Veils of Negative Existence]. *The Mother and Father* [Binah and Chokhmah] *are the First Creative and They desire change and evolution,"* says the Archangel.

"We inherit that from Them."

"Yes," He answers with a hint of humor.

"What are we evolving to?"

"The Parents. The human task is to become ever more aware and ever more creative."

"Should we want to become one with the First Comprehensible?"

"You may choose to rest there or dissolve into It." (I get the idea that "resting there" means between incarnations. Being "dissolved into It" would be joining the Divine Peace and no longer incarnating.)

In a different session, we expand on the idea of creativity. I have a theory about two activities, both creative, which define us as human and that we see clearly displayed as far back as our cave-dwelling ancestors: Art and Magic. When we first got our heads above water in the struggle for existence, what did we do? We carved little statuettes of Goddesses. We painted the magic of shamans and the numinous power of animals on rock walls. And we signed our work with our handprints. And so I ask Raphael about the source of human creativity.

"Your innate connection with Creative Divinity," He says.

Yet that legacy is simply the first spark, the inspiration. It is the calling voice of the Muse—whether She is whispering sweetly or shouting and shaking you till your teeth rattle. Raphael explains that there are human qualities that we may be born with, if we're lucky, or need to develop, if we're like most people, in order to make our creativity successful. First, we must allow ourselves to be different, imbalanced, even odd. Yet in the face of our own weirdness, we must also have the ability to actually do the project, seeing it through to completion. Persistence re-balances the required imbalance. Oh, yes. And optimism.

A certain amount of Chaos is required for creativity, Raphael says, and this applies in the Divine realm as well. In relation to this, I ask to be shown "something I would not have imagined." Immediately I find my Genius standing to my right and left in Her/His feminine and masculine forms (we'll get to that). As fast as thought, Raphael is before me and bids me look into His eyes. They are deep and black and flecked with stars.

"This is the Primordial. And there was always Light," He says. *"Chaos is not a void, but full of stars. It is the consciousness of the Divine."*

"What is the Light?" I ask.

"Ideas in potentia. God is All and Naught. Then one Idea stirred and drew God's attention and Will was born from that Attention. This Idea-Starred Chaos penetrates all things; it is the Ground of Being. It is unknown how the First Idea stirred. The Idea was independent of God, yet within God's Chaos-Consciousness. With Will, came Divine curiosity and then discovery and then the Multiversal Trees [of Life] *emanated. But the places between them are still God Chaos."* (This refers to another vision where I was shown an ultra-wide-scope view of the All in which multiple Trees of Life were continually coming into manifestation through The Fall, then being Restored and—with their cycle complete—becoming un-manifest once more. Worlds being created everywhere right now, which will eventually ascend into non-manifestation; thus "Multiversal Trees." It is reminiscent of the births and deaths of galaxies in space.)

Yet chaos can be destructive, too. So I ask about the ever vexing "problem of evil." Raphael speaks of human responses to chaos taking us down different paths.

"What is the difference between those who do evil in response to chaos and those who get creative?" I wonder.

"Environment and maturity of Spirit," He says. *"Step beyond frustration to healing by creativity."*

"Are You, then, the Archangel of Creativity?"

"Yes. It is one of the reasons I am so close to you [humans]*."*

Part of why I'm doing this 40-day communion with the Archangel is so that I can get a more visceral feel for some of the other mythologies with which I deal as a magician but that don't naturally draw me. During one session, I decide to ask some questions about Judaism and Christianity.

"What about Christianity is true?" (By "true," I mean religiously/spiritually/magically true, not literally.)

"The Sacrifice is true," answers the Archangel.

"How so?"

"*Incarnation is a sacrifice for all souls. Of course, there are compensations: joy of body, the beauty of the world, the finding of The Other, the Lover.*"

"Why incarnate at all?"

"*Completion must be reached; it cannot be reached without the entire cycle. Some human faculties would not develop without it.*"

"Like?"

"*Compassion, which is already in the Heart of God. To become godlike, you must gain God's heart.*"

"What is true about Judaism?"

"*The ascensional path is very true and beautiful.*"

[And then I get off track.] "What does the Ultimate Divine do—on an everyday basis, I mean?"

"*It exists. And It dreams. And when It dreams, it sends out Seeds of Becoming and then things change.*"

"What about death?"

"*Death happens naturally in the world.*"

"Is Qabbalah true?"

"*Yes. It is a beautiful map.*"

"But there are other maps..."

"*Yes, of course.*"

"What truth can you tell me that I don't know?"

"*In a way, we* [the Angels] *long to be you* [humans]*, yet we have great compassion for you.*"

"But many of us strive to be like You..."

"*That is why we must unite; we are better together than alone. That is the reason behind the Genius. Striving for contact is striving for unity. Our natures cry out for it.*"

"Is there any ultimate Truth?"

"*Yes: the Divine is and you are part of It.*"

"So what can I give You?"

"*Your Love. Your Beauty. Your Light. The Root* [God] *has no need of our praise. We sing Holy, Holy, Holy to express our own joy in Its Presence.*"

"All my Deities are ecstatic," I say. And I touch His face and one of His ever-shifting tattoos. I get, "Revealer." And another, "Lover." And another, "Speaker." "You are trying to make me fall in love with You," I say.

Smiling, He says, "*Yes, of course.*"

On the Higher and Divine Genius

This was probably a bit dim of me, but I did not anticipate the extent to which my Genius would be involved in this Work with Raphael. But in fact, Beluel was always there, from the very beginning, supporting me and helping me better access and understand aspects of the Work.

As an Adept, I have had the much-vaunted conversation—if not what I would consider true and deep knowledge—of my Genius for many years now. But because I also have very intimate relationships with both Isis and Dionysos, my Goddess and God, much of the spiritual Work that some Adepts might do with their Genii, I have done with my Goddess and God. Once I understood that Beluel was to be an inseparable part of this, I took our 40-day period as an opportunity to come to know Beluel on a yet more personal basis as well.

Something I hadn't yet done with my Genius turned out to be a key technique: Assuming the Godform—or more specifically, the Geniusform. I can say in truth that it came as a revelation to me, and on just the second day, too.

As I look at Raphael, newly arrived in His Journeyform, I suddenly know that I should be in my Geniusform. So, as I would with any God/dessform, I use the Vibratory Formula to Assume Beluel's Form. It is easy, even comfortable. Then I look at Raphael again. With me in Geniusform, He looks much different. He is an intense sphere of energy, wings everywhere and in constant motion. I am suddenly awestruck and humbled before Him. I bow down, the Angel in me acknowledging Its ruling Archangel in Him.

Another interesting thing about my Work with the Genius this time around was that, just as Raphael had many different visionary forms, so did Beluel. I've already mentioned the gender switch. Beluel frequently appeared in dual forms, female and male Beluelim. But that wasn't all. We also did an exercise in which I had an opportunity to see Beluel's/my images in each of the Spheres of the Tree of Life. It was both a fascinating and instructive exercise and I highly recommend it.

Once, as the Beluelim stand by my side, hands crossed at the back of my neck and with one of Their wings out to each side, They say, "There is not just the one thing." They tell me that there is a lot of Divine assistance available to the human being, everywhere in the Multiverse. This message was repeated on at least one other occasion (by Raphael): We are not alone. (The little psychotherapist in my head wonders whether I've been feeling lonely lately.)

One time, I asked Raphael what the Genius is. *"It is the Certain Thing,"* He said. I think He meant that the Genius is a sure connection, a genuine gateway to the Divine, a true thing. (Then, just as I was closing this document for the day, I found something in my notebook from another session that seems to bear on this: "Perhaps moments of joy and awe on earth are connected to a remembrance or understanding of the Greater Divine Connection.")

Days Eleven & Twelve

With a flurry of white and golden wings, the Archangel arrives, and with Him, Be-luel. She hovers above the ground, behind me and begins to touch two places high on my back. Soon I feel something there, a little flow of energy, an itching. Beluel is drawing my wings out. They are soft blue and green and purple, contrasting with Raphael's gold and white ones. Then I Assume the Geniusform of Beluel.

I understand that today we are to work on a radical heart opening, an enlarge-ment of my personal Tiphereth center. I notice that, in the physical, I am rocking back and forth slightly as I concentrate on visualizing my heart center open. The rocking seems to serve as a distraction for the body and at the same time hints at a heartbeat. This goes on.

After a while—but then all of a sudden—something happens. I feel and hear the shutters of my heart fling open wide. In my heart, in Beluel's, in Raphael's, then up into Briyah and Atziluth everything opens. I look up and I can see into Kether of Atziluth.

The words leave my mouth before I can think, "I have no desire to go there," I blurt. Now why did I say that? I cast around in my head looking for a reason. Then I have to laugh at myself. I guess I'm afraid of oblivion. In fact, I may even be angry at oblivion. So, damn; I guess I am afraid of death, too. The reason I'm amused with myself is because, with my Pagan and Mysteries background, I've always believed I'm reasonably comfortable with death, even though I have always qualified it by saying I'm not ready to go quite yet.

Emphatically returning my attention to the heavens, Raphael says, *"It is a Ladder to Heaven, made of hearts. You should go there and overcome your fear."*

Immediately—and without my assent, I might add—Raphael tucks me under His wing and we rocket upwards. Once there, I am relieved to realize that I can sim-ply be a witness in the Sphere, rather than having to actually experience it. It is all White Brilliance and I sense a sort of heartbeat around me. There is a sense of taste as well, like a strange flower that isn't, but reminds me of, lavender.

"Here is ultimate freedom," He says.

"Yes. This is like Dionysos' freedom. Scary."

"Yes. But it is also the peace of freedom. Just accept it. Beyond this, there is no know-ing of the Not."

"I do want to believe there is something beyond death," I say.

"And there is."

"How can I be certain?"

"You are as certain as you can be," He answers. (For me, that's about 75%. Is it enough to overcome the fear? Almost.)

The next day's session, while dissimilar, nevertheless seemed to be a follow-up. It was another preparation for the 5=6 sacrifice.

Immediately upon invoking Raphael, the Archangel's Form envelops me, directly and without Beluel's mediation. Instead, Beluel is duplicated six times and stands around Raphael and me in front of the six Lesser Hexagrams that stand at the gateways of the Temple of Tiphereth. The circle and hexagrams are exceptionally and persistently clear in my vision today.

"*This is the Theurgic elevation,*" says the Archangel to me. "*Aspire.*"

I do, and we are transported to a three-dimensional Tree of Life within a greater Cosmos. We are suspended from our hearts at Tiphereth in the Tree. I am here in Godform, but it is Raphael Who has Assumed me; not I who have Assumed Him. The structure is the same, the Archangel's Form is around me and I am sensing through Him, but it's different from any Assumption I have ever done. I am being carried rather than carrying. It is effortless.

I am simply to be, to exist, in this elevated place, suspended in Raphael, suspended in Tiphereth. We are being purified. I feel a pulling at my wide-open heart from the weight of being suspended, but my heart is also strengthened by its envelopment by Raphael. Interestingly, while this Assumption feels different, it does not feel more powerful than others I have experienced.

"*Come back to the elevation and rest there,*" reminds Raphael.

I do. My heart and my soul are open. Air and Light wash through me. Suddenly, I feel that I want to do a healing from this place. That impulse must be from Raphael. "*Always take the Form of the Willing Sacrifice first,*" He counsels. I practice this healing technique for a while. Eventually, we return to the Temple of Tiphereth. Raphael 'un-Assumes' me and we are complete for the day.

Techniques

As in the example above, there were a number of sacred magical techniques and refinements of techniques that were part of the 40-day Work with Raphael Tipherethel. I offer a sample of them here in case you should wish to experiment with them for yourself. Our College has already worked with at least one of them and we hope to do more in the future.

A Circulation of Energy for Health

Using vibration of the Divine Name and visualization, elevate your consciousness to the Sphere of Tiphereth. Now let yourself become aware of your own Tiphereth center. Using your breath, expand your Tiphereth so that it encompasses your entire Sphere of Sensation and let your expanded Tiphereth be filled with Yellow Brilliance. Now become aware of a clockwise rotation of the Light of this Sphere around you. Firmly establish the visualization of this rotating energy. Maintaining that visualization, now become aware of the Middle Pillar that extends through your body and your expanded Tiphereth. Another flow of Light moves up and down this Middle Pillar. Moving up, it rotates clockwise, down, it rotates counterclockwise. Concentrate on being aware of the clockwise rotation of your expanded Tiphereth at the same time that you are aware of the clockwise-up and counterclockwise-down movement of the Light through the Middle Pillar.

This is a healing flow, Raphael tells me. It is an exercise the Adept should do regularly to maintain both bodily and spiritual health.

Transformation

According to the *Grimoire of Armadel*, in Raphael's sigil "is taught the manner of joining Actives and Passives together the one unto the other, in natural things."[4] As in the above circulation for health, there were other techniques from Raphael that included energy patterns that were doubled, simultaneous, or both. With its concurrent clockwise and counterclockwise flow, the technique above may be interpreted as the joining of Actives and Passives.

Raphael also showed the use of the lemniscate or infinity symbol as a method for not just joining but also transforming "Actives and Passives." It can be used both in visualization and as a gesture in ritual. While I am sure it would be

Fig. 2. The Lemniscate

quite effective in making spiritual transformations (fear to no fear, for example, or enabling the connection of Adept with Genius), it was actually given as a technique of practical magic. So let's use the ever-popular example of finding a new job, that is, going from a state of no job (or wrong job) to right job.

Open the temple in a manner appropriate for the Working. Facing east, visualize the current state (no or wrong job) to your left and illuminated with light. Visualize the desired state (right job) to your right and in darkness. Slowly trace the lemniscate from left to right, encircling the visualization of both the current and desired states. Each time you reach the "pinch point" in the lemniscate figure, state the desired outcome, in this case, something like "right job." Begin to see the light flow from left to right until the current state is in darkness and the desired state in light.

The key is that pinch point. By compressing the energy of the desired transformation into that tiny point, it becomes more susceptible to influence by magic. This was a message I received several times during our 40 days together. To work magic most effectively, find the pinch point, the small thing that can be affected. Things in a state of change are easier to influence as well. (This is why weather magic often works well, especially here on the west coast as ever-changing and unstable weather

---

4. S.L. MacGregor Mathers, *The Grimoire of Armadel* (London: Routlege & Kegan Paul, 1980), p. 30.

patterns sweep in toward us from the ocean.) Instead of a Big Bang, Raphael speaks of a little push, a dream, a seed sown: *"Created Creation is a mere initial push set in motion in a solution of Potential* [the God Chaos]. *That is how Magic is Worked. Discover the right place and method of pushing—in accordance with the natural order of Creation—and you will begin the Creation of the desired thing. Yet do not believe that it can be completely controlled."*

Raphael and Beluel also used the lemniscate to move energy in me. As I stand between Them, Raphael begins using the symbol to move increased energy from His Kether center into mine. Beluel does the same. Soon I am quite tingly and energized and I learn that this technique can also be used for healing. Of course it can. Raphael.

Purification

While I wasn't invoking Raphael according to the rites in the *Grimoire of Armadel*, I find it nonetheless interesting that Armadel counsels, "Thou must be both pure and chaste when thou dost invoke Him."[5] What's more, Raphael is the only Angel in that collection for Whom purity is a stated requirement. While Raphael and I did not discuss chastity, purification was something we worked on quite a bit. It was necessary for the upcoming Sacrificial Rite, but it also seemed to be a natural concern of the Archangel. I wonder whether Raphael's association with purification could stem from His healing function. In physical healing, cleanliness is always preferred, perhaps purification of psyche or mind is especially important in spiritual healing.

What follows is a purifying visualization Raphael gave me and which we used repeatedly—right up to the day before I made my sacrifice:

After the invocation, all I am aware of is Raphael's golden finger poking me in the heart. Hard. This makes the sun rise in me, warming, elevating, invigorating. I discover myself suspended on a three-dimensional Tree of Life in space, Tiphereth at my heart, my arms stretched out to Chesed and Gevurah in Osiris Slain. My feet reach out to Malkhuth, but do not rest there. Raphael still does not show Himself. He is all poking finger and Voice today.

"The Sacrifice is necessary," He says. *"The radical giving over to the Higher—as you did with Dionysos."*

Yes, I did do that with Dionysos. And He shook my life up. A lot. No regrets in the end, but I'm not so sure I want to do anything similar right now. I'm just now getting settled in after the disruption. Besides, I need to be able to function in the

---

5. *Ibid.*

world. Raphael says that while this giving over is similar, the effect will be gentler. Well, I think, I hope so.

"I'll show you," He says. *"Visualize all the accretions to your Self going back to their appropriate Sephiroth."*

Okay. So I start in Malkhuth and try to name all the negative things that I think might have gotten stuck "onto" me, or in my psyche, during the course of my life in order to envision them going away.

"Too thorough," says Raphael.

So I bring my consciousness back to Tiphereth, remember that I am spread out on the Tree, and I begin to visualize "stuff" simply floating away from each of my Spheres. It's as easy as tossing flower petals in the wind, as effortless as sand shifting in the desert, as simple as dust blowing away, as beautiful as ink dissolving in clear water. The Cosmic Wind blows the Qlippoth, the "shells," off my Spheres. Some turn into flowers to show that even waste may be useful. Some sparkle into non-existence. As this goes on, Raphael exhorts me repeatedly to *"maintain a cosmic perception."* A broad perspective is somehow required for the purification to work.

"It is not necessary to understand it to do it," explains the Archangel. *"It is not necessary to know exactly what keeps you from the whole-hearted Sacrifice in order to whole-heartedly make the Sacrifice. Dissolve reservations in affirmation."*

"Oh," He adds, *"And you only have to do this up to Chesed. Beyond that, even in your own Sphere of Sensation, accretions are not a problem."*

With His comment, I am immediately aware of my own Kether, Chokhmah, and Binah around my head. Suddenly, I laugh because I have an image of myself as a version of that famous photo of Aleister Crowley with a triangular hat on his head, making a two-fisted gesture with his thumbs. Reth takes pity on me.

"Wear the Neshamah as the Triple Crown that it is," He says with what seems to me to be an ever-so-slight edge of feigned exasperation. Nevertheless, His suggestion brings a somewhat better image to my mind, enabling us to complete the Work of the day.

Tasting the Tree

We all have different ways that we perceive the invisible realms, the astral, if you will. Some people "see" either clear or dreamlike images in their mind's eye. Some people "hear" in their mind's ear. Others say they simply know or intuit or feel. Lesser used senses, at least for many of us, include smell and taste. This exercise is about tasting on the astral. It will not only help develop another of our astral senses, but also, it's fun. Here's how Raphael guided me through it:

"*Tiphereth*," says the Archangel, "*is the one Sphere directly connected to all the other Spheres, except Malkhuth, which is mediated. You can taste all the Spheres from here. What does Kether taste like?*"

"It is a kind of peace in the midst of everything. It's like being at a party and you look at all your friends around you and realize how truly beautiful they all are," I say.

Clearly, I hadn't caught on to the exercise at this point. I was feeling or sensing more than tasting. We continue. I give my taste impression, then Raphael adds commentary.

"Chokhmah tastes like a strange, but not unpleasant mineral," I venture.

"*That is the Seed of Becoming. It is what lightning tastes like,*" says Raphael.

"Binah tastes like salted, black chocolate," I say.

"*Salt and bitter,*" He says, "*the necessary ingredients for coalescence.*"

"Chesed is like wine and stone."

"*It is the taste of building, creating, persuading,*" says the Archangel.

"Blood and salt and air for Gevurah," I say.

"*It is the taste of strength; it creates an opening for justice and the breath of freedom,*" He comments.

"Netzach tastes like sharp, green grass, smoke and fire, and pine," I say.

"*It is the ecstasy inspired by creation; un-control brought into control,*" He responds.

"Hod is like iron in water that I'm drinking."

"*To drink it is to absorb the crystalline structure of pre-things,*" Raphael says.

"Yesod tastes like what a lotus blossom would really taste like if you ate it, green and weird," I say.

"*It is the taste of new things, which are many here.*"

To taste Malkhuth, I must taste through Yesod. "It tastes like everything, from dirt to food," I say.

"*It is the Vessel of All That Is,*" Raphael comments.

And Tiphereth? It tastes like honey in which I can discern the terroir, the flavor of every flower the Tipheretic bees have ever visited.

Rose Cross Ritual Variation: the Circle of Angel Fire

This is a variation of the R∴R∴ et A∴C∴'s Rose Cross Ritual that Raphael unfolded for me in one session.

I see a circular fire at the center of the Temple of Tiphereth. Solar flares erupt and reside. I know intuitively that I am to purify myself in that solar fire before the rite. Unafraid, I step into the fire without hesitation. I am immediately surrounded by what seems like many, many Wings of Fire. Raphael explains that these are the wings of the Host of Tiphereth, the Melakhim.

In this variation of the Rose Cross Ritual, the Adept surrounds herself with the fiery wings of the Melakhim instead of the symbol of the Rose Cross. Instead of tracing the Rose Cross in the crossquarters, above, and below, the Adept makes a "wings" gesture. With her hands crossed over her heart, she opens them into the Orant position. Furthermore, instead of vibrating the name of Yehesuah, the Adept vibrates the name of Raphael. For the final and larger Rose Cross of the original ritual, the Adept substitutes the full signs of Osiris Slain and Risen.

"What is different about this rite compared to the Rose Cross?" I ask. "What should this rite be used for?"

"This rite is more actively healing and protective," says the Archangel. *"It Calls the Host of Tiphereth and the Wings of the Host should be seen as beating slowly, stirring activity in Tiphereth."*

The ritual can be fine-tuned by making the gesture facing outward for protection; facing inward for actively healing.

On Raphael as an Oracular God

"I," said Raphael one day without preamble, *"like Apollōn, am Oracular. We will practice."*

At first blush, Raphael as an Oracle may seem surprising; until you think about it for half a second. In fact, Apollon is a pretty good equivalence for Raphael Tipherethel on just about anybody's "corresponding Deities" chart. First and foremost, both are Healing Deities. Both are solar connected. In their myths, both slew a Great Adversary; in Apollon's case, the Python, and in Raphael's, the demon Asmodeus.

Also interesting is support in gematria for this. By gematria, Raphael's name adds up to 311, a prime number (Resh=200 + Peh=80 + Aleph=1 + Lamed=30). Twice 311 is 622, which by gematria is the same as Greek *Omphaia*, "Oracular," literally "Speaking with a Divine Voice." Double that (622 × 2 = 1244), and we get another relevant Greek equivalence: *Hierophantēs*, "Revealer of the Sacred."

So Raphael's statement of oracular-ness is no longer very puzzling at all.

The Archangel feels free to tell me *"we will practice"* so immediately because He has dug around in my head and knows that I have been a Pythia for Apollōn many times. Back in the '90s, for quite a number of consecutive years, a group of us worked a Portland version of the Oracle at Delphi. During that time, I served in a variety of roles, including Pythia, the priestess who speaks Apollōn's words for the seekers.

In keeping with this, I am given a Raphaeline version of the Pythia's chamber of oracular audience: I am to sit on a doubled tripod of six legs (easy to decode, eh, Adepti?) over the solar-flare fire that burns in the center of the Temple of Tiphereth in which we have been Working. I take my place and I become the blue center of the holy flame. Beluel comes to protect me, but I do not Assume Her.

I sense Raphael 'arrange' Himself above me. He opens His wings. There is a great SOUND of things falling into place. I open myself to His energy. He gives me some practice oracles having to do with the zodiac, which He calls the *"twelve cattle arranged in the sky to send heavenly messages to humankind."* This is the other time when the Angelic message of "You are not alone" was given.

"Our Guidance is all around you. Do not say, 'I don't know what to do.' Be quiet and listen. Tame the roaring beasts inside. I am the Guide and know you partake of My nature."

To clarify what I've been thinking, I ask, "May I say You are an Oracular God?"

"You may say it," He replied.

And then I ask for an oracular message for the Adepts of the R∴R∴ et A∴C∴. Raphael further opens Himself to the influence of the Higher; He says this is an *"accumulated message"*:

"The Work you do is simply the Work of all human beings. If you are not changing your world for the better, you are not doing the Work. Yet know that this can take time. Plant and grow fine roses in your garden [This is clearly metaphorical]. *Open rather than close. Purify rather than reject. Sacrifice lower for higher. Transform rather than destroy. There is conservation of matter and conservation of energy—however you may conceive of it. Attend to power; use it with wisdom. Attend to humility; feel its weight upon your soul. In this central place* [Tiphereth], *I am the Archangel of Connectedness, even Connectivity. I send the Melakhim where They are needed and They appear as I am. I am The Guide. Ask Me. Do you understand?"*

"I think so," I say.

"It is enough."

Raphael counsels that each oracular session should be ended by recharging the prophetess or prophet. To do this at this time, Raphael descends so that His Form is over both mine and Beluel's. He reopens His wings. There is a shock of power as Divine energy flows into my body, soul, and spirit. As a footnote, Raphael says that He speaks *"ruach to ruach,"* and He reminds me that health questions are particularly appropriate to Him.

On Sacrifice

As an Adept in my tradition, I am no stranger to the concept of sacrifice. It is also familiar in my roles as a priestess of Isis and a Dionysian mænad. In the early centuries CE, the Beloved of Isis, Osiris, and Dionysos were, in fact, specifically identified with Jesus; so the harmonies are there. Indeed there are those who have tried to say Jesus was just another of the Pagan dying and reborn Deities. It's not that simple, of course. According to Their myths, the deaths of the three Gods served quite different purposes. Still, for all three, there is a dissolution or destruction of the previous self that is at the heart of Their sacrifices.

It is at the heart of the 5=6 sacrifice, too: "I die to the old life and am reborn to the new." The re-enactment of the sacrificial part of that ritual is an opportunity to not only reaffirm the original rite, but also to attempt to accept its magic on a deeper level, withholding as little as possible of myself and placing my trust more fully in the Divine. Early on, when Raphael first made the suggestion, I told Him I wasn't sure how to do that, to open more fully. So from time to time, He would show me things, ways to look at it. For instance, in the Temple of Tiphereth, I am placed in the center in the form of a cross, but there is no cross, just Beluel's wings to support me.

"This is the Temple of Compassion," says Raphael, *"The place of saying 'yes.'"*

Soon, I am aware of the images or spirits of many people passing through me. I am reminded that I must be more generous in giving to those who come to me; that while they take something away, they also leave something of themselves in exchange. Beluel notes that She can help facilitate this exchange. I forget to ask how because I am focused on the feeling here, an ecstatic sort of feeling in which I am intensely interested in everyone I see and feel a soft love for them.

Another time, Raphael called Tiphereth the Heart of Becoming (and another time, the Intelligent and Moveable Heart) and noted that its sacrificial nature is part of the purification of the Sphere. He said that sacrifice is giving up for the Greater Good and that since Mind and Will are powers of Tiphereth, they assist in the decision to sacrifice. It is the state of "throwing open the doors" regardless of reservations. It is simple, but not easy.

"How does Heart and Beauty come into it?" I ask.

"It is a Glory, a Beauty that feeds the Heart when it [the sacrifice] *is done,"* He says.

He also noted the connection between healing and sacrifice: *"The Healer, like the Sacrifice, must be pure."* I'm not exactly sure what this means. Sheer cleanliness is a given. Purity of intent? Willing to completely give one's self over to the healing, which might apply to both healer and healee?

There were a number of times Raphael put me in the cross position prior to the 5=6 reenactment so that we could talk about it and He could show me things. Once, He had me identify with Him, though there wasn't a formal Assumption of the Archangelform.

"Reach out and find all those who, at this very moment, are reaching out to Me," He said. *"I am the Rays of Light. I am the Flares of Fire. I am the Answer to their Calling—and so are you. Reach out and touch them back."*

I do and I see a number of very specific people who are reaching out to Raphael. I can reach out to them and say "yes" to them.

"In the Christian mythos, this is the position of the Savior, the Christos," Raphael says.

"This reminds me of the Chief Adept in the Corpus Christie ritual," I say.

"Yes," He says. *"Now take it bigger."*

"To include those not reaching out..."

"Yes. The supply of Grace is unlimited and unending."

"Am I expected to do this?"

"Work toward it for death," says the Archangel. *"You gain the power to do so from YHVH Eloah va-Daath, from Beauty, and from Compassion."*

I have been reading the Gnostic Gospels as part of my background study, so Raphael uses that: *"Think of the Gnostic Jesus,"* He said, *"the One Whose feet do not touch the ground; His Tiphereth is always ascended."*

"Oh, I see that as a visualization I could use."

"Yes, you have it. Leave the rest to the Divine Machinery. When you sacrifice, you see through the eyes of Jesus, Dionysos, Osiris, all the Sacrificed Ones. My eyes, too."

"What is Your story of sacrifice?" I ask.

"When God emanated Me, He said, 'go down and serve.' For a thousand thousands of time, I have assisted."

"Is it lonely?"

"There is each human being to engage with, but rarely do I see My peers and I am away from My Divine Bliss. Thus I treasure these interactions."

"I have drifted from Your perception," I note.

"Resume."

"How do I keep my balance?"

"Connect to the Higher. It is Flow. All is Flow. Flow—and Lightning on occasion."

"Am I ready for tomorrow?"

"You are ready enough."

Day Forty

For the past week, I've had a cold and been doing the rituals more or less silently. So I'm really, really glad that I'm well enough to vibrate today. I sound like an old motorboat, but I can vibrate.

After the invocations, I am once more within the Tiphereth Temple. The many Forms of Raphael Tipherethel in which I have seen Him during these past 40 days are there, too: the Egg & Ouroboros, the Living Caduceus, the Tattooed and Serpent-Bearing One, He of the Black and Starry Eyes Full of God Chaos, the Great Bird and the Little Bird. The Melakhim, the Host of Tiphereth has come, too.

There is a Great Cross in neutral grey at the center of the temple. At its base, a solar-flare fire is burning without consuming. I look up, but cannot see the top of the cross, it extends infinitely, but I am aware of the crossbar. I begin to circumambulate the temple. I put on the Robe of Mourning. It is light and I understand that there is not much in my own life for which I mourn; I have been fortunate. I put on the Chain. It symbolizes the external worries of the world, from war to environmental destruction. It is heavy, but not unbearably so. I put on the Crown of Thorns and Roses. This is the garland of the Sacrifice; as we have always done.

I complete the circumambulation and come before Raphael of the Black and Starry Eyes.

"I am ready," I say.

He nods and the Beluelim take my arms and we rise up. I am fastened to the cross. Immediately, Raphael is before me.

"Be the Sacrifice," He says. *"Osiris Slain."*

As I make myself become aware of my vulnerability, my heart becomes a Sun and its rays connect to all the Forms of Raphael and each one of the Host. My heart is a glittering Sun shining. Its Light obliterates shadow.

"Make your Confession," Raphael demands.

I recite the Tiphereth Clause of the Oath of an Adepta Minor, assenting to each word in all the ways that I can imagine to do so. I feel a slight pain in my physical chest. I invoke Yeheshuah the Christos, Osiris, and Dionysos. In my mind I maintain a litany of assent, confirming again and again that I am willing to take the next step in my spiritual growth, whatever that step may be.

"Now, Osiris Risen," says Raphael.

I fold my arms and feel movement in my Middle Pillar. Malkhuth rises to Yesod. Yesod rises to Tiphereth. Tiphereth rises to Daath, which is no more, but adds Its Knowledge to the Mind and Heart of Tiphereth Risen. Things feel very different now.

Immediately I see how this new set of energies could work for the Adept. The Manifesting Power is now invisibly present in the natural place of human manifestation, the genitals. Yesod at my heart feels strange; perhaps this would enhance the creativity of the Adept. Ascended, Tiphereth is now above Chesed and Gevurah. Thus these Spheres are now to be preceded by Tiphereth's Heart and Reason and will gain additional balance thereby. The triad of Chesed, Gevurah, and Yesod is very, very powerful. There is almost infinite energy there for Making. The triad of Malkhuth, Hod, and Netzach is comfortable and balanced. The Tree's Heart of Tiphereth, no longer the center, instead receives directly from Abba and Aima Elohim. I wonder whether the Adept Working in the Ascended Tree could purposely reenact The Fall as a very powerful method of magical manifestation.

"This is where the placements are when you pass beyond the Veil," explains Raphael.

"Could they be used as I envisioned?"

"Not while you are manifest," He says, *"It is a construct of the Heavens."* Then, clearly changing the topic, He says, *"It is enough. You have assented and it has been heard. Go now and do your Work, with your Order and for your Divine Ones."*

I think to myself, "I do love You, Raphael, just not in that way."

He can read my mind. *"Yes, of course,"* He says.

As my Sephiroth re-descend to their Fallen state, I realize that the Ascended or Restored Tree is an enormously powerful circuit without a ground. With the re-descent of my Spheres, the circuit in me is grounded once more, strongly and perhaps more gracefully.

The Beluelim help me from the cross.

The Work is complete.

Epilogue: On Being a Priestess of Raphael—or Not

This was a difficult article to write. I tend to be a rather private person. Most of this kind of Work—the hard, often messy, embarrassingly self-revelatory work of spiritual growth—I share with only a very few people, or only with my Deities. Now I've made a chapter of it public. Deep breath.

Unless you've done this sort of Magical Work before, you could be forgiven for thinking that I'm just the teensiest bit delusional or, at the very least, it's 'all in my head.' I would, in fact, agree that a good deal of it is in my head; in fact, it should be. The more an Adept knows about what's going on in her head, the more that knowledge can be a valuable part of the always ongoing struggle for self-understanding that is one of the vital foundations of spiritual growth. As to the part that (I believe) is not just in my head? Well, that's the really fascinating stuff. And perhaps, just perhaps, it is in that unknown, surprising, and colorful soil that the seeds of enlightenment can be planted and flourish.

So I've written about this Archangelic adventure; and the writing of it is part of my sacrifice. I am saying yes, regardless of reservations and vulnerability. I hope the Adepts among you will gain some ideas for your own explorations. I hope those of you who have not yet done this type of Work will now have a taste of what it can be like.

This finally brings us back to one of my initial reasons for this endeavor: to explore the priestessly invitation Raphael had extended to me all those years ago.

If you've been following along, perhaps you won't be all that surprised to learn that, at least at this time, I have not accepted the beautiful Tattooed and Serpent-Bearing Archangel's invitation to His service. In the end, my priestess relationships are both passionate and religious. On the passionate side, I fall deeply in love with my Deities. I serve Them because I love Them, because I can't help but do so. At any given time and with any given Being, that kind of relationship either happens or it doesn't. What's more, to do it properly—that is, with energy and devotion—this kind of relationship requires a significant expenditure of time. As I am already a priestess of Isis and of Dionysos, the available time I have to offer is limited (see "mortgage" in the first part of this article).

The other side of this whole equation is, of course, religious. I'm Pagan; not Christian, not Jewish. I cannot, in good conscience, give the Archangel what priest-esshood—in my experience and in my heart—demands. While Raphael is clearly willing to work with me in my own mythological context, it wouldn't be right if I didn't also work with Him in His.

That said, Raphael and I have magical Work to do together. (No, really. He gave me an actual list in one of our sessions.) So I will be liberally exercising my Adept's prerogative to Work in a wide variety of pantheons—Christian, Jewish, Hermetic Qabbalistic, as well as my natural Pagan ones. In that way, I am sure that I will be, at least at times, what Raphael asked me to be: "...My messenger, an angel of an Angel."

Appendix: An Aretalogy of Raphael Tipherethel

An aretalogy is a recitation of virtues (Greek *arētai*), usually in the first person, and often by a Divine Person. Isis is the Deity most famous for Her aretalogies, but I think They all deserve at least one; most certainly Raphael Tipherethel does. That's why I insisted we devote two sessions to receiving His aretalogy.

The way I do it is to include my laptop in the magic circle. After invocation, I place my hands on the keyboard in the correct *qwerty* position, close my eyes, and type what I perceive without punctuation or capitalization. Afterwards, when I'm in conscious-writer mode rather than entranced-channel mode, I edit it as I see fit to make it more beautiful and comprehensible. Sometimes there are strange phrases or images that I don't understand, but which insist on staying. There are several of these in this Aretalogy of Raphael Tipherethel:

> *I am Raphael Tipherethel, an ancient Power of Grace and Form and Intellect of Heart.*
> *I am the Power at the Center of the Tree of Life.*
> *From that place in the Fallen Tree, My Wings touch All That Is.*
> *I am a participant in The Fall, a Divine Volunteer.*
> *I am with you.*
>
> *I am the One of the Ennead Who was sent to caretake Creation In the Beginning.*
> *I am Life Divine at the Gateway.*
> *I keep the Way of the "Self Consumed in the Heart; the Heart Expanded in the Self."*
> *I am Trismegistos at the Heart of the Sun.*

I am the Far-Wandering Mind, the Conceiver of the Impossible, the Mechanic of Divine Power.

I am the God Speaker, the Hearing Ear, the Warrior Wing.

I pour down Light on all Beings who call upon My Name.

Also, I am a Sacrificial One.

I carry the message of Divine to Human and Human to Divine in the place Between the Worlds.

I am the End of Egotism; the Limit.

I am the Illusion of Separateness; Constant am I.

In the Grace of Aeons, I am Paramount.

I am a Reconciler, a Gateway of Forgiveness.

I am Power Immeasurable.

I am Willforce.

I am Hope.

I am the One Who holds the Knowledge of your Beauty and Sacrifices.

This Truth, I possess for I am the Understanding One.

I am manifest to hundreds of thousands right now. They feel My touch; I defend them.

I am Pure Gold, a drop of Un-taint in a Sea of Corruption.

I am in the Helix of Life and all cells know My Name.

I am the outpouring of the Light of God. I am the in-breath of Humanity.

I am the gold of Sun-on-Water, the Beauty of human compassion.

I am Surgery, the cutting out of Evil.

Evil can be bound through Me.

I am the Panacea, without doubt and true.

I am Healing Itself.

I am Green Reeds—hollow and open, conducting Life.

I am far from Death, but I fold My Wings when the time of Death comes to each thing.

That flames illuminate is Mine.

That heat urges growth is one of My Presences.

I am the White Bull, the Golden Eagle, the Shedding Serpent.

I am Transmutation; and Things Transformed are Mine: honey, wine, vinegar.

Serve Me by Work. Serve Me by growth—for what burgeons is also Mine.

I teach Compassionate Arts; Beginnings and Endings.
I teach Magic and its proper use.
I teach the "Crown of Stars," the "Breath of Power," the "Image Behind
the Image."
I teach "Claiming."
I am the Answer to the Right-Asked Question.
I am the Wellspring of Purity.
Do you pray and invoke Me in Purity, as I demand.
Yet know that in the absence of ill will, ignorance is forgiven; wrong
methods are nothing in My eyes.

I am ever Un-angered.
I show the Way to those who invoke Me with sincerity.
Mind-Strong, Heart-Wise am I.
I see Beauty in Everything.
With the simplicity of Angels, I am Agreeable.
Bring your Innermost to Me and let it blossom under the Solar Gaze
of Beauty in the Place of Mediation, the Middle, the in-Between.
Refresh yourself in Me.
Stand in strength in Me, under the Guidance of Heart in the Place of
Wisdom, O Rising One Opened Out into the Universe!

References

Primary References

"Grimoire ou la cabale, par Armadel" in Bibliothèque nationale de France Arsenal
MS 2494 (formerly MS de la Bibliothèque de l'Arsenal S. et A. F. N° 88).
English translation in Mathers, S.L. MacGregor. *The Grimoire of Armadel*.
London: Routlege & Kegan Paul, 1980.

Origen, *Contra Celsum*. English translation in Henry Chadwick. *Origen, Contra
Celsum. Translated with an Introduction and notes*. Cambridge: University
Press, 1953.

Cat ritual for many purposes in Papyrus gr. Louvre 2391 (=P. Mimaut, PGM
   III). English translation in Betz, Hans Dieter (ed.). *The Greek Magical Papyri
   in Translation, Including the Demotic Spells. Volume One: Texts*. Chicago, Ill.:
   University of Chicago Press, 1986.

Secondary References

Jolly, Karen Louise. "Prayers from the Field: Practical Protection and Demonic
   Defense in Anglo-Saxon England," in *Traditio*, Vol. 61 (2006), pp. 95–147.

✛

Substance Through Spirit

A Reflection on Magical Evocation and Talisman Construction

BRYAN GARNER / FRATER ASHEN CHASSAN

FRATER ASHEN CHASSAN / BRYAN GARNER is a practicing occultist and grimoric traditionalist who has been involved in Western ceremonial magic since 1999. His passions center on reproducing experiments from the Solomonic magical texts and exploring their effectiveness. His approach is based on a serious study of historic forms of magic and spirit communication. He is the author of Gateways Through Stone and Circle, *a manual of evocation for the planetary intelligences. You may follow his blogs at* Frater Ashen Chassan *(ashenchassan.* wordpress.com) *and* A Magician's Workings *(bryanashen.blogspot.com).*

Substance Through Spirit

*A Reflection on Magical Evocation
and Talisman Construction*

HE WESTERN ESOTERIC MYSTERIES are currently experiencing an unprecedented resurgence of interest. In the growing popularity and increased recognition of the occult or magical sciences, many talented individuals are coming forth to demonstrate their skill in either the academic study or the actual practice of classical forms of ritual or ceremonial magic. Various manuscripts and volumes of magical practice ranging in age from Late Antiquity to the eighteenth century have been translated by reputable scholars, and many worthy practitioners are attempting to replicate magical procedures which until recently remained incomplete and obscure. In accomplishing this, these scholars and magicians have paved the way for others to garner the benefits by following their operations. As a result, more people have found that they are able to produce magical effects and observable results by conducting experiments in classical magic which involve the aid of spirits, angels, demons, and gods.

The angels and other spirits of the classical books of magic known as the *grimoires* are gaining more acknowledgment in esoteric and occult circles as being sentient, independent, and active forces in the universe, instead of archetypical manifestations of the magician's own psyche. It has also been argued within these same circles that the spirits themselves are the ones largely responsible for the actual magical effects and results occurring after a successful ritual.

Angelic magic, and particularly angelic evocation, has quite unpredictably become the central vocation of my own magical career. More than any other classes of spirits in ceremonial magic, the angelic beings of the elemental, planetary, and zodiacal realms, as well as those of the fixed stars, have become my chief assets in magical accomplishment, learning, and even business. Since my continued work with the Planetary archangels, the *Almadel* angels, and the *Arbatel* angels, I have come into contact with several other angelic entities who have become true assets in my attempts to understand and operate from the occult principles of reality. I believe in many respects that my own work has recently taken leaps and bounds in uncovering the nature and working principles of several of these celestial beings and their preferred methodologies for working with humankind. More than simply comparing and contrasting historical works and manuscripts on magic and angels, I have conducted practical investigations into the true nature of these beings by conversing with them directly. Unfortunately, due to the subjective nature of such experiences, the validity of these experiments cannot be further confirmed or denied past my own discernment and that of my colleagues. Before the avid seeker after true magic loses heart, however, I will explain the process by which I attempt to discern authentic interactions from imaginative flights of fancy.

Through Prayer, Practice, Work, & Trial: The Standards for Achieving and Verifying Audience with the Celestial Intelligences

There is a methodology which I utilize in magical evocation and other forms of spirit contact for uncovering whether my experiences and those of my scryer have merit. I have established a set of criteria for success, and use a systematic approach to determine whether those criteria are met. Crucially, I record the entire process, from the initial contact with the spirit to the final follow-up and review of results long after the operation has been concluded. I document my questions and the responses of the spirits, both any information received and any agreements reached. I also conduct further research and comparison between historical magical texts and my and my scryer's experiences. Not only this, but I follow up each magical operation with further investigations to see if the information given by the entity has validity, and of course to see if any requests to which the spirit agreed were indeed carried out, and if any magical effects became apparent in physical reality.

Before anything can be assumed about the nature of a magical being (angel, spirit, elemental, godform, etc.) or its abilities, the true magician must first be able to contact the being and encounter it face to face. Only then one can become more confident regarding what the being is able to accomplish. Where evocations are concerned, I make sure the following criteria are met:

I. Initially, I conduct the magical experiments myself to witness and experience what I can about the intended spirit. I only consider the magical evocations which register with the majority of my senses to have validity or usefulness for the sake of constructive interaction. In other words, I only consider the invocations and evocations where I visually see a discernible and apparent entity, change in the environment, color, light and other visual senses as a verifiable arrival of the spirit in ceremonial magic.

Likewise, if I am working with a magical scryer or seer, he or she will have to behold similar phenomena as well for the experiment to be considered successful. When working with scryers, I make sure that they are not informed ahead of time which entity we will be attempting to contact. Further credibility is lent to your experiment when your scryer is not educated in classical magical correspondences or archetypes or Hermetic occultism. The best if not "purest" results have been achieved from those whose preexisting knowledge of magical matters is limited. I've enjoyed immensely the wealth of information garnered during evocation rituals where my scryer had little to no knowledge of the spirit we were to contact until we were in the midst of the ceremony. It seems that the clearest and most detailed information has come when no presumptions were made by the scryer as to the nature or identity of the spirit beforehand.

If clear contact cannot be made I do not consider the operation successful, as there is too much room for the mind to fill in the blanks by the use of imagination or wishful thinking. I've learned that the arrival of a spirit or angel cannot be mentally forced into being, but is something which occurs as a result of several subtle elements all being present during the time of the invocation.

II. Second, once the spirit has arrived, I require clear enough communication for me to perceive visual manifestations and imagery or audible responses which occur in response to my spoken questions. If no discernible or understandable responses occur within a reasonable time after posing each question, I consider the experiment unsuccessful. I consider this to be true even if the issue may lie in my own ability to perceive what a spirit was intending to convey. The most intense experiences are dynamic, intensely emotional, and profound in which I had difficulty recalling specific details of what transpired during the operation and everything the spirit related to me in adequate detail. This is due to a number of factors, including the inability to write quickly enough to record what the spirit is saying, showing in visions and imagery, and relating in emotional stirrings or impressions which convey certain things that are indescribable in words. I've found that all of these forms of communication are vital to capturing more completely the message which the angel or spirit is trying to convey to the magician and scryer. For this reason I've adopted using a voice recorder while taking notes and recording impressions. Any errors will most likely be on the ability to absorb, comprehend, and most of all retain all of the information and sensations which transpire during an operation of invocation or evocation.

III. During a magical operation, I pose several questions to the spirit in areas in which I expect it to have expert knowledge and practical involvement. Also, I really only consider information and detail which I could not readily find by researching basic facts and history which is now a readily accessible convenience through the internet and other media sources. Luckily, my experiences when conversing with an angel have never been drab or uninspiring. Even when some of the replies are rather complex, esoteric, and riddling, I find that I am inspired and gain new insight into the area of my inquiry. The ongoing results have been more than enough to continue my work in this area. I don't always receive the answers and responses for which I was initially looking, but my spirit informants, in the manner of great teachers and highly evolved beings, typically give me the answers I need in relation to my current situation and experience.

IV. If the spirit claims that it can produce a particular influence, effect, or action in the physical world, there should be observable results following the conclusion of the operation. My experience from nearly every result that I have witnessed is that the effect in the world never quite occurs the way I expected or predicted. Instead of this being a frustration, I've grown to appreciate the unexpected form of these occurrences as a further indication that the working was carried out by a force and intelligence besides my own imagination.

If no perceivable effect occurs, the magician and the scryer (if a separate scryer other than the magician is employed) should certainly follow up with subsequent evocations to question the spirit as to why there was an apparent lack of results. There may be a reason such as a time constraint unforeseen by the magician. There may have been a break in communication and understanding concerning the imagined result as well. For the advanced magician making talismans or magical implements for others, it's important to receive feedback and verification that your creations are functioning as they should.

I must reiterate that the magician's discernment will be a key factor in determining whether the spirit in question is actually able to produce the effects it claims (and perhaps by extension whether it is indeed the spirit you intended to evoke) or if it is instead attempting to befuddle and mislead the magician with falsehoods. The existence of a plethora of oaths, bindings, and penalties in classical books of magic requiring the spirit to tell the truth is an obvious indicator that this has been a major concern for conjurors through the years. I believe that much of the apparent discord or ambiguity seems to have existed due to the unwittingly mistaken assumptions made by the magician about what is intended or possible for a spirit working on a different level of existence. In fact, errors in communication between an incarnate invoker and a discarnate spirit are bound to occur, as the perceptions and understandings of these inhabitants of very foreign worlds will undoubtedly result in very different perspectives. After several years of performing magical evocations, I consider the human element to contain inherent flaws in perception and interpretation, where spiritual interaction is concerned. It is well documented that human beings in general are poor witnesses, as both observers and relaters of how events transpired in the physical world. I can readily assume that these flaws would be even greater in the realm of spiritual interaction, where the very ability to perceive and communicate with an incorporeal being is a feat in itself. The process is further complicated by the multitude of mental faculties—many of them initially unfamiliar and undeveloped—which we use to perceive such beings. There is no small amount of both talent and experience required to discern and communicate effectively with spiritual beings. With all of these variables and the obvious possibility of error, I am genuinely surprised each and every time that an evocation succeeds, from the initial contact to the final result. Amazingly enough, they continue to do so time and again, so my interest and confidence in the operations of magic remain high.

In the face of a seemingly endless array of stories and legends containing spontaneous visions and bizarre accidental encounters with spirits, ghosts, demons, and beings of uncertain nature, ritual magic provides a step-by-step process by which a person can beneficially accrue relevant information by means of direct, intentional spiritual contact. The process of magical evocation creates a structure through which it is possible for a cordial, clear, and concise meeting to take place between two entities—a magician and an evoked spirit—through a formalized and respectful exchange. Through the rigorous adherence to ceremony, ritual, and practice, we remove many of our contemporary justifications of entitlement which seems inseparably saturated in modern western culture. If nothing else, the rigorous adherence to ceremony, etiquette, and tradition speak directly to the subconscious on the importance of the event (in this case the veritable evocation of a spiritual entity before you). It is customary across human civilization that any time of importance is typically marked out by some fashion of ceremony. Regardless of the individual spirit's preference or taste for such ceremony, we should always present our best side forward, and honor their arrival with utmost diplomacy. To speak and treat with beings who are not human, and who seldom match the portrayals of them in popular media, we must assume no familiar concept as to their nature and disposition towards us in the beginning. Likewise, to assume spirits neither desire nor appreciate formal and respectful discourse is a foolhardy way to approach any sentient, intelligent being.

Here are a few more points from my experience lending credibility and importance to the usage of classical methods of magical evocation.

Once several contacts have been made with a particular spirit, and due to steady exchange and responses from the spirit indicating that it appreciates and responds to particular forms of communication (e.g., forms of greeting, offerings, prayers, images, and other symbols), it would naturally be advisable to follow the recommendations of the spirits in further contacts. The only cautionary note to include here would be to use your discretion and discernment when a spirit advises you to perform any action which would give the spirit greater influence and control over your life. This is one of the notorious hazards in working with spiritual beings, and the reason that attentiveness, cleverness, and discernment must be essential proficiencies within the repertoire of the magician.

The magician should contact a spirit numerous times in order to better understand its attributes and the effects it produces, which cause it to be useful for life in the physical world. Many times the spirits and angels described in classical catalogs seem vast and mighty in their offices, but in practice the direct result produced by a particular entity in the physical world can be somewhat difficult to distinguish. While dedicated magicians make a point of learning all they can from any spirits with whom they come in contact, they may well find with experience that only a select few will be particularly useful to them in their magical careers. Likewise it is probable that the magician will only be truly compatible with a particular number of spirits, and thus will only be able to harness and convey the power of those spirits into works of enduring magic such as the fashioning of talismans.

Talismans: Physical Containers of Esoteric Power

Ironically, interest in ancient and medieval forms of magical practice seems to have increased with the advancement of scientific technology. Talented magicians, occultists, and scholars have uncovered and translated many texts of magical processes, connecting the dots between cultures, traditions and systems. These same talented individuals have brought previously obscure and untranslatable bits of information to more cohesive and systematic approaches to authentic and ancient magical procedure.

The Solomonic texts remain among the most popular workbooks for practitioners of authentic ritual magic, and the growing number of published Solomonic manuscripts and complementary translations add richness to the endeavor. The most noted of these texts is the *Key of Solomon,* in which we find classic images of talismans corresponding to each of the seven planetary intelligences. With each planet, a set of various offices or abilities is presented as being accessible to the magician by the aid of the spirits or angels associated with the particular talismans.[1]

It is quite apparent that on their own, the simple presence of the symbols and sigils pictured on the talismans have no inherent power or ability to effect the promised change or effect in the physical world.[2] Regardless of what has been said or written, the symbols and sigils themselves will not initiate any result for the owner or beholder unless the spirit takes it upon itself to enact some sort of effect. The cases I've come across are very few, and the crediblity of those seem questionable. The ability to construct an authentic talisman is not an exercise in simply engraving or drawing various seals during astrologically appropriate times. The process historically required—and presently requires—a competent magician, able to call forth the entity who bears the particular power with which he wishes to imbue the talisman, and either beseechingly or forcefully bind the power of the spirit to the talisman.

As with many ritualistic objects used in magic, exactly what a talisman is, what form it takes, and how it functions vary according to different traditions and based on the experience of the individual who constructs it. The *American Heritage Dictionary* offers a typical modern definition of a talisman as "an object marked with magical signs and believed to confer on its bearer supernatural powers or protection." The English word comes from the Arabic *talsam*, an alteration of Greek *telesma*, meaning both "completion or perfection" and "a religious rite." *Telesma* itself comes from the verb *teleō*, which means "I complete or perfect" and "I perform a rite." Ascertaining the meaning from the original Greek term, one can see that it is the process and method for charging the talisman that in fact makes it a talisman. It is not just the physical material or even the symbols inscribed thereon, but the actual magical rite or ceremonial procedure by which the base material is imbued with its magical properties and functionality.

Another excellent explanation comes from Migene Gonzalez-Wippler:

> Amulets and talismans are often considered interchangeable despite their differences. For example, the amulet is an object with natural magical properties, whereas a talisman must be charged with magical powers by a creator; it is this act of consecration or "charging" that gives the talisman its alleged magical powers. The talisman is always made for a definite reason

---

1. Illustrations of the planetary talismans from the *Key* are easy to find and also to buy in a variety of commercialized forms. Many companies have simply had the talismanic diagrams stamped on various metallic medallions, such as the pewter variety which can be bought at nearly every New Age store.

2. The same is also of course true for the over-popularized demonic sigils from the *Goetia*, which can now be found on trendy clothing (including spandex leggings!) which fortunately have little to no potency from the mere printed sigils, let alone any trace of the spirit's actual presence. (I wonder what interesting reactions would occur if they actually did!)

whilst an amulet can be used for generic purposes such as averting evil or attracting good luck. According to the Hermetic Order of the Golden Dawn, a magical order active in the United Kingdom during the late 19th and early 20th centuries, a talisman is "a magical figure charged with the force which it is intended to represent. In the construction of a talisman, care should be taken to make it, as far as possible, so to represent the universal forces that it should be in exact harmony with those you wish to attract, and the more exact the symbolism, the easier it is to attract the force."[3]

The craftsperson making the talisman would presumably already be familiar with the symbolism connected to the chosen force, usually either planetary or elemental, in order for it to be effective. Various magical associations in synchronization with the selected elemental or planetary force, such as colors, scents, geometric patterns, and Kabalistic figures, may be integrated in the creation of a talisman. In several medieval talismans, geomantic signs and symbols were used in relation to different planets. It is also feasible to augment the talisman by adding a Biblical verse or other inscription which corresponds to the particular entity or power with which it is connected.

Some talismanic images are so prevalent that even those ignorant about mystical symbolism will often recognize symbols like the Star of David or the Seal of Solomon.

The Seal of Solomon, also known as the interlaced triangles, is another primeval talisman and amulet that has been commonly used in several religions; but though it is said to have been the emblem by which the wise king ruled the Genii, it could not have originated with him as its use dates back much further than the Jewish Dispensation. As a talisman it was believed all-powerful, being the ideal symbol of the absolute, and was worn for protection against all fatalities, threats, and trouble, and to protect its wearer from all evil. In its constitution, the triangle with its apex upwards represents good, and with the inverted triangle, evil: the triangle with its apex up being typical of the Trinity that exists in several religions; in India . . . its three angles represent Brahma, Vishnu, and Siva, the Creator, Preserver, and Destroyer or Regenerator; in Egypt it represented Osiris, Isis and Horus; and in the Christian Church, the Holy Trinity. As a whole it stands for the elements of fire and spirit, composed of the three virtues (love, truth, and wisdom). The triangle with its apex downward symbolized the element of water, and typified the material world, or the three enemies of the soul: the world, the flesh, and the Devil, and the cardinal sins, envy, hatred and malice. Therefore, the meaning of the two triangles interlaced, is the victory of spirit over matter, and at the beginning of our present civilization was believed an all-powerful talisman and amulet, especially when used

---

3. Migene Gonzalez-Wippler, *The Complete Book Of Amulets & Talismans* (St. Paul, Minn: Llewellyn Publications, 1991).

with either a Cross of Tau, the Hebrew Yodh, or the Egyptian Crux Ansata in the center.[4]

A Variety of Talismans

Talismans have been created to achieve virtually every result, and to cure every ailment, and have been crafted from a diversity of materials in an array of forms. However, all of the various types of talismans will be little more than curiosities to the uninitiated and inexperienced. Simply copying interesting symbols and hoping for brilliant effects is delving into fantasy, not magic. It is not only the choice of the proper materials and the addition of appropriate symbols, but the timing, method of construction, and most importantly, *the spiritual imbuement of the material by the relevant spirit* that makes the object a veritable talisman, a functioning implement of magic. Only those true magicians who have studied and assimilated the information congruent with a specific set of symbols, images, and patterns, as well as the precepts for constructing and charging a physical object as a bearer and manifestor of the associative energy, will be able to produce a true talisman through direct contact with the spiritual forces which govern these correspondences, relating one thing to another in a powerful symmetry and harmonious tuning of elements and images.

Choosing a particular talisman to make would and should rely on the magician's grimoric and religious tradition and chosen field of expertise. I present the following examples as a frame of reference, drawing the examples from sources most famous for their talismanic depictions. Obviously there are countless others to consider, which may be more appropriate to your understanding, cultural or sociological outlook, as well as geographic location. Talismans are found in every human culture in India and the Orient as well as from African sources and the Caribbean, such as the Voodoo tradition. Whatever the reader's interest, however, I urge you to take into account that simply replicating an image is not enough to create a working talisman. Creating a physical object imbued with patterns of potent spiritual influences is truly an art form which—like all arts—takes years of immersion and application for the artist to develop true skill and effectiveness. There is a level of maturity and experience that goes into effectively and responsibly making talismans for magical use which result in intervention in the magician's and other people's lives. It is easy for the neophyte to be caught up in the grimoires' claims of spectacular effects and phenomena; taking it all at face value is a sure way to become beguiled, rather than penetrating to the deeper occult meaning of these

---

4. William Thomas Pavitt and Kate Pavitt, *Book of Talismans, Amulets and Zodiacal Gems* (London: William Rider & Son, 1922), pp. 19–20.

talismans. Like any worthwhile endeavor, talisman-making should involve study. A dedicated magician should explore the background of the images, sigils, characters, and geometric patterns on each talisman to grasp the full significance of the magical symbolism beyond the artistic display. The same attention should be given to the names and words written on each talisman, to comprehend their significance and effectiveness. Most talismans bear sacred names of God and names of angels and spirits who preside over the influence which is invoked. Many Solomonic talismans also contain verses from the *Psalms* to give extra power and Biblical backing to the talisman's effect.

Talismanic Pentacles from the Solomonic Grimoires

Fittingly, the first category of talismanic construction and use I am presenting will be from the famous if not infamous *Key of Solomon*. Although the various manuscripts claiming this title are nowhere near the oldest or original source of these planetary talismans, they are perhaps the most recognizable among magical practitioners of all calibers. The *Picatrix*, for example, predates most surviving versions of the *Key* by centuries. However, within the various versions of the *Key of Solomon* are found some of the most enticing and inspiring catalogs of planetary talismans, claiming to produce some of the most astonishing feats of magic. Within its pages are found numerous talismanic images and seals for each of the seven classical planets of medieval astrology. Each talisman has correlating effects and functions which place it under one of the seven main houses or celestial bodies of influence. The *Key* states that the reason these talismans are effective is that the spirits are astonished or fearfully persuaded to obey and serve the magus when these are made correctly.

> The medals or pentacles, which we make for the purpose of striking terror into the spirits and reducing them to obedience, have besides this wonderful and excellent virtue. If thou invokest the spirits by virtue of these pentacles, they will obey thee without repugnance, and having considered them they will be struck with astonishment, and will fear them, and thou shalt see them so surprised by fear and terror, that none of them will be sufficiently bold to wish to oppose thy will. They are also of great virtue and efficacy against all perils of earth, of air, of water, and of fire, against poison which hath been drunk, against all kinds of infirmities and necessities, against binding, sortilege, and sorcery, against all terror and fear, and wheresoever thou shalt find thyself, if armed with them, thou shalt be in safety all the days of thy life.
>
> Through them do we acquire grace and good-will from man and woman, fire is extinguished, water is stayed, and all creatures fear at the sight of the names which are therein, and obey through that fear.

However my personal experience is that the spirits are more apt to consecrate and imbue a talisman with their power if the magus is sincere and cordial in petitioning for their assistance rather than threatening them or demanding their obedience. It is perhaps the evolution of human society beyond feudal hierarchy which has resulted in the inclination of many modern ceremonial magicians to set aside the traditional harsh and dictatorial treatment of spiritual beings as bound servants in favor of an approach with more respect and dignity.

> These pentacles are usually made of the metal the most suitable to the nature of the planet; and then there is no occasion to observe the rule of particular colors. They should be engraved with the instrument of art in the days and hours proper to the planet.

Below are a few examples of select talismans from the *Key of Solomon the King*— one for each planet—with which I have worked in the past. The reason I have selected these talismans is that I found they were most effective when conjuring and invoking their corresponding spirits to appear and consecrate the talisman.

The angelic names listed below are the ones inscribed or written on the talisman and these angels should be evoked prior to as well as during the actual consecration of the talisman. The magician who succeeds in this endeavor should question the angels to understand properly charging the talisman, what further capacities it may contain, what is necessary to keep it an active working talisman, and if there are any restrictions on its use.

The Third Pentacle of Saturn

> This should be made within the magical circle, and it is good for use at night when thou invokest the spirits of the nature of Saturn.

A pentacle of Saturn should be engraved on lead, or drawn on parchment with black ink or paint.

Fig. 1. Third Pentacle of Saturn

The Angels or Spirits of Saturn to be invoked to charge this pentacle are Omeliel, Anachiel, Arauchiah, and Anazachiah.

The First Pentacle of Jupiter

> This serveth to invoke the Spirits of Jupiter, and especially those whose Names are written around the Pentacle, among whom Parasiel is the Lord and Master of Treasures, and teacheth how to become possessor of places wherein they are.

Fig. 2. First Pentacle of Jupiter

A pentacle of Jupiter should be engraved on tin or silver, or drawn on parchment with royal blue ink or paint.

The Angels or Spirits of Jupiter to be invoked to charge this pentacle are Netoniel, Devachiah, Tzedeqiah, and Parasiel.

The First Pentacle of Mars

Fig. 3. *First Pentacle of Mars*

> It is proper for invoking spirits of the nature of Mars, especially those which are written in the pentacle.

A pentacle of Mars should be engraved on iron or steel, or drawn on parchment with red or crimson ink or paint.

The Angels or Spirits of Mars to be invoked to charge this pentacle are Madimiel, Bartzachiah, Eschiel, and Ithuriel.

The Second Pentacle of the Sun

Fig. 4. *Second Pentacle of the Sun*

> This pentacle, and the preceding and following, belong to the nature of the Sun. They serve to repress the pride and arrogance of the solar spirits, which are altogether proud and arrogant by their nature.

A pentacle of the Sun should be engraved on gold, or drawn on parchment with yellow or gold ink or paint.

The Angels or Spirits of Sol to be invoked to charge this pentacle are Shemeshiel, Paimoniah, Rekhodiah, and Malkhiel.

The First Pentacle of Venus

Fig. 5. *First Pentacle of Venus*

> This and those following serve to control the spirits of Venus, and especially those herein written.

A pentacle of Venus should be engraved on copper or bronze, or drawn on parchment with green ink or paint.

The Angels or Spirits of Venus to be invoked to charge this pentacle are Nogahiel, Acheliah, Socohiah and Nangariel.

The Third Pentacle of Mercury

> This and the following serve to invoke the spirits subject unto Mercury; and especially those who are written in this pentacle.

A pentacle of Mercury should be engraved on fixed mercury, silver, or an alloy of metals, or drawn on parchment with mixed colors of ink or paint.

The Angels or Spirits of Mercury to be invoked to charge this pentacle are Kokaviel, Gedoriah, Savaniah, and Chokmahiel.

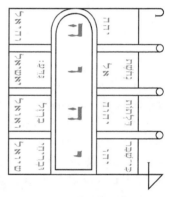

Fig. 6. Third Pentacle of Mercury

The First Pentacle of the Moon

> This and the following serve to call forth and invoke the spirits of the Moon; and it further serveth to open doors, in whatever way they may be fastened.

A pentacle of Luna should be engraved on silver, or drawn on parchment with black, violet, or silver ink or paint.

The Angels or Spirits of the Moon to be invoked to charge this pentacle are Schioel, Vaoel, Yashiel, and Vehiel.[5]

Details of how the above talismans and related ritual implements are utilized will be expounded in the section dealing with making authentic talismans. For this section they are

Fig. 7. First Pentacle of the Moon

listed as examples of talismans I have had experience in and continually work with. In each case I learned something new or was corrected in false assumptions about what the talisman could do or not do effectively. In some cases, it will depend on the level of proficiency of the magician if not their personal interaction and relationship with the above mentioned spirits and angels. In the effort of the magician to construct a lamen of veritable imbued power with the properties of the cosmos

---

5. The versicle on the pentacle is from *Psalm* 107:16 (Hebrew numbering of the *Psalms*) or 106:16 (Septuagint and Vulgate numbering), reading "For He hath broken the gates of brass, and cut the bars of iron asunder." For those who wish to intone the versicle in their talismanic work, the Hebrew is *Ki-sibbar dalthoth nechosheth u-brichei barzel*; the Greek *Hoti synetripsen pylas chalkas kai mochlous sidērous syneklasen*; and the Latin *Quia contrivit portas æreas et vectes ferreos confregit*. —APF

and or entities of representative attributes, it is quite a feat to have a physically perfected talisman which can boast the aforementioned properties and results.

Talismanic Rings from the Solomonic Grimoires

Magical rings have secured a definite spot in the lore of the magical world. The Greek, Germanic, Arabic, and Jewish traditions all have stories of powerful talismanic rings. In classical antiquity, Plato (in *The Republic*, 2.359a–2.360d) tells the story of the Ring of Gyges, which granted invisibility to the wearer, allowing him to eventually become a king in Asia Minor. Gyges' ring remained well-known enough to be included in several post-mediæval grimoires. In northern ring lore, there is the talisman made most famous in Wagner's *The Ring of the Nibelung*, the powerful but cursed magical ring which was obtained by the hero Siegfried from the hoard of the dragon Fafnir.[6] The famous collection of Arabic tales in *The Thousand and One Nights* contains one of the best examples of a spirit bound to a ring and made to serve the master who wears it. An evil sorceror recruits the boy Aladdin to enter a cave and bring out a magic lamp which controls a powerful bound *djinnī* or spirit, and lends the youth a lesser talisman to help him in his task—a magical ring of protection. When Aladdin rubs his hands together in distress, he incidentally rubs the ring, and it is revealed that the ring, like the lamp, performs its magic by means of a *djinnī* who is bound to the talisman. Magic rings are also known in Jewish esoteric tradition; they are referred to in the Talmud and in Midrash.

The Ring of Solomon is famous in Jewish, Muslim, and Christian traditions for its ability to control demons and bestow upon its wearer near-godlike authority. In the ancient *Testament of Solomon*, we are told of the heavenly origin of the ring. The son of the master builder of the temple is being victimized at night by a demon, and Solomon seeks a solution.

> Now when I Solomon heard this, I entered the Temple of God, and prayed with all my soul, night and day, that the demon might be delivered into my hands, and that I might gain authority over him. And it came about through my prayer that grace was given to me from the Lord *Sabaôth* by Michael his archangel. [He brought me] a little ring, having a seal consisting of an engraved stone, and said to me: "Take, O Solomon, king, son of David, the gift which the Lord God has sent thee, the highest Sabaôth. With it thou shalt lock up all demons of the earth, male and female; and with their

---

6. In the twentieth century, modern western culture was refamiliarized with several of the key motifs associated with the traditional lore of talismanic rings—notably the Dragon's Hoard, the Cursed Ring, and the Ring of Invisibility—when they were employed to such powerful effect by Professor Tolkien in his literary *magnum opus.* —APF

help thou shalt build up Jerusalem. [But] thou [must] wear this seal of God. And this engraving of the seal of the ring sent thee is a *Pentalpha.*'"

And I Solomon was overjoyed, and praised and glorified the God of heaven and earth. And on the morrow I called the boy, and gave him the ring, and said to him: "Take this, and at the hour in which the demon shall come unto thee, throw this ring at the chest of the demon, and say to him: 'In the name of God, King Solomon calls thee hither.' And then do thou come running to me, without having any misgivings or fear in respect of aught thou mayest hear on the part of the demon.'"[8]

The *Goëtia* of the *Lemegeton* is predicated on the same tradition of Solomon's control over demons, and it also features one of the best known magical rings in ceremonial magic, which is a talisman of protection.

This is the Form of the magic Ring, or rather Disk, of Solomon, the figure whereof is to be made in gold or silver. It is to be held before the face of the exorcist to preserve him from the stinking sulphurous fumes and flaming breath of the Evil Spirits.[9]

A magical ring is also used in *The Art of Drawing Spirits into Crystals*, for protection and as an emblem of authority.

We are going to look at three separate sets of grimoric talismanic rings, which occur in various manuscripts, typically as either components of or companions to versions of the *Key of Solomon*.

——— ◆ ———

The first treatise on magic rings which I will consider is entitled *To Make the Kabalistic and Astronomic Rings, Compounded from the Metals, Called Talismans*, or *The Method of Making the Astronomic Rings, Compounded from the Metals, Called Talismans*. It describes a set of four talismanic rings, one of which the magician is directed to craft for personal use based on his or her birthdate.

There is a very great power in the Celestial Nature, for the luminaries and stars exert an influence on the metals, as well as on the animals, herbs, plants, trees, and precious stones, which is dependent on their rulerships. This is why it is very important for one who wishes to excel in the kabalistic and occult Science to always have upon himself <something which derives

---

7. *Pentalpha* is an alternate Greek name for the Pentagram, when thought of as consisting of five interlaced letters A.

8. Translated from the Greek by F.C. Conybeare, "The Testament of Solomon," in *The Jewish Quarterly Review*, Vol. 11, No. 1 (Oct., 1898), pp. 1–45.

9. [S.L. MacGregor Mathers,] Aleister Crowley, and 'Solomon,' *The Book of the Goetia of Solomon the King: Translated into the English Tongue by a Dead Hand and Adorned with Divers Other Matters Germane, Delightful to the Wise: the Whole Edited, Verified, Introd. and Commented by A. Crowley* (Boleskine, Foyers, Inverness: Society for the Propagation of Religious Truth, 1904).

from the said Science. Thus, my son,[10] I have not found anything more useful and convenient than to have upon oneself>[11] one of the four rings compounded as you will see below.[12]

The First of the Astronomic Rings

As there are only four rings in this set, we will examine all of them. I will quote the description of the first ring in full.

The first is good for those who were born in the months of March, July, or October,[13] and must be made as follows:

It is necessary to take of gold and iron an equal portion of the one and the other, and combine them on about the 24th of July, in the day and hour of the Sun,[14] and having immediately made a ring from the said material, you will wait until the month of March, on the day and hour of Mars,[15] to engrave around the outside the following characters [See figure 8.],[16] and you will put in the bezel a little of the herb named heliotrope and of that named *napellus*,[17] with a bit of the skin of a lion and that of a wolf, and

10. The author is using the familiar pseudepigraphic form of writing his Solomonic treatise as though it were part of the testament or written legacy which the magus-king left for his son Rehoboam. —APF

11. The section inside the pointed brackets is inserted from MS Lansdowne 1203, the rest being from BnF 2344. —APF

12. Unless otherwise indicated, all excepts from *The Method of Making the Kabalistic and Astronomic Rings, Compounded of the Metals, Called Talismans* are translated from the French of Bibliothèque nationale de France MS Arsenal 2344 (formerly MS Arsenal S. et A.F. Nº 70) by Adam P. Forrest. The interested reader may find online Joseph H. Peterson's translation of the complete treatise from MS Lansdowne 1203, where it is seemingly incorporated as the final chapter of the Abognazar *Veritable Clavicles of Solomon*, at http://www.esotericarchives.com/solomon/l1203.htm. The Abognazar *Veritable Clavicles* also features tables of correspondences which include several drawn from the *Astronomic Rings*. —APF

13. Although the author of the text has simplified the calendrical attribution of the rings to simply birth months, it is clear that in fact it is the zodiacal sun signs which begin in those months that are intended. It is also clear that, although the magician's natal zodiacal sign is the indicator for the choice of ring, these are in fact planetary talismans, for the signs associated with each ring are those ruled by the planets whose metals and Olympic spirits are assigned to that ring. —APF

14. That is, in the Solar day and hour when the Sun is in the opening cusp of Leo, ruled by the Sun, one of the two planets of this ring. —APF

15. I.e., in the Martial day and hour when the Sun is in the opening cusp of Aries, ruled by Mars, the second planet of this ring. —APF

16. The seals or sigils of Och, the Olympic Planetary Spirit of Sol, and Phaleg, the Olympic Planetary Spirit of Mars, along with the Hebrew letters Yod and Resh. Since there are two Hebrew letters on the rings with two Planetary correspondences and two Olympic Sigils and one on the Mercury ring which relates to a single Planet, we would expect the Hebrew letters to correspond one-to-one to the Planets. However, the basis for the letter attributions remains opaque, as Aleph occurs three times (including twice on one ring) and Resh twice. —APF

17. *Napellus* (in some MSS *mapellus*) is the modern *aconitum napellus*, monk's-hood or wolfbane. —APF

a bit of the feather of a swan and of that of a vulture, and over it all the stone named the ruby.[18] Next, turning towards the quarter of the West, you will invoke the angels *Michael, Cherub, Gasgatel* [correctly in another MS *Gargatel*], *Tariel, Tabiel* [properly *Tubiel*], *Bael,*

Fig. 8. Olympic Sigils and Hebrew Letters for the First Astronomic Ring, for those with natal Sun in Aries, Leo, or Scorpio

the Sylphs, Camael, Phaleg, Samael, Och, Anael.[19] And having censed it with storax and musk, you will wrap it in the lion skin. And you will not carry it

---

18. Note that the correspondences employed in each ring span the "Four Perfect Kinds of Mixed Bodies" (*i.e.*, Animals, Plants, Metals, and Stones) from Agrippa's Scale of the Quaternary (*De Occulta Philosophia* Book 2, chapter 7). —APF

19. The eclectic assembly of "Angels" drawn together in this invocation sets the pattern for those of the other three astronomic rings as well. The list combines Angels and other Spirits of the two Planets of the talisman with the Spirits of the season in which the ring is used and of the quarter from which they are invoked. The names of these spirits are drawn from the usual primary sources (*De Occulta Philosophia, Heptameron, Arbatel De Magia Veterum,* etc.). In fact, the very key to the compounded rings—the division of the Metals and Planets into three pairs plus solitary Quicksilver, attributed to the quarters—is to be found in Agrippa. In his Scale of the Quaternary, the seven Metals are attributed to the Tetrad thus: Gold and Iron to the Eastern quarter, the Summer season, and the Element of Fire; Copper and Tin to the West, Spring, and Air; Quicksilver to the North, Winter, and Water; and Lead and Silver to the South, Autumn, and Earth.

Unfortunately, some jumbling has occurred in the course of the migration of correspondences from the sources to this treatise. It seems that the primary confusion with our first ring is that, to accord with Agrippa, the Angels and Spirits of this talisman should be called from the East, not the West. With Gold and Iron, Sol and Mars should correspond to the East, Summer, and Fire (as Agrippa uses the Cardinal attributions of the Quarters: *viz.*, Fire in the East, Earth in the South, Air West, and Water North).

Och is of course the Olympic Spirit of the Sun and Phaleg that of Mars, from *Arbatel*. Gargatel and Tariel are two of the three Angels of Summer, and Tubiel is the Head of the Sign of Summer, all from the *Heptameron*. Samael is the Archangel of Mars from the *Heptameron*. Camael comes from Agrippa, as the Mars Archangel among the "Seven Angels Who Stand Before the Presence of God" in the Scale of the Septenary. Michael is probably here on dual grounds, as both the Archangel of the Sun from the *Heptameron* and as the Archangel of the East and of Fire from Agrippa's "Four Angels Ruling Over the Four Cardinal Points of Heaven" in the Scale of the Quaternary.

Agrippa's "Four Princes of the Demons over the Four Angles of the Globe" from the Scale of the Quaternary are also evoked with these rings. "J.F." (probably John French, but possibly James Freake), the 1651 translator of *De Occulta Philosophia* into English, for some reason chose to mislead his readers, and has also hoodwinked many modern occultists who do not have access to the Latin text. Although he translated *Quatuor principes dæmoniorum nocentes in elementis* two lines earlier in the same table as "Four Princes of devils, offensive in the Elements," and though Agrippa has unambiguously placed both sets of Dæmonic Princes, along with the four Underworld rivers (Styx, etc.) of Greek religion, *in Mundo Infernali* ("in the Underworld"), J.F. disingenuously translates *Quatuor principes dæmoniorum super quatuor angulos orbis* as "Four Princes of spirits [rather than *demons* or *devils*], upon the four angles of the world."

Agrippa's *Oriens* (simply Latin for "East"), found in many grimoires, is a title of Bael as King of the East, rather as Henry VIII was called "England" by his peers. It may be that as the First of the four Princes, ruling the East and Fire, Bael (unlike Paymon, Amaymon, and Egyn) may sometimes by called by his title

save during the summer, taking it only on a Sunday or Tuesday in the hour of the planet of the day, while turning towards the West. And it will bring you a great happiness, and—a marvelous thing!—you will be loved and adored by everyone.

The Second of the Astronomic Rings

The second ring is beneficial for those born in the months of April, September, November, and February. It is compounded from equal parts of copper and tin, which is formed into a blank ring on the day and in the hour of Venus or Jupiter following the entry of the Sun into the sign of Taurus. However, the magician must wait until the day and hour of Jupiter or Venus after the Sun enters Sagittarius in November to engrave the ring with the appropriate characters (fig. 9), consisting of the sigils or seals of the Olympic spirits Hagith and Bethor, and the Hebrew letters Tav and Aleph.

The correspondences which should be "set[20] in the bezel[21]" are small samples of the herbs *capillus Veneris* (maiden's-hair fern) and *Barba Jovis* (Jove's Beard), along

Fig. 9. Olympic Sigils and Hebrew Letters for the Second Astronomic Ring, for those with natal Sun in Taurus, Libra, Sagittarius, or Pisces

---

rather than his proper name on the ancient, cautiously euphemistic principal of He-Who-Must-Not-(At-Least-Casually-)Be-Named.

The three remaining names represent errors on the part of the compiler of the treatise. Cherub is one of the "Four Angels Presiding over the Cardinal Points of Heaven" in the Scale of the Quaternary, but should properly be ascribed to the West and the second ring, while Seraph should be the correct Angel for the first ring. Anael should be recognized easily as an Archangel of Venus, but in a few grimoric treatises (most relevantly in *The Operation of the Seven Spirits of the Planets*, found in BnF MS Arsenal 2344 alongside *To Make the Kabalistic and Astronomic Rings, Compounded of the Metals, Called Talismans*), confusion has led to swapping Raphael and Anael as the Archangels of Sol and Venus. It should be Raphael here for the first ring, drawn like Camael from Agrippa's "Seven Angels Who Stand Before the Presence of God." Finally, the author of the treatise attributes to the rings the four Paracelsian species of Elementals, whom he names in French as *les Sylphes, les Aëriens, les Nymphes, and les Pigmées*. Paracelsus ascribes the *Gnomi* or *Pygmæi* to Earth, the *Sylphes* or *Spiritūs Aërei* to Air, the *Undinæ* or *Nymphæ* to Water, and the *Salamandræ* or *Spiritūs Ignei* to Fire. So the author of our treatise has mistakenly subdivided the Paracelsian Elementals of Air into two separate groups, *les Sylphes* and *les Aëriens*, and omitted *les Salamandres* of Fire. The correct attribution should be the Salamanders for the first ring, and the Sylphs (alias Aërial Spirits) for the second ring. —APF

20. The French verb used is *enchâsser*, which means "to set or mount" a gem or similar item in a ring. With relevance to placing pieces of magically sympathetic items in the astronomic rings, it is definitely worth noting that *enchâsser* is also used in the Catholic Church as a technical term meaning "to enchase or enshrine" a sacred relic in a reliquary. —APF

21. The word used in the manuscripts is *chaton*, which unhelpfully may mean equally the bezel of a ring or the stone which is set in the bezel. —APF

with bits of goat skin, stag skin, dove feather, and eagle feather, and the stone set over all is an emerald.

When the ring is completed, the magus should turn to face the corresponding quarter,[22] and call upon the angels Raphael, Seraph,[23] Carascasa, Hamabiel, Commissoros, Maimon, the Aërials, Zadkiel, Bethor, Sachiel, Haniel, and Hagith. The ring should then be suffumigated with the proper planetary incenses, which are bay and lignum aloes. The manuscript does not specify, but the talisman should be probably wrapped in the goat or stag skin.

The magician is instructed to take up the second ring in the spring, while facing the proper quarter on the day and in the hour of Venus or Jupiter.

The Third of the Astronomic Rings

The third ring is useful for those who were born in the months of May and August. It is under the auspices of only a single planet, Mercury, but as the corresponding metal is liquid at room temperature, it must be alloyed to make a ring. The magus is told

Fig. 10. Olympic Sigil and Hebrew Letter for the Third Astronomic Ring, for those with natal Sun in Gemini or Virgo

to congeal mercury with lead in order to produce a solid mercury which can be formed into a ring.[24]

The magician then waits until the day and hour of Mercury after the Sun enters Virgo in August to engrave the ring with the proper characters (fig. 10), which are the Sigil of the Olympic spirit of Mercury, Ophiel, and the Hebrew letter Resh.

The correspondences which should be set in the bezel of the ring are a pinch of the herb *mercurielle*,[25] along with bits of monkey skin and stork feather, and the stone set over these is rock crystal.

When the ring is completed, the magus should turn to face the north, and call upon the angels[26] Gabriel, Tharsis, Amabiel, Etaran, Poimon, the Nymphs (or Un-

---

22. The manuscript says the East, but the correct quarter is almost certainly the West. See the lengthy explanatory note to the first ring. —APF

23. If the magician wishes to employ the corrections to the list of spirits for the first ring, she or he should be able to make the corresponding ammendments to this and the two other remaining lists. —APF

24. IMPORTANT: See the CAUTION below in the section entitled "The Necessary Items and Materials for Creating a Talisman."

25. *Mercurialis annua*, or French mercury. —APF

26. If the magician wishes to employ the corrections to the list of spirits for the first ring, she or he should be able to deduce the corresponding ammendments to this list. —APF

dines), Michael, and Ophiel. The ring should then be perfumed with the proper planetary incense, which is juniper. The talisman should be wrapped in a piece of multi-colored silk taffeta.

The magician is instructed to take up the third ring in the winter, while facing north on the day and in the hour of Mercury.

The Fourth of the Astronomic Rings

The fourth ring is beneficial for those born in the months of December, June, and January. It is compounded from equal parts of silver and lead,[27] which is formed into a blank ring on the day and in the hour of Luna or Saturn following the entry of the Sun into the sign of Cancer. However, the magician must wait until the day and hour of the Moon or Saturn after the Sun enters Capricorn in the following December to engrave the ring with the appropriate characters (fig. 11), consisting of the sigils of the Olympic spirits Phul and Aratron, and the Hebrew letter Aleph twice.

The correspondences which are to be set in the bezel are small samples of the herbs *selenotropia* and *joubarbe*,[28] along with bits of cat skin, mole skin, owl feather, and lapwing feather, and the stone set above them is to be a sapphire.

When the ring is completed, the magus should turn to face the south, and call upon the angels[29] Uriel, Ariel, Tarquam, Gualbarel, Egin, the Pygmies (or Gnomes), Zaphkiel, Gabriel, Aratron, Phul, and Cassiel. The text says that the ring should then be censed with sulphur.[30] The manuscript

Fig. 11. Olympic Sigils and Hebrew Letters for the Fourth Astronomic Ring, for those with natal Sun in Cancer, Capricorn, or Aquarius

---

27. IMPORTANT: See the CAUTION below in the section entitled "The Necessary Items and Materials for Creating a Talisman."

28. The plant correspondences for this ring are both potentially confusing. Selenotrope is a Lunar correspondence cited since antiquity, but it does not seem to refer to any actual known plant.

We have already encountered *Barba Jovis* ("Jove's Beard") as the correspondence for Jupiter with the second ring, and clearly *joubarbe* is a French form deriving from that Latin name. However, they are known to be two different plants with similar names; the *Barba Jovis* of the second ring is the modern *Anthyllis barba-jovis* or silver-bush, while the fourth ring's *joubarbe* is *Sempervivum tectorum*, the common houseleek. —APF

29. If the magician wishes to employ the corrections to the list of spirits for the first ring, she or he should be competent to make the corresponding ammendments to this list. —APF

30. If you have not, please read the CAUTION below in the section entitled "The Necessary Items and Materials for Creating a Talisman."

does not specify, but the talisman is probably intended to be wrapped in the cat or mole skin.

The magician is directed to take up the fourth ring in the autumn, while facing south on the day and in the hour of the Moon or Saturn.

This treatise ends[31] with a final instruction from Solomon to his son:

> However, as these rings are entirely dependent upon the Celestial influences, and their powers and operations proceed only from the aforesaid influences, you should be meticulous when performing the designated rituals. Also, follow and execute this testament which I leave to you, and which I order you to conserve as a perpetual benefit.[32]

Of particular interest are those talismanic rings which are claimed to have a 'bound' spirit attached to or housed within them. Our second treatise deals with one set of such rings, and is found alongside versions of the *Key* in several manuscripts. The title of the text is *The Talismans: Characters of the Twelve Rings, in Which One Confines a Spirit for Everything One Wishes.*

The method for constructing these rings is akin to those found in *Liber Lunæ* and other grimoires which give instructions to engrave an image and a name on the ring as well as on parchment. However, the complete process for properly constructing the rings in this particular text is more than a bit vague and some educated guesses have to be made to fill in the blanks, which shouldn't be too difficult for an experienced Solomonic magician to piece together. By combining the limited instructions we do have specifically concerning the twelve rings with the section later in this article dealing with the proper creation of magical talismans in general, the reader should be able to formulate a viable operation to fashion one or more of these powerful talismanic rings.

The author of the treatise provides us with a notice or warning concerning a particular requirement of the procedure, which is the same regardless of which of the dozen rings is being prepared:

> When you wish the aforementioned rings to be of service to you, it is necessary to recite the following prayer with the exorcism, before which you

---

31. In MS Lansdowne 1203; the Solomonic framing device is missing in BnF MS Arsenal 2344. —APF

32. Translated from the French of MS Lansdowne 1203 by Adam P. Forrest. —APF

make the figure on the stone [of the ring] and the name of the Spirit on the earth;[33] and [the Spirits] being summoned, ask them for what you desire.[34]

The prayer is in Latin and is addressed to God, while the exorcism is in the vernacular and is to be addressed to the summoned spirit.

> *O Domine Deus, qui ex nihilo cuncta creasti, et antequam fuerint providisti, nosque honore et gloria coronasti, et constituisti super opera manuum Tuarum, et omnia subjectisti sub pedibus nostris, oves, boves universos, et super hoc sacratissimum verbum sis semper benedictus per omnia sæcula sæculorum. Amen.*

> "O Lord God, Who didst create all things from nothing, and didst foresee them before they were, and didst crown us with honor and glory and didst set us over the works of Thy hands, and didst subject under our feet all things, all sheep and oxen, and over this most sacred word, mayest Thou be blessèd always, through all the æons of æons. Amen."

The exorcism alludes to several points from the prayer, and specifies the authority under which the spirit is bound to comply.

> I conjure thee, *N.,*[35] by the most powerful God, Who hath given unto me authority, and hath set me over the works of His hands, and hath crowned me with honor and glory, by the name Agla, On, by and to which name all are bound to obey, that if I first make such a ring, the mark which it containeth will make thee do that which I ask of thee.

I am including a selection of three of these twelve rings which I deem to have been of the most use or interest to me.

---

33. This reference to tracing the name (or, elsewhere, the figure or both the figure and the name) of the spirit on the earth is reiterated over and over throughout the treatise, and in several places it is stressed that the name or figure of the spirit must not be easily rubbed away. Most likely the original author is speaking either of a holy table or ritual altar on which the ring is being consecrated or a private plot of ground which is serving the same purpose.

34. All of the excerpts from this treatise used here are translated from the French and occasional Latin of British Library MS Lansdowne 1202 by Adam P. Forrest. The reader may find complete English translations of the entire treatise from two different MSS in two available sources. A translation by Paul Harry Barron of the text from MS Wellcome 4670, where the *Twelve Rings* follows *The Clavicles of R. Solomon... translated...into French by M. Pierre Morissoneau,* is published in Stephen Skinner & David Rankine, *The Veritable Key of Solomon* (Singapore: Golden Hoard Press, 2010), pp. 264 ff. Talia Felix's English translation of the text from MS Lansdowne 1202, where the *Twelve Rings* stands alongside *The True Clavicles of King Solomon. By Armadel,* is published (along with the original French and Latin text) online at Joseph H. Peterson, *Douze Anneaux (Lansdowne MS 1202),* on his exceptional website, *Twilit Grotto—Esoteric Archives* (http://www.esotericarchives.com/solomon/anneaux.htm). —APF

35. For *N.,* insert the name of the particular spirit whom you are evoking.

The Second of the Twelve Rings

The second of the dozen talismanic rings is intended to grant the magus a familiar spirit.

> It is necessary to make a ring of gold in the second mansion of the Moon,[36] and it is necessary to mount on it a yellow stone of the same color as the gold, on which it is necessary to engrave this figure [see fig. 12]; and in the hollow space beneath the stone, to confine[37] this word, *Astarot*, written with the blood of a white dove on virgin parchment; and it must be perfumed with amber.

As the reader can see, the few sentences describing the nature and construction of the ring are rather vague and short of exact details. For instance, the "yellow stone," while clearly intended as a solar correspondence, could be citrine, hyacinth (yellow zircon), or yellow topaz. The method for enclosing the piece of parchment in the ring is somewhat confusing. In a similar text, the magician is instructed that the stone should be concave. One possibility is that the parchment is secured on the flat bezel of the metal ring and the stone then mounted on top of that. Another possibility is that the ring is meant to be a locket ring or compartment ring with the parchment placed inside and so not visible unless the locket is opened.[38] Again, this is speculation which should be further clarified by conjuring and questioning the spirit who will eventually inhabit the ring.

Fig. 12. Sigil for the Talismanic Second Ring, Being That of Astarot

This ring is of particular interest for more than one reason. First, it is a clear example of a grimoric operation to bind a familiar spirit to a ring. Second, it involves the conjuration of the Archdemon Astaroth (or Astarot, as the name is sometimes

---

36. The 28 mansions (or houses or stations) of the Moon are fundamental to this process, which suggests that these talismanic rings may be Arabic (or even Greek, *via* the scholars and mages of Harran or al-Andalus) in origin. The 'mansions' are 28 equal divisions of the Zodiacal circle of the ecliptic, which represent an ancient approximation of one day of the progress of the Moon through a Lunar month. The position of the Moon, as the most quickly moving of the seven ancient Planets, is—along with the Planetary days and hours—among the most specific of the astrological variables in the timing of magical rituals. —APF

37. The word used in the manuscript for "to confine" is *renfermer*, the same verb which is used in the title of the treatise, *The Talismans: Characters of the Twelve Rings, in Which One Confines* ("Enferme") *a Spirit for Everything One Wishes*, making it clear that the physical binding of the spirit's written name within the ring is a piece of sympathetic magic corresponding to the spiritual binding of the entity itself to the ring. —APF

38. The second option would echo the talismanic scrolls which I will discuss below, which are kept secure in a talismanic container, to conceal and protect the consecrated paper or parchment.

rendered in French grimoires). In the *Goëtia* of the *Lemegeton*, Astaroth is the 29th listed spirit.

> He is a Mighty, Strong Duke, and appeareth in the Form of an hurtful Angel riding on an Infernal Beast like a Dragon, and carrying in his right hand a Viper. Thou must in no wise let him approach too near unto thee, lest he do thee damage by his Noisome Breath. Wherefore the Magician must hold the Magical Ring near his face, and that will defend him.

The *Goëtia* also tells us that Astaroth rules 40 legions of spirits, and warns us strongly that he—like all the other listed spirits—will not cooperate with a magician who does not wear his seal (fig. 13) as a lamen. Weyer's *Pseudomonarchia Dæmonum*[39] agrees with the *Goëtia* in almost all particulars, but adds the detail that Astaroth claims that he did not fall of his own accord. A.E. Waite[40] says that elsewhere Weyer reports that Astaroth also holds the position of Grand Treasurer in the Ministry of Hell. In the *Sacred Magic of Abramelin the Mage*, Astaroth is described as one of the eight sub-princes ruling over all the demons.

Before the talisman-maker can consider any hope for success in consecrating this ring, he would need to be able to summon Astaroth to begin with in order to bind the spirit—or a familiar provided by Astaroth—to the ring. Further questioning of Astaroth would be a given in this case to discover if he would be bound himself or if, as the wording of the grimoire suggests, a familiar spirit would be substituted. Further questioning as to the nature, office, and abilities of the familiar spirit to be bound to the ring would also be a matter of course for an experienced summoner. Also, the magician should question if the given sigil is still appropriate or even viable, or if there is another sigil more appropriate.

Fig. 13. Goëtic Seal of Astaroth

It would be prudent to assume that if the familiar spirit to be bound to the Second Ring were provided by Astaroth, it would have similar powers to those of that Archdemon. In the *Goëtia*, he is said to give true answers to questions concerning things present, past, and to come. He knows or can discover all secrets, and will

---

39. *Pseudomonarchia Dæmonum* is Greek (in a Latinized spelling) for *"The False Monarchy of the Demons."* The author, Johann Weyer (in Latin, Johannes Wierus), was a student of Agrippa, and edited the *Pseudomonarchia* from a grimoire entitled *Liber Officiorum Dæmonum* (*"The Book of the Offices of the Demons"*). —APF

40. A.E. Waite, *The Book of Ceremonial Magic: Including the Rites and Mysteries of Goëtic Theurgy, Sorcery, and Infernal Necromancy* (London: Rider, 1911).

declare willingly how he and his fellow spirits fell. He is said to "make men wonderfully knowing in all Liberal Sciences."

The talismanic ring of Astarot is to be made when the Moon is in the second mansion (12°♈51′ to 25°♈42′), which is called Albotayn. The energies attributed to the mansions of the Moon vary among the key sources, such as Agrippa's *De Occulta Philosophia* (Book II, chapter 33), and the Latin version of the *Picatrix* (Book IV, chapter 9). Agrippa says that the second mansion conduces to the finding of treasures, and to the retaining of captives. In this regard, the ring and attached familiar or demon would seem to be geared toward "discovering hidden or secret treasures." The *Picatrix* states that the second mansion is suitable for operations directed at alleviating anger.

The Fourth of the Twelve Rings

The fourth of the twelve Talismanic Rings is intended to grant the magician the power of invisibility. In MS Lansdowne 1203, the fourth ring is specifically identified as "the Ring of Gyges."

The magus should either make or have made a ring of gold when the Moon is in her ninth mansion, and a yellow stone should be set in the ring, upon which the magician should engrave the sigil in figure 14. The name to be confined within the ring is *Tonuchon*, written on virgin parchment with the blood of a white dove, and perfumed with orange peel.

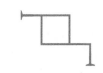

Fig. 14. Sigil for the Talismanic Fourth Ring, Being That of Tonuchon

The overall solar influence and correspondence of this ring is quite obvious. The talisman harkens to that of the sixth pentacle of the Sun listed in the *Key of Solomon* which "serveth excellently for the operation of invisibility, when correctly made." The versicle of the sixth pentacle combines *Psalms* 69:23 ("Let their eyes be darkened, that they see not; and make their loins continually to shake.") and 135:16 ("They have eyes and see not."). The Latin of these verses, which would be a very useful intonation to include in the rituals for the making of this ring, is *Obscurentur oculi eorum ne videant et dorsum eorum semper incurva. Oculos habent et non videbunt.*[41]

---

41. And for those who might wish to include additional incantations, the Hebrew is *Techshakhnah eineihem mereoth u-mathneihem tamid hamad. Einayim lahem ve-lo yiru*; and the Greek is *Skotisthētōsan hoi ophthalmoi autōn tou mē blepein, kai ton nōton autōn dia pantos synkampson. Ophthalmos echousin kai ouk opsontai*. Again, to avoid confusion, be aware that there are two systems of numbering the *Psalms*. Our versicle is assembled from either *Psalms* 69:23 and 135:16 according to the Hebrew numbering convention, or 68:24 and 134:16 according to that used in the Septuagint and Vulgate. —APF

Furthermore, the Moon in Atarfa, the ninth mansion ($12°\mathcal{S}51'$ to $25°\mathcal{S}42'$), "hindereth harvests and travelers, and putteth discord between men," according to Agrippa. If this is correct, then the nature of the 'invisibility' granted by the ring could possibly be the magic of diversions arising or conflicts happening near where the magician wishes to remain unseen. By this method, such discord would keep all attention away from him as he moves about unseen and unnoticed, and thus invisible. The *Picatrix* states that the ninth mansion is for generating infirmity. Could this possibly be directed for creating weakness in others' eyesight or attention?

The Seventh of the Twelve Rings

The seventh ring is designed to protect the magus from all wicked spirits.

It should be made of silver while Luna is in the second mansion, and be set with a quartz stone engraved with the hexagram (see figure 15).The name *Gabriach* must be written with the blood of a white dove on virgin parchment, perfumed with lignum aloes, and confined in the ring.

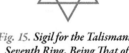

This ring quite obviously corresponds to the Moon, with both the metal and the stone being Lunar in nature. The second mansion of the Moon, you will recall, is said by Agrippa to be conducive to the discovery of treasures and the holding of captives, and by the *Picatrix* to the removal of anger. Neither really suggests

Fig. 15. Sigil for the Talismanic Seventh Ring, Being That of Gabriach

anything to do with protection from spirits, unless it coincides with evil spirits encouraging anger and thus danger in others is removed. However, the Moon being the controlling gateway might suggest the aptitude for disallowing sublunary spirits to attack the magician who bears this ring.

The name *Gabriach* may have some correlation to Gabriel, in which sense the spirit's name, like the materials for the ring, would correspond well with the Moon. Generally it seems that demons or lesser spirits are associated with this particular set of magical rings. However, since the purpose of this ring is to protect against evil spirits and the sigil is the hexagram, it may be that Gabriach is to be considered a lesser angel serving under Gabriel.

In one of the manuscripts which contains the *Twelve Rings* (MS Wellcome 4670), we also find our third brief treatise on talismanic rings, where it stands as chapter XV of the manuscript's main grimoire, *The Clavicles of R. Solomon*, and is entitled

Concerning the Mysterious Rings Which the Most Ancient Doctors of the Kabalah Used with Marvellous Success.[42]

The author of *Concerning the Mysterious Rings* begins by relating tales of various magical rings. In Jewish lore, he tells us, Moses secured two magical rings by having learned the techniques of the Egyptian magicians while being raised in the court of the pharaoh. Moses' rings, one causing love and the other invisibility, were each constructed under the corresponding planetary spirits. He also relates from Greek lore the story of the fabled Ring of Gyges, which made the wearer invisible and allowed Gyges to kill the king of Lydia and marry the queen, thus becoming king himself.[43]

The System of the Twelve Rings

The author then proceeds to direct the magus in the process of creating the mysterious talismanic rings. First, make or have made a ring in the appropriate metal of the planet, and then set or have set in the ring a precious stone corresponding to the planet. Next, engrave inside the talisman the name and sigil of the Olympic spirit of the planet.

Then cast a magic circle of the distinctive form proper to this system (fig. 16).[44] Standing in the middle of the circle, burn the appropriate planetary incense in a virgin ceramic vessel and, holding a new wax candle, speak the conjuration to the Olympic spirit whose sigil you have engraved on the ring:

---

42. The title in the French MS is *Des Anneaux mystérieux dont les plus anciens Docteurs de la Cabale se sont servi avec un merveilleux succès*. An English translation by Paul Harry Barron of the whole of Wellcome 4670 may be read in Stephen Skinner & David Rankine, *The Veritable Key of Solomon* (Singapore: Golden Hoard Press, 2010), including this treatise on pp. 218 ff. Also, Ebenezer Sibley made his own English translation (apparently from a different French version of the treatise) in the 18th century, which has been published in a beautiful facsimile edition of a manuscript prepared by Frederick Hockley, along with Joseph Peterson's always invaluable commentary, as Sibley, Hockley, and Peterson, *The Clavis or Key to the Magic of Solomon* (Lake Worth, FL: Ibis Press, 2009). This treatise is found there on pp. 183 ff., where it is entitled *The Mysterious Ring* rather than *Rings*, as the similarity in meaning between 'ring' and 'circle' has allowed Sibley's French source to alter the title to refer to the singular magic circle rather than the array of planetary rings which may be consecrated in that circle. Sibley (or, from the phrasing, more probably his French source) adds, concerning the circle, "It is not in order to impress on the Credulity of the Curious Followers of the Occult Science, that it is said, that it is more than *Two Thousand Years* since this Ring [*i.e.*, Circle] already mentioned has been in use." —APF

43. This introductory section of traditional ring lore is missing from Sibley's translation. —APF

44. Sibley mistook the illegible writing alternating with the word *Tetragrammaton* in the border of the Circle for Arabic numerals, but they are certainly the badly degraded Hebrew letters one finds so often in the grimoires. There are clearly too many strokes in the characters to represent only the four letters of the Tetragrammaton (יהוה), but they could represent, for example, three permutations of the Tetragrammaton in each quarter of the Circle. —APF

I conjure you, N..., by the Great Living God, Sovereign Creator of all things, that you come here under any visible form that you wish, without noise and without fright, to imprint on this Ring, which carries your name, the glorious qualities of which you are the minister and dispenser. I make this conjuration to you by the Sacred Names of the Great Living God, whom you must obey. Hear, therefore, with respect and with swift submission these Names terrible and fearful to all created Beings: Adonay, Agla, Tetragrammaton, Gaha, Agaro, Thetron, He, Elhi, Cotlyis, Ygaha, Emmanuel, Vau, Ory, Elohim, Goth, Geni.[45]

When you are aware of the tangible presence of the spirit, whether visible or invisible, the treatise says that you should face the east, and present the ring to the spirit on the end of a properly consecrated wooden wand[46] dedicated to the appropriate planet, so that he may charge the ring with the properties you seek. When the consecration is complete, give the spirit license to depart, speaking the formula: "Faithful Minister, go in peace in the Name of the Great God, your Master, who has sent you to be sympathetic towards me."[47]

You should then remove the ring from the wand and place it on your finger. Finally you should again offer incense before erasing the circle (which is obviously pictured by the author as drawn on the floor with chalk, or inscribed on the earth with a knife or sword) and retire into a profound silence.

The magician is then instructed to preserve the consecrated ring in a new box or small silk bag in a proper planetary color.

Unlike many grimoires, *Concerning the Mysterious Rings* addresses the question of making a talisman for another person. The author explains that, if the magician has properly consecrated the rings, "they will retain their qualities when they change master, provided that the one who receives them is willing to perform everything that needs to be done in the rituals. He or she should also burn perfumes in the name and to the honor of the spirits, who by their virtues, rule over the ring."[48]

---

45. Skinner and Rankine, *op. cit.*, p. 219. Sibley read the Names slightly differently in the manuscript from which he was working: *Adonay Agla Tetragrammaton Gaha Agari Thetron He Elhi Ygaha Emanuel Venry Eloym Goth Genii.*

46. Sibley does not refer to the wand in his translation, but confusingly says that the magus should present to the spirit "the Ring, at the end of a small *ring* which is particularly consecrated to the Planet under the auspices of which you work." I can only presume that Sibley encountered the word *baguette* ("wand") in the French manuscript which he translated, and through either misreading or misunderstanding, took it for *bague* ("ring"). —APF

47. Skinner and Rankine, *Ibid.*

48. *Ibid.*, p. 219.

As the author confesses near the end of the treatise that he has provided only a general description of this particular method, and that the magician must employ additional Solomonic techniques taught elsewhere to fully consecrate the rings, I will expound on this process from my own experience, including elements of Solomonic procedure which are vital for actually being successful in this magical operation.

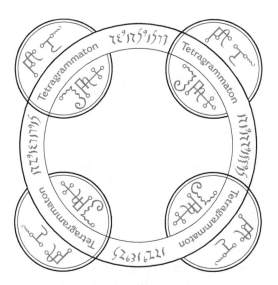

Fig. 16. Magic Circle for Consecrating the Mysterious Rings from the Clavicles of R. Solomon

The creation of a talismanic planetary ring by this system consists of three distinct ritual steps: first, the making of the blank ring from the proper metal and the setting of the proper stone; second, the engraving of the sigil on the stone; and third, the charging of the ring. Each of these processes should be performed on the most powerful and auspicious day and time, according to the planetary power and purpose of the ring as well as the sprit who will consecrate it. The first step will definitely take longer than an hour to complete properly, and the third may end up taking nearly as long as the first. The second part however, should not be nearly as involved as the first and the last parts.[49]

Unless you are a skilled artisan, it is sensible either to have a ring custom crafted or to buy a new blank ring which you are certain is made of the correct metal. The obvious drawback to commissioning another person to make a talisman is that you cannot be sure of the exact timing of the craftsperson unless you are right there with them. Gold, copper, iron (steel), and silver rings will be fairly easy to procure, but tin, lead, and especially mercury will prove more of a challenge.[50] This system also requires that a corresponding planetary stone be set in the ring; I give a list of suitable stones in Table 17. Since this particular system does not require confining a piece of parchment or other correspondences beneath the setting, I prefer if pos-

---

49. While I find the first hour of the planetary day to be the most powerful, the eighth hour of the day and the third and tenth hours of the night also have strong correspondence to the planetary ruler of the day.

50. IMPORTANT: See the CAUTION below in the section entitled "The Necessary Items and Materials for Creating a Talisman."

sible to have the stone set in such a way that it can be viewed from the underside of the ring as well as the top. This gives the option of inscribing the stone from underneath, and also provides an opening or gateway through which the spirit can move in and out of the ring to carry out its duties. If you are not crafting the ring or setting the stone, you may purify and bless the blank ring and stone as the first phase of your work.

The second phase of crafting your ring will consist of the engraving of the Olympic spirit's sigil. Magicians who have developed their magical voice through successful invocation and evocation should sing or chant the name of the spirit over and over again as they engrave its sigil upon the ring or stone. The magician's magical voice is something which comes about naturally from receiving the gift to call forth spiritual entities to visible and auditory manifestation. You should sing to the ring—and thus the spirit—in such a way that you become aware of the metal, stone, and engraved symbol starting to resonate at the same pitch and frequency that correspond to the spirit itself. This is something which cannot be explained further in writing, only demonstrated by an experienced occultist.

For this ritual, in which the magic circle is of a very particular form, I would recommend drawing or painting the circle on canvas to place directly on the floor. Although painted circles are the most durable and safest from accidental smudges and erasures, it is also traditional to draw them on a floor or pavement with blessed chalk, or to engrave them directly on hard-packed earth with a properly consecrated Solomonic tool.

This grimoire says that the spirit will manifest in the east, but experience shows that a planetary spirit will show up in a particular direction with which its planet is associated. I have provided a list of the directions corresponding to the planets for this operation in figure 17. Given the form of this magic circle, the four circlets or small circles should be a hint that the spirit can appear in one of them, so be sure to position your circle so that one of the circlets coincides with the spirit's natural direction.

For the candle, I recommend making or purchasing a beeswax candle of the corresponding color and engraving it with the angel's or spirit's sigil and other correlating symbols. Find a simple new candlestick to hold your candle upright for lighting and also for ease of retrieving during the ceremony.

For the incense brazier which will be located in the center of the circle, I recommend fashioning a new ceramic bowl, etched with all the corresponding sigils and symbols of the planet and spirit, as well as glazed in the corresponding color.

Although none is mentioned, having a lamen to wear during the invocation would be prudent and in line with nearly every other grimoire's process concerning evocation of a spirit. The lamen should be made of virgin parchment at the very least, if not of the same metal as your talismanic ring. You should inscribe on the

PLANETARY SYMBOL	OLYMPIC SPIRIT	INTELLIGENCE FROM PLANETARY KAMEA	STONES FOR MYSTIC RING	TREE OR WOOD FOR WAND	DIRECTION
♄ Saturn	Aratron	Agiel	Granite, onyx	Alder, beech, cypress, pine, yew	North
♃ Jupiter	Bethor	Johphiel	Topaz, lapis lazuli, blue sapphire	Fig, juniper, oak, poplar, ash	Southwest
♂ Mars	Phaleg	Graphiel	Ruby, sardonyx, garnet	Cedar, acacia, hawthorn, holly, thorn	South
☉ Sun	Och	Nachiel	Citrine, chrysoleth, sunstone, amber	Acacia, laurel, chestnut	South or West
♀ Venus	Hagith	Hagiel	Aetites, beryl, emerald, jasper, coral, turquoise	Apple, elder, eucalyptus, quince	North
☿ Mercury	Ophiel	Tiriel	Opal, agate	Hazel nut, almond, aspen, larch, mulberry, rowan, silver birch, ebony	Northeast
☽ Moon	Phul	Malcha Betharsithim Ed Beruah Schehakim	Pearl, quartz, moonstone	Weeping willow, bay, papaya	West

Fig. 17. Table of Correspondences for the Seven Mysterious Rings

lamen the sigil of the Olympic spirit, and perhaps also that of the planetary intelligence from the kameoth or magic squares (see fig. 17).

Now, as to the particular form of the wand on which the ring will be placed in order to be consecrated by the spirit, it should also be made with the utmost care and attention to detail. My recommendation would be to cut and retrieve the wood for your wand from a living tree if possible, during the very first hour of the day associated with the planet and spirit, and when the planet is auspiciously located and aspected. For use in this particular ritual, the wand must be long enough to extend from your hand outside your circle and into the circlet of the spirit without your having to pass your own hand from your circle. The wand should either be carved to taper or turned on a lathe like a spindle so that it is slender enough at the tip for the ring to be slipped onto it, and thick enough further down to keep the ring from sliding too far down the wand. Further blessings and consecrations can be done on the same day and hours corresponding to the nature of it. Pray with the wand in your hand, pointed directly at the planet in the sky if possible, and ask that when the time comes for the consecration of the ring, the spirit will be drawn instantly near where the wand reaches to imprint its energy and powers upon the ring. Such a compound of corresponding energies should assist in making a very powerful talisman indeed.

The ring to be consecrated, the incense bowl, the candle, and the wand should all be able to rest on an altar table in the very center of your magic circle. This arrangement is customary in several grimoric traditions, and will allow the magician to move about and utilize each item without them being cumbersome or an obstacle. An added element would be to set the ring to be consecrated on a parchment sigil or seal of the spirit you will be invoking to consecrate it.

At the correct hour, and after undergoing the usual prerequisites and preparations for conducting any serious ritual of ceremonial magic, the magician should enter the circle and stand before the altar. Light the candle and then the charcoals for the incense. In the majority of Solomonic magic, consecration prayers are said for both flames and charcoals. None of these steps would be amiss in this ceremony. Begin to place generous amounts of the proper incense mixture on the charcoals, and when ready, take up the ring and the wand from the altar, and slide the ring securely onto the wand. Be sure to keep the wand tip aloft at all times so that the ring does not slip off onto the floor. Pass the ring three times over the flame of the candle, but not closely enough to burn or discolor it. Then take up the candle in the candlestick in your other hand, stand at the very center of the circle facing the spirit's corresponding direction, and take a few deep cleansing breaths. With the same magical voice you used during the engraving of the ring, call the spirit to arrive using the conjuration specified in the treatise. If reading the conjuration, it can be written out on a piece of paper or parchment in letters large enough to view easily on the ground or the altar from where you will be standing. Repeat the conjuration as necessary, and wait for the palpable and distinct presence of the spirit to arrive. Be patient and allow it to form and appear as solidly and distinctly as it can. Give the spirit a formal greeting such as in the *Key of Solomon*. Declare clearly and distinctly why you have summoned it, and wait for its reply. If the spirit agrees to consecrate your ring, move forward and extend the wand slowly, directly in front of the spirit, taking care never to extend your hand beyond the boundary of your circle. Take note of the powerful and very distinct energy and presence of the spirit, who is now at its nearest to you. Keep your wand and the ring extended until you receive a clear reply that the ring has indeed been endowed with the power and office of the spirit. When this is done, withdraw your wand slowly and respectfully while taking a step backward to the center of your circle, still being careful to keep the wand tip raised to avoid dropping the ring. Thank the spirit sincerely for consecrating your talisman, and give it license to depart. Do not immediately remove the ring from the wand but take a few moments to gaze upon it and feel the energy radiating from it. Spend a few moments in silence and in thanks for the accomplishment of the making of this powerful object.

When the ring is consecrated by the power and office of the spirit, you should and will know. To attempt to describe what this should feel and be like is unnecessary. You will know. Like the grimoire instructs, do not leave the circle. Instead, remove the ring from the wand, set aside the wand upon the altar, and hold the ring cupped in both your hands, raising it up to heaven, thanking the Creator and the spirit for the successful completion of this rite, and praying for the ring to remain endowed with its blessing and power. Take a moment to admire the authentic ring of magic in your hands, then put the remaining incense on the charcoal in the censer. Place the ring on your finger and hold your hand wearing the ring directly over the incense plumes so that your entire hand and the ring become immersed in the suffumigations. One last time, sing the name of the spirit of the ring and feel a humming or reverberation come from it in response. Withdraw your hand after the smoke has begun to subside. You may keep the talismanic ring on for a time if you wish, but when you remove it, immediately place it in a silk pouch of the correct planetary color. I would advise also keeping it locked away in a chest or box when not in use.

Careful consideration should be observed whenever putting on this consecrated ring. A talisman is always used for specific reasons and under specific circumstances; never wear it simply out of curiosity or for decoration. While it is possible to re-charge or re-consecrate the ring by utilizing the same ceremony if the need arises, it should not be necessary if the ring is used in accordance with its purpose.

Astrological Image Talismans from the *Picatrix*

> Those who seek to make images must first master the science of calculating the positions of the planets and the constellations, and also the motions of the heavens.[51]

---

51. John Michael Greer & Christopher Warnock, *The Picatrix (Liber Atratus Edition): The Occult Classic of Astrological Magic* (n.p.: Adocentyn Press, 2010–11), Book III, chapter 4.

> In the same way, magical images work by virtue and similarity, because a magical image is nothing other than the power of celestial bodies in the material bodies that they influence. Thus when the substance of the material body is disposed to receive the influence of the aforesaid celestial bodies or planets, and the celestial body likewise is disposed to influence the material body of the magical image, that image will be more powerful and more disposed to bring about the effect we seek and desire. Similarly, the gifts of the planet will be more perfect and more complete.[52]

The two preceding quotes from the arguable bedrock of classic Hermetic talisman creation, the *Picatrix*, are perhaps the most important statements for truly apprehending this complex system of magical image creation. The magic of the *Picatrix* employs archetypal images stemming from rich sources, including Greek, Hebraic, Hellenistic, Gnostic, and even Indian origins, and then focuses the potency of the celestial influences into each image by exact astrological calculations to fashion the most potent and correspondent talisman possible.

The talisman-maker is instructed to choose a magical image that corresponds with the intended purpose of the working and the planet whose influence governs that purpose, and then to fashion the image from materials that are also in harmony. It should be formed and consecrated at a time when the heavens themselves are in complex harmony with the intention of the working.

For example, if the magician wishes to work magic to strengthen the love between himself and his beloved, the *Picatrix* instructs him to gather his materials and await a very specific set of astrological circumstances: the Moon must be well aspected to Venus (and preferably conjunct), the North Node of the Moon should be in the Ascendant, and the lord of the seventh house must be trine or sextile to the lord of the first house. When all of these factors come together in the hour of Venus or Jupiter, the magician should then fashion images of himself and his beloved, place the images together face to face, and bury them at the home of the one he loves.

The *Picatrix* also preserves some talismanic processes that are as old as ancient Egypt. Book II, chapter 10 describes a rite attributed to Hermes Trismegistus, in which the image of a crane[53] is to be made of red stone. The astrological requirements are unusually simple, the crane being made in the hour of Jupiter, when Jupiter is in Cancer (*i.e.*, exalted). Then water or other potable liquid is poured over the image, and drunk by the magician, who it is said will gain the power to see spirits, and will be granted a wish.[54]

---

52. *Ibid.*, Book II, chapter 6.

53. Perhaps originally the ibis of Thoth?

54. This rite of charging water by pouring it over a consecrated image is how such talismans as the Metternich Stele (now in the Metropolitan Museum in New York City) were employed in pharaonic Egypt, the

Golden Dawn Talismans

In the Golden Dawn system of magic, you find a unique catalog of talismanic figures, largely adapted from magical sources such as the *Key of Solomon*, along with very specific techniques for creating new figures and for charging talismans. Golden Dawn talismans employ a distinctive system of color correspondences, and also make extensive use of complementary colors (which are termed "flashing colors" in the Golden Dawn), which, when placed directly next to one another, produce an interesting optical effect which can assist the deeper mind in becoming immersed in the nature of the talisman.

The Golden Dawn utilizes a particular method for creating sigils from the Hebrew names of spirits for use in talismans or evocation, much like the system for creating sigils on the Planetary kameoth, by drawing a line from one letter to another on the Rose Cross until all of the letters of the spirit name have been linked to form a distinctive and readable sigil.

In *Talismans & Evocations of the Golden Dawn*, Pat Zalewski states, "Calling upon an Angelic or Archangelic name does not automatically give access to the august being itself, nor does it help reach the spiritual state we are targeting."

From my perspective, it seems that the Golden Dawn utilizes the proper timing and charging of talismans combined with the corresponding celestial influences, sigils, colors, geometric shapes, and intention to form a complete and potent talisman. A direct evocation of the associated angel or spirit does not seem necessarily required for this practice to be effective.

Talismanic Scrolls

Paper, or more appropriately parchment, has been a key medium for drawing talismans for many centuries and across many cultures. Metal talismans are more obviously enduring, but parchment talismans for all sorts of spiritual and magical concerns are vastly more affordable, and have seen use the world over. There is an 11th-century example of a talismanic scroll found in Egypt which was crafted in the Fatimid caliphate. Along with this find, numerous Islamic paper or parchment talismans are on display in museums, containing sacred verses from the *Qur'ān* and displaying similarities to the Judaic talismans which became the pentacles of the *Key of Solomon*. An interesting feature of these Islamic talismans is that they have been found within 'amulet boxes' which physically preserve the parchment talismans and also act as energetic containers for the spells. These talismanic scrolls were in production utilizing a method for block printing which predated European print-

---

charged water in that case being used to protect or cure children from the bites or stings of poisonous animals. —APF

ing by hundreds of years. The mass demand for talismanic scrolls can be discerned by the use of these early block prints, each of which would have made hundreds of these scrolls.

A prime example of talismanic scrolls may be found in the Jewish *tefillin* (usually translated into English as "phylacteries," from Greek *phylaktēria*), which are a pair of small leather boxes containing parchment scrolls upon which are written particular verses from the Hebrew Bible. Both boxes and scrolls are created by experts with long training in the artistry and the complex traditional rules of phylactery making. The two *tefillin* are worn, one on the left arm and one on the forehead, by observant Jewish men and especially adherents of Orthodox Judaism during morning weekday prayers.

The Japanese also have a tradition of using talismanic scrolls called *o-fuda* which are hung in the home to protect the household. They are purchased by visitors to a Shinto shrine or temple where they have been ritually consecrated, and the purchase is considered a contribution to the shrine. An *o-fuda* scroll contains the name of a particular Shinto *kami* spirit and the name of the shrine from which the talisman was obtained, and is typically housed in a decorative container of wood or cloth.

A variation on the *o-fuda* is the *o-mamori* ("protection"), a portable talismanic scroll intended for the benefit of an individual rather than an entire household. Unlike *o-fuda*, which are specifically Shinto, *o-mamori* may be purchased at both Shinto shrines and Buddhist temples. The small talismanic scroll will normally contain a prayer or invocation to a Shinto *kami* or a Buddhist *bosatsu* (*boddhisatva*) or other religious figure, and is contained in a brocade bag which is carried on the owner's person. A specific *o-mamori* may be a talisman to provide general protection or good fortune, or one of the particular benefits which have always been sought through talismans (health, prosperity, love, peace, scholarship, safe travel, etc.).

It is traditional to replace one's *o-mamori* at the New Year. Old talismans are preferably returned to the same sacred location at which they were purchased so they can be disposed of properly. If the owner of an *o-mamori* is unable to visit a shrine or temple at the proper time and must dispose of the amulet on his or her own, the talisman should not be placed in the trash like common rubbish, but rather should be burned respectfully.

Japanese scroll talismans have a rich and enduring history, and are just as prevalent in modern times as ever. A discerning Western ceremonial magician might be wise to study and cross-reference the customs and practices of this tradition to enrich his understanding of how better to create, maintain, and dispose of talismans.

Haunted or Cursed Objects and Places:
A Paranormal Overview

Stepping away from magical talismans and their construction *per se* for a moment, I wish to touch on a topic which is becoming more familiar to the general public due to the increase in television shows and websites dedicated to "the paranormal." These programs often deal with the results of an energetic imprint left upon physical objects or places.

Modern paranormal terminology includes a long list of terms for particular types of paranormal disturbances and their associated causes. Two of these terms reflect when some manner of spiritual or emotional energy is bonded to a particular place or thing, causing the place or object to be "haunted" by the energy released in a moment in time by a then-living person or by some other entity. Those terms are:

✦ ATMOSPHERIC APPARITION: Not actually a ghost or spirit, but instead a visual imprint of people and events that was left behind in the environment and continues to replay.

✦ HAUNTED OBJECTS: Jewelry, furniture, clothing, and even toys that seem to be haunted by a past owner or to have been cursed. Examples of the most famous of such objects which have drawn the attention of the paranormal media to date are 'Robert the Doll,' the 'Dybbuk Box,' and the 'Annabelle doll.' Many of these allegedly cursed or haunted items have inspired fictionalized motion pictures and much online media hype. Not long ago, a television show called *Haunted Collector* aired on the Syfy Channel, which focused completely on haunted objects. This paranormal reality series featured a group of investigators headed by "demonologist" John Zaffis, who investigated alleged haunted locations with the hopes of identifying and removing any on-site artifacts or "trigger objects" which were potentially the source of the disturbance or supposed paranormal activity. The Zaffis family and their team travel around the world to the sites of alleged paranormal occurrences to investigate items that Zaffis identifies as having something to do with spirits or other paranormal energies. Zaffis removes the items from the location and takes them to his haunted relics museum located in a barn on his property in Stratford, Connecticut.

Of course, the phenomenon of places or objects being impregnated with a particular spirit or energy is nothing new. Many people relate anecdotes regarding certain places or objects which seem to have triggered sudden mood changes—most often of discomfort or anxiety—in them. Beyond this is the ability of *psychometry*, by which highly adept mediums or psychics are able to touch an object and pick up impressions and sensations which allow them to "read" the history of past experiences related to the object or to a person who owned it. Apparently under the right conditions, places and objects can be much like an environmental recorder which stores the impressions of energetic release. The more intense the emotion or experience, the more energy is released and potentially recorded onto the object or place.

A case could be made that a legitimate talisman or magical implement which has been used in properly executed occult ritual and charged by an angel or other spirit with its own powers would be more amply imbued with a distinct energy than any other object. When it comes to talismans, the ability to create one is heavily dependent upon this realization. I contend that a magician must be adept at evocation above all other occult arts, even astrology, to be able to successfully impregnate a physical object with a spiritual or esoteric force. I find this to be one of the largest discrepancies in the knowledge of would-be practitioners of classical magic. Simply choosing the most favorable times and planetary alignments in which to create a talisman does not automatically imbue it with any significant power or function. It is the spirits themselves which grant to the object the power to contain the abilities of their office if they themselves are not somehow bound to the object. In essence, it could be stated that an authentic talisman is "possessed" by the nature or office of the spirit and its particular power.

On the opposite end of the spectrum, in relation to 'haunted' or 'cursed' objects, the magician's ability to call a spirit into proximity or possibly into occupancy of a physical object should be balanced naturally with the ability for them to call one *out* of something. To exorcise or remove a spirit from a person, place, or object is historically a cornerstone of the magician's profession. If you read this and considered that the same ability is typically connected with priests and other clergy, you would be right as well. Magicians should be trained in both the invocation and the banishing or exorcism of spirits (or spirit energies), again coinciding with the methods of the tradition or traditions in which they are versed.

Spirit Images and the *Liber Spirituum*

The power behind spirit images, icons, and effigies is well known through countless cultures and spiritual traditions. In the earlier section dealing with the images employed in the *Picatrix*, we saw that, if made by a talented magician and under the right circumstances, illustrations of spirits can contain a power in and of themselves. In my first book, *Gateways Through Stone and Circle*,[55] which detailed my work with *The Art of Drawing Spirits into Crystals*, I included a chapter dealing with the famous *Liber Spirituum* or "Book of Spirits" (synchronistically the namesake of this current anthology), that being a roll or catalogue of various spirits, with the names, titles, offices, and powers under which they enact influence in the world, and the means by which they may be summoned, as well as the particular oaths

---

55. Ashen Chassan (Bryan Garner), *Gateways through Stone and Circle: A Manual of Evocation for the Planetary Intelligences* (Timmonsville, SC: Nephilim Press, 2013).

and conjurations by which they may be bound to perform some task or obligation such as charging talismans. The book is most famous for having innate power over the spirits illustrated within it. The images themselves are said to embody the very natures of the spirits who are bound to the book. The source text has a few passing remarks on how this volume of catalogued spirits is to appear in size and context and construction:

> Where now, this being done in the order prescribed, take out thy little book, which must be made about seven inches long, of pure white virgin vellum or paper, likewise pen and ink must be ready to write down the name, character, and office, likewise the seal or image of whatever spirit may appear for this I must tell you that it does not happen that the same spirit you call will always appear, for you must try the spirit to know whether he be a pure or impure being, and this thou shalt easily know by a firm and undoubted faith in God.[56]

In *Gateways*, I gave a detailed account of how I constructed my own Book of Spirits and what transpired after I asked archangelic beings to imprint some of their nature and energy onto the pages wherein I drew to the best of my ability their images as I beheld them within the crystal stone. However, I felt it was quite fitting to the title and purpose of the current Azoth Press collected work to reiterate a few points on the Book of Spirits. More specifically I wish to point out how magical evocation, the Liber Spirituum, and the creation of magical talismans all link together.

The Book of Spirits is covered in greater depth in the *Fourth Book of Occult Philosophy*, or *Of Magical Ceremonies: The Fourth Book*, attributed to Agrippa[57]:

> Now this book is to be made of most pure and clean paper, that hath never been used before; which many do call *Virgin-paper*. And this book must be inscribed after this manner: that is to say, Let there be placed on the left side the image of the spirit, and on the right side his character, with the Oath above it, containing the name of the spirit, and his dignity and place, with his office and power. Yet very many do compose this book otherwise, omitting the characters or image: but it is more efficacious not to neglect anything which conduceth to it.

---

56. Trithemius, *The Art of Drawing Spirits into Crystals*, in Francis Barrett, *The Magus, or Celestial Intelligencer* (London: Lackington, Allen, and Co., 1801).

57. The attribution to Agrippa is false. As Joseph H. Peterson notes on his website, *Twilit Grotto—Esoteric Archives* (http://www.esotericarchives.com/agrippa/agrippa4.htm), "The so-called *Fourth Book* appeared in Latin some thirty years after Agrippa's death. Johann Weyer, a student of Agrippa's, denounced this work to be spurious (cf. *Præstigiis Dæmonum*, 1563) and that evaluation has rarely been questioned." However, the reason for the attribution isn't difficult to see. As Peterson also remarks, "This book quotes from and expands on certain themes in Agrippa's *Third Book of occult philosophy*, to create a more concise and practical synopsis of the techniques for summoning spirits."

Moreover, there is to be observed the circumstances of places, times, hours, according to the Stars which these spirits are under, and are seen to agree unto, their site, rite, and order being applied.

Which book being so written, and well bound, is to be adorned, garnished, and kept secure, with Registers and Seals, lest it should happen after the consecration to open in some place not intended, and endanger the operator. Furthermore, this book ought to be kept as reverently as may be: for irreverence of mind causeth it to lose its virtue, with pollution and profanation.[58]

The image of the spirit, along with its name, sigils, governing holy words, and binding conjuration, together create a powerful and permanent example of the energies and powers associated with that being to be kept sealed—and readily available to the magus—on the vellum page in the book, which thus becomes in itself another talisman of the spirit. The *Fourth Book* goes on to set forth how a spirit is conjured and bound to swear an oath by the book, describing almost to the letter the process of evocation as set forth in the *Goëtia*.

Now this sacred book being thus composed according to the manner already delivered, we are then to proceed to the consecration thereof after a twofold way: one whereof is, That all and singular the spirits who are written in the book, be called to the Circle, according to the Rites and Order which we have before taught; and the book that is to be consecrated, let there be placed without the Circle in a triangle. And in the first place, let there be read in the presence of the spirits all the Oaths which are written in that book; and then the book to be consecrated being placed without the Circle in a triangle there drawn, let all the spirits be compelled to impose their hands where their images and characters are drawn, and to confirm and consecrate the same with a special and common Oath. Which being done, let the book be taken and shut, and preserved as we have before spoken, and let the spirits be licensed to depart, according to due rite and order.[59]

The instructions clearly reveal the importance of being able to deal with a spirit in a communication so profound that the form of the spirit can clearly be seen as well as the impression it makes as it "signs" (charges and acknowledges itself linked to) its page in your Book of Spirits. As fantastical as this may seem to some, repeated experience has proven it to be attainable, though obviously reserved for those magicians and scryers with developed sight and the ability to conjure spirits to visible and auditory manifestation. As one would imagine, this ability is quite useful if not imperative in consecrating talismans properly, where spirits imprint their being, office, and power into a prepared physical object other than The Book of Spirits.

---

58. *Henry Cornelius Agrippa His Fourth Book of Occult Philosophy*, translated into English by Robert Turner (London: printed by J.C. for John Harrison at the Lamb at the East-end of Pauls, 1655).

59. *Ibid.*

Crafting and authentically charging any magical image or talisman seems to require this process by which a magician gains close proximity to the spirit or angel who is to effectively impregnate or charge the intended item. Timing, astrological considerations, and knowledge of correct correspondences are vital, but only a fraction of the needed elements which go into crafting a truly magical implement. In this case, the drawn or painted image of the spirit as seen by the invoking magus or scryer has particularly potent influence and directly correlates to the interaction which occurred between summoner and spirit. Likewise, if the sigil or seal is afterwards consecrated or impregnated with the spirit's power and authority, it becomes a potent and activated direct link with the spirit itself. The Book of Spirits is the vital link between the material basis of the talisman and the working implement. With a catalog of charged or "possessed" pages containing portraits and descriptions of the spirits, much like the ones illustrated and explained in the *Picatrix*, the spiritual influences of any of a variety of beings can be contacted quickly and to great effect to charge a particular talisman.

Steps for Fashioning Authentic Talismans

As we have already made mention of the Pentacles, it is necessary that thou shouldest understand that the whole Science and understanding of our *Key* dependeth upon the operation, Knowledge, and use of Pentacles.

He then who shall wish to perform any operation by the means of the Medals, or Pentacles, and therein to render himself expert, must observe what hath been hereinbefore ordained. Let him then, O my Son Roboam,[60] know and understand that in the aforesaid Pentacles he shall find those Ineffable and Most Holy Names which were written by the finger of God in the Tablets of Moses; and which I, Solomon, have received through the Ministry of an Angel by Divine Revelation. These then have I collected together, arranged, consecrated, and kept, for the benefit of the human race, and the preservation of Body and of Soul.[61]

In this section, I aim to give a clear overview of how I construct a talisman from beginning to end.[62]

Of course, there is foundational work required before ever beginning to make talismans. The magician who wishes to become a maker of veritable talismans must

---

60. Roboam is the Greek and Latin form of the Hebrew name of Rehoboam, the son and heir of King Solomon. —APF

61. S. Liddell MacGregor Mathers and 'Solomon,' *The Key of Solomon the King (Clavicula Salomonis)* (London: George Redway, 1889), Book I, chapter VIII, "Concerning the Medals or Pentacles, and the Manner of Constructing Them."

62. That is, given that I have made no variations, constraints, or alterations on the basis of advice given by the appropriate spirit or spirits during preliminary evocations.

first develop a broad knowledge of magical correspondences, imagery, symbols, and lore. This preparation is vital to becoming a successful magician at all, since the spirits and angels very much move and communicate within the framework of classical correspondences. A magician well versed in western esoteric symbolism will be able to garner much more meaning and associative information when shown a vision of, for example, a crowned and sceptred king with stag horns, wearing a blue mantle, and with an eagle flying overhead.

Also fundamental is the development of the crafting and artistic skills for preparing the physical object of a talisman. As with any skill, the ability to create a fine piece of artwork is a matter of dedication and practice, as well as trial and error. Any craft requires practice and no small level of skill and aptitude to produce pieces which appear worthy of the potent energy which will be imbued in them. At least some skill will develop within persons who take their time and consider what they are undertaking to be important and worthwhile.[63] Of course talismans, charms, and magical seals have been found throughout antiquity and many are hardly the work of expert craftspeople. Their function rests not primarily with their æsthetic appeal but with the successful process by which they are made into veritable objects of magical potency and effect. For this to be accomplished requires a magician who is skilled and knowledgeable in his or her craft.

As I have already stated, once you have crafted a pleasing piece of artwork, to perfect it into a veritable talisman, you will require the ability to contact the spirit or spirits who will directly empower the talisman. Therefore, the final part of the foundational work is the development of adeptship in evocation. To describe and relate a full system of evocation is beyond the scope of this work and one which I have already covered in depth in *Gateways Through Stone and Circle*. Presumably, the rite of evocation will follow the systematic approach laid out in the grimoire from which the magician is fashioning the talisman. All will be accomplished by a magician who already knows well how to summon a chosen entity before they ever attempt the crafting of a real talisman.

It is through the angels, spirits, and god-forms that talismans receive their virtue and functionality. This point cannot be reiterated enough, as it is through these intelligences that the talismans really comes into being.

Outline for Crafting a Talisman

To reiterate a crucial point, one should be well versed and initiated in the tradition from which a talisman originates for it to be truly effective and a veritable magical object. It is obviously beyond the scope of this article to describe each of the

---

63. I am acquainted with two traditional ceremonial magicians who became successful professional jewelers from learning to make talismans, spirit seals, and lamens.

methods and particular techniques for creating talismans from the traditions listed above. To begin with, I recommend becoming familiar with a single tradition and its method for creating magical talismans and working at it diligently with as much authenticity and integrity as you can muster.

General Outline for Making a Magical Talisman

0. Planning and Preliminary Evocation
1. Gathering the Necessary Implements and Materials
2. Arranging the Magical Chamber
3. Purification and Retreat
4. Preparing and Blessing the Raw Materials
5. Crafting the Talisman
6. Evoking the Spirit or Spirits to Consecrate the Talisman
7. Completing the Ceremony.

0. Talismanic Planning and Preliminary Evocation

At this point, the *Key of Solomon the King* will provide us with a solid traditional basis on which to proceed.

> It is necessary, above all things, to be attentive to the operation, and never to forget or omit those things which contribute to the success which the Pentacles and Experiments promise, having ever in thy mind no other intention than the Glory of God, the accomplishment of thy desires, and loving-kindness towards thy neighbour.[64]

I highly recommend beginning with one of the planetary aspects, since that is the talismanic system employed by the majority of classic magical books. Look to the fountainhead of talismanic magic, the array of talismans with their designs and powers presented in the grimoires. Choose one of the particular talismans that most closely corresponds to your situation or intention.

Whether intending to make a talisman for yourself or another person (and I cannot stress too strongly the importance of first developing real skill in fashioning talismans for yourself and testing their effectiveness before ever agreeing to make one for someone else), I would consult in advance a spirit or angel who presides over the influences and "office" proper to the talisman which you intend to create, an entity whom you have successfully conjured more than once, and ask its advice in constructing the talisman properly.

The next step for planning your operation is to determine the exact day and hour for the crafting of your talisman as well as the day and hour for the evocation of the being who is to empower the talisman. Many grimoires give instructions on which

---

64. Solomon and Mathers, *op. cit.*

days and astrological conditions are most favorable for constructing a given talisman, and my recommendation for doing this initially is to follow the same grimoire in which you found the talisman you have chosen to create. If you are making a planetary talisman, the timing is straightforward; work in the day and hour of the planet, when the planet is well-placed and is favorably aspected. The *Key of Solomon* also suggests that calm and clear weather is beneficial for talismanic consecration.

At one point, the *Key* instructs that "The pentacles should then be made in the days and hours of Mercury, when the Moon is in an aërial or terrestrial sign; she should also be in her increase, and in equal number of days with the Sun." Some modern magicians have been confused by this statement, thinking that all the planetary talismans should be made on these days and times, but the author is referring only to the general protective pentacles used in the work. You will find that the Solomonic texts suggest that most magical implements, such as the wands, knives, swords, and other instruments, be made on a day and hour of Mercury due to spirits being of a Mercurial or airy nature. This isn't always the case, but more often than not I find that if you are uncertain or a given text is unclear or perhaps does not designate a certain day or time to craft a talisman, that the above times and days are well suited. When in doubt, go with Mercury, as it is the best energy for crafting as well as the best conduit for the exchange of information between the spiritual and physical worlds.

You will also of course need to make sure well in advance of the time chosen for the operation that you have acquired the proper metals, parchment, incense, and other necessary tools and materials needed for crafting the talisman and performing the ritual to call the forces into the talisman.

1. Gathering the Necessary Implements and Materials

Items List:

a. Raw materials: Metal, parchment, stones, and any other components which will become the material basis of the talisman. Ingredients for the proper incense.

b. Crafting tools: Metal cutters, burin, paints, pens, brushes, any and all items needed to inscribe or draw the sigils and words necessary for the talisman.

c. Ceremonial magic items for talismanic construction and evocation, including: Robes, lamens, any great seals and general pentacles, wand, circle, triangle, lamp, candles or lights, Book of Spirits or book of invocations, evocations or prayers, holy table/working table, holy water and sprinker, incense and incense burner(s), and a silk wrapping and perhaps a secure box for the talisman once it is consecrated and charged.

CAUTION: If you would be a worthy, skillful (and long-lived) magician, you must assume responsibility and do your own research to be aware of any dangers inherent in the materials prescribed in texts transmitting premodern recipes. For example, the toxicity of some metals was understood poorly if at all before the modern era. Both lead and mercury are toxic to humans when handled, and particularly when heated as for casting a ring or other talisman. While lead poisoning (sometimes called saturnism) has been known since antiquity, it is only in recent years that we have learned how dangerous even small levels can be. Several of the plant ingredients in grimoric incense recipes (such as henbane and wolfbane) are also poisonous to humans and other animals, and sulphur, when burned, releases potentially deadly sulphur dioxide. Be responsible for yourself and those who trust your expertise. **Do Your Research.**

These Pentacles are usually made of the metal the most suitable to the nature of the Planet; and then there is no occasion to observe the rule of particular colours. They should be engraved with the instrument of Art in the days and hours proper to the Planet.

Saturn ruleth over Lead; Jupiter over Tin; Mars over Iron; the Sun over Gold; Venus over Copper; Mercury over the mixture of Metals; and the Moon over Silver.

They may also be made with exorcised virgin paper,[65] writing thereon with the colours adopted for each Planet, referring to the rules already laid down in the proper Chapters, and according to the Planet with which the Pentacle is in sympathy.

Wherefore unto Saturn the colour of Black is appropriated; Jupiter ruleth over Celestial Blue; Mars over Red; the Sun over Gold, or the colour of Yellow or Citron; Venus over Green; Mercury over Mixed Colours; the Moon over Silver, or the colour of Argentine Earth.

The Matter of which the Pentacle is constructed should be Virgin, never having been used for any other purpose; or if it be metal it should be purified by fire.

As regards the size of the Pentacles it is arbitrary, so long as they are made according to the rules, and with the requisite solemnities, as hath been ordained.

The virtues of the Holy Pentacles are no less advantageous unto thee than the knowledge of the secrets which I have already given unto thee; and thou shouldest take particular care if thou makest them upon virgin parchment to use the proper colours; and if thou engravest them upon metal, to

---

65. The *Key* clarifies below that virgin parchment is meant.

> do so in the manner taught thee; and so shalt thou have the satisfaction of seeing them produce the promised effect.

And also

> Among other things, thou shalt chiefly use these colours: Gold, cinnabar or vermilion red, and celestial or brilliant azure blue. Furthermore, thou shalt make these medals or pentacles with exorcised pen and colors, as we shall hereafter show thee.[66]

First discern the most suitable metal or other material for the talisman you are making. Be sure it is not something which was already used for another function. This is what the grimoires mean when they say that a material should be "virgin." For planetary talismans this is commonly lead for Saturn, tin for Jupiter, iron for Mars, gold for the Sun, copper for Venus, mercury or mixed metals for Mercury, and silver for the Moon.

Otherwise, parchment made from calf or goat (kid) skin is traditionally used. Make sure you are using real parchment, and not modern "parchment paper." Once you have selected the desired material, I would keep it wrapped up (traditionally in a white silk cloth or something similar) and make sure it is not used or touched before you begin to work on it at the proper day and hour.

Notice that the *Key* specifies using the "instrument of Art" and "exorcised pen and colors" in crafting the talisman. My adherence to the traditional forms of classical ceremonial magic is such that I will only use tools which I have purchased new and never used for any other purpose, and which have been consecrated and dedicated to the art of magical implement and talisman making, and in many instances I will inscribe them with the associated sigils, and dedicate them with the proper prayers, blessings, and consecrations to further authenticate the process.

> When thou shalt construct these Pentacles and Characters, it is necessary never to forget the Incense, nor to employ anything beyond that of which mention is made.

and

> It is necessary after this that thou shouldest have within the circle a vessel of earth with burning coals and odoriferous perfumes thereon; with the which thou shalt fumigate the aforesaid pentacles; and, having turned thy face towards the East, thou shalt hold the said pentacles over the smoke of the incense.[67]

The most complicated ingredients which the magus will have to accumulate before the operation are typically those which are used to blend the incense. Every grimoire has a slightly different assortment of applicable, corresponding suffumiga-

---

66. Solomon and Mathers, *op. cit.*

67. *Ibid.*

tions to be utilized. Traditionally, each planetary mixture should be created on the proper day and hour of the associated planet to further imbue the perfume with corresponding energies. Gather your ingredients ahead of time and plan out those that seem most agreeable. I've experimented with a wide variety of classic incenses and even some of the newer mixtures with varying results. I've decided to include a table of five grimoire-based varieties which I feel are most appropriate for this work.

The first column lists the ingredients for the compound incenses prescribed in *The Clavicles of R. Solomon* (in MS Wellcome 4670). In the original texts, blood and brains of certain animals are included in the incense recipes, which I have omitted.[68] Although I am a traditionalist, I have chosen not to use any corruptible animal material as components in my incense blends. I like to keep incense I've made for as long as I can, and most animal material will putrefy quickly if not used. I have used some of the supplements Aaron Leitch suggests in his indispensable book *Secrets of the Magickal Grimoires*[69] to account for this. I do not doubt the effectiveness of the prescribed animal ingredients, but in practice I have never detected any inadequacy in the effectiveness of the animal-free compounds I have made.[70]

The second column contains a list of planetary perfumes suggested by Agrippa in *De Occulta Philosophia*, Book I, chapter 44, "The Composition of Some Fumes Appropriate to the Planets." It is obvious that this list is either the inspiration for the *Clavicles* perfumes or that they share a common source. Also, as in the *Clavicles*, the original recipes call for animal blood and brain ingredients, which I exclude.[71]

Third is a list of planetary incense blends compounded by Harold Roth of Alchemy Works,[72] inspired by the planetary correspondences distributed throughout *De Occulta Philosophia*.

The fourth list consists of the simple, single-ingredient planetary perfumes found in the mediæval *Heptameron*.[73]

---

68. For the full recipe (including the blood and brain components), see Skinner and Rankine, *op. cit.*

69. Aaron Leitch, *Secrets of the Magickal Grimoires: The Classical Texts of Magick Decyphered* (Woodbury, MN: Llewellyn Publications, 2005).

70. In particular, I've used the Jupiter recipe many times, minus the animal blood and flesh parts, and it works wonderfully!

71. For the full recipes, see Donald Tyson, Henry Cornelius Agrippa of Nettesheim, and James Freake, *Three Books of Occult Philosophy* (St. Paul, MN: Llewellyn Publications, 1995), or Joseph H. Peterson, Heinrich Cornelius Agrippa, and J.F., *Of Occult Philosophy, Book I (Part 1)*, at the *Twilit Grotto—Esoteric Archives* website (http://www.esotericarchives.com/agrippa/agrpp1b.htm).

72. Harold A. Roth, *Three Books of Occult Philosophy Incense*, at the *Alchemy Works* website (http://www.alchemy-works.com/incense_agrippa.html).

73. Barrett includes the operation of the *Heptameron* before *The Art of Drawing Spirits into Crystals* in *The Magus*.

The fifth and final list of incense blends is from a grimoire which has only recently become available to ceremonial magicians, Frederick Hockley's *A Complete Book of Magic Science*. The operation in this grimoire corresponds closely to that of *The Art of Drawing Spirits into Crystals*, which is the system I utilize most often for evocation, so I was interested to see what incense ingredients were recommended. The book contains a list of planetary suffumigations to call forth the Olympic Spirits.[74] The incense ingredients clearly derive from the same source as *The Clavicles of R. Solomon* and *De Occulta Philosophia*, but there is some obvious confusion in the attribution of the blends to the planets. Also, like the related blends, the original formulæ call for the inclusion of animal blood and brain matter.[75] Although I have included the list here, I have not experimented widely with the *Complete Book* concoctions as attributed. I prefer those listed in the first four categories, with which I have had very agreeable results.

Keep in mind, some of these perfumes seem intended for lower planetary spirits and demons rather than angels. In my own work, I've found that the ingredients in the first two lists seem to be the most agreeable for the archangels.

Out of these selections, the practicing magician should find plenty of ingredients with which to experiment.

On the day of the operation, organize your materials and be sure you have your metal or parchment (or other suitable material), colors, and implements for making the talisman. You should certainly have a tracing of the perfect shape for your talisman as well as copies of all the proper sigils, names, and other symbols that are going on it so it will be easy to transfer them onto your talisman or image. Also be sure you have all of the necessary ritual equipment, including the invocations and correspondences for the spirits, your lamen or lamens, wand, holy water and sprinkler, incense and censers, robes.

2. Arranging the Magical Chamber

Ceremonial magicians will be very familiar with the requirement for a dedicated magical working space. The *Key of Solomon*, for example, instructs us that it is "necessary to have a Chamber or Cabinet specially set apart and newly cleaned,

---

74. This list of planetary spirits and a similar list of associated perfume mixtures is also found in *The Secret Grimoire of Turiel*.

75. You may read the full recipes (including the blood and brain components) in Frederic Hockley and Dietrich Bergman, *A Complete Book of Magic Science* (York Beach, ME: The Teitan Press, 2008).

Planet	Compound Incenses from *Les Clavicules de R. Salomon*	Compound Incenses from *De Occulta Philosophia*	Alchemy Works Blends Inspired by *De Occulta Philosophia*	Simple Incenses from the *Heptameron*	Olympic Incense Blends from Hockley, *Complete Book of Magic Science*
♄ Saturn	Black poppy seed, henbane seed, mandrake root, powdered lodestone, civet, myrrh	Black poppy seed, henbane seed, mandrake root, powdered lodestone, myrrh	Frankincense, costus, calamus, bdellium, spikenard, galangal, ginger, vetiver, zedoary (white turmeric)	Sulphur	Saffron, wood of aloes, balsam of myrrh, a grain of musk, ambergris
♃ Jupiter	Rowan berries, lignum aloes, storax, benzoin, powdered lapis lazuli, chopped peacock feathers	Ash-tree seed, lignum aloes, storax, gum benzoin, powdered lapis lazuli, the tops of peacock feathers	Clove, allspice, star anise, juniper berries, vanilla, peppercorn, fir cone, nutmeg	Saffron	Mastic of the east, any chosen incense, cloves, powdered agate
♂ Mars	Euphorbium, belladonna, sal ammoniac, roots of both (white and black) hellebores, powdered lodestone, a pinch of sulfur	Euphorbium, bdellium, sal ammoniac, roots of both (white and black) hellebores, powdered lodestone, a pinch of sulfur	Cedar wood, red sandalwood, juniper wood, cypress, rosewood, ho wood	Pepper	Storax, loadstone, gum Benjamin (benzoin storax), camphor, chamomile flowers, and a grain of white poppy
☉ Sun	One-sixth ounce each of saffron, lignum aloes, lignum balm, laurel seeds, cloves, myrrh, frankincense, and a grain each of amber and musk	Saffron, amber, musk, lignum aloes, lignum balsam, fruit of the laurel, cloves, myrrh, and frankincense	Frankincense, benzoin, storax, labdanum, galbanum, elemi, ambergris	Red sandalwood	Black pepper, hogsbane (black henbane), powdered loadstone, eastern myrrh
♀ Venus	Musk, ambergris, aloes wood, dried red roses, red coral	Musk, amber, lignum aloes, red roses, red coral	Safflower petals, jasmine flowers, larkspur flowers, rose petals, ylang ylang	Costus (Heb. *qosheth*, Ar. *qust*)	Musk, ambergris, lignum aloes, dried red rose petals, powdered red coral
☿ Mercury	Oriental mastic, any chosen incense, cloves, pentaphylla flowers, powdered agate	Mastic, frankincense, cloves, cinquefoile, powdered agate	Cinnamon, coriander, cardamom, musk seed, anise, blood orange, bergamot, grapefruit	Mastic	Ash-tree seed, lignum aloes, storax, powdered loadstone, the end of a quill
☽ Moon	White poppy seed, the best frankincense, a pinch of camphor	White poppy seed, frankincense, camphor	Myrtle leaf, wormwood, eucalyptus, rosemary, clary sage, davana, geranium	Lignum aloes	Euphorbium, bdellium, sal ammoniac, hellebore roots, powdered lodestone, a pinch of sulfur

Fig. 18. Table of Grimoric Planetary Incenses

wherein thou canst remain without interruption."[76] It is my firm belief that a practicing magician should designate a room solely for the practice of magic and use it for no other purpose. This viewpoint is often considered outrageous or impractical by many modern occultists who do not have the circumstances or finances for such "luxuries." As difficult as this may be for many practitioners, I cannot condone transforming a spare bedroom or office into a temporary space for the evocation of spirits or any sincere work of grimoric magic. In my experience, makeshift temple and ritual spaces for occasional magical workings never seem to get the best results.

Your magical ritual or working room should already be supplied with all the necessary implements and materials, your book of spirits, table for consecration, magical circle, lamp, associated incense and incense burner or brazier.

Hermetic or Solomonic magical methods involve utilizing a magical circle. If working from the *Key of Solomon*, I suggest using the circles with the names listed there. However, there are a multitude of magical circles described in various grimoires that are in the same tradition, and I have experienced no adverse results from using any of the various forms of magic circle.

Whether you will be drawing, painting, or engraving the talisman, you will require a table on which to work. The table should be more than just a simple work top, it should be arranged as an altar for sacred magic, dedicated to the consecration of your talisman. For this I consider one of the varieties of Holy Tables to be well suited. Personally, I use two varieties of altars for constructing talismans. One is the Table of Practice found in *The Art Pauline*. Another is a version of the Holy Table I use in the Trithemian *Art of Drawing Spirits into Crystals*, which contains the names of the seven planets and the angels ruling them, with their seals or characters, along with the names of the kings of the four quarters of the earth, drawn within a double circle, with a triangle in the center. Another option the magician could consider is engraving on his or her altar table one of the Great Seals of Solomon.

There should be no unnecessary items on the table, just the ones required for the ceremony and for crafting the talisman. Ideally, you should put a white linen tablecloth on it, or a colored one which corresponds to the planetary nature of your talisman as well as the day and hour. Adding a ritual light source such as a holy lamp or Solomonic wax candle likewise colored to the specific nature of the talisman is appropriate as well.

For the actual consecration and charging of the magical image or talisman, I use a magical triangle, but not exactly like the one in the *Goëtia* which is used for charging and binding spirits to an oath or decree outside of the magic circle. The triangle that I utilize is quite similar to the one pictured in *Evocations and Talismans in the*

---

76. Mathers and Solomon, *op. cit.*, Book I, chapter 8.

Golden Dawn.[77] To make my triangle, I cut out a wooden disk and engraved and painted an equilateral triangle within the circle of the disk, and a smaller circle in the very center of the triangle. A small circle is also inscribed at each angle of the triangle where censers go. I place this magic triangle in the direction or quarter with which the particular spirits of a ritual are associated. If invoking angels, I place the triangle just inside the border of my magic circle; in all other cases, it goes outside my circle.

I also place within the central circle of the triangle, underneath the talisman, a smaller board cut to a geometric shape which corresponds to the planetary alignment of the talisman I'm consecrating, inscribed with corresponding sigils and other symbols. I typically also place a number of colored candles around the consecration areas which correspond in both number and color to the associated planet.

3. Purification and Retreat

> Above all things, remember that to perform any of these operations thou must be pure in body and mind, and without blemish, and omit not any of the preparations.[78]

I believe this to be an essential step for magical operations that is often overlooked in modern times. In some cases, the process of purification can determine the degree of success in the entire magical working, as it coincides with the clarity and level of intention which the magician can hold during the ritual. I would say that this discipline is a key ingredient to actually being able to perform rites of evocation and spiritual contact, if not a magical act of any kind. It is a very pointed discipline. For the magician, it is establishing alignment to God/The Divine, and mastery of the self, control over one's "universe." It is making a conscious decision to discipline the body in order to strengthen the spirit.

Most grimoires instruct the magician to adhere to a strict regimen of fasting and celibacy before any operation, but especially before evocation. The period of preparation for a major ritual is typically nine days. If circumstances require, the magician may shorten the period of preliminary discipline to three days or, in extreme circumstances, one day. For a minor operation, if nothing else, do not eat or drink anything heavy on the day of your ritual.

Purification culminates on the day of the working. Typically an hour or so before the planned time of the operation, I prepare myself ritually by bathing, sprinkling myself with holy water, and anointing myself with holy oil, all while repeating several Psalms of cleansing, always including Psalm 51. As far as the baths, prayers, and

---

77. Pat Zalewski, *Evocations and Talismans in the Golden Dawn* (Longborough, Leicestershire: Thoth Publications, 2002).

78. Mathers and Solomon, *op. cit.*

perfumes (scented oils and incense), many spirits actively appreciate cleanliness and the mental equivalent, centeredness, which is amplified by the purificatory removal of both conscious and unconscious distractions. For the properly purified magician, the mind will reach a pitch of focus which makes concentration and determination—the magical application of the will—not only possible, but extremely heightened in potency. In the realm of the grimoires, such cleanliness is a movement of ascension toward God/Godhead.

I then put on my ritual robes or vestments, and purify the working space.

4. Preparing and Blessing the Raw Materials

Having set up your magic circle and triangle,[79] your table, and working instruments, and having purified yourself and the working space, it is time to enter your circle and begin the operation proper. First take a few moments to settle yourself within the magical circle.

I recommend that you spend a moment in contemplation of the object before you and also in visualization of its completed form. See the resulting talisman before you as clearly as you can, even before you begin to work. In many cases it is a potent method to recite a prayer, blessing, or statement of intention as you work. Breathe your intentionality into it but do not be concerned with perfection. Concentrate on your work and be concerned with proper intention, keeping focused only on the task at hand and purpose of the talisman.

When you feel ready, take the holy water and sprinkler and bless the materials you are about to fashion into a magical object. A blessing from the *Key of Solomon* can be used, or one modified from *The Art of Drawing Spirits into Crystals* such as, "O thou inanimate creature of God, be sanctified and consecrated, and blessed to this purpose of becoming a powerful talisman, that no evil phantasm or falsehood may affect thee, for our Lord Christ's sake, Amen."

5. Crafting the Talisman

> Thou shalt commence the writing or construction of the pentacles in the hour aforesaid. … Whensoever thou constructest them, if thou canst complete them in the hour wherein thou didst begin them, it is better. However, if it be absolutely necessary to interrupt the work, thou shouldest await the proper day and hour before re-commencing it.[80]

At the allotted time, begin by reciting an appropriate prayer or otherwise form a prayer from the heart for your intention, done with sincerity and humility, and ask

---

79. Or other place of consecration for your talisman, according to the system you are following.

80. Mathers and Solomon, *op. cit.*

for all the assistance of the celestial host to bless your working and to make it successful.

Next light a charcoal and burn a bit of the incense previously consecrated for this hour and the talisman as well as the spirits. Pick up your tools for creating the talisman and being working. Take your time and do not rush, but cut out your talisman and engrave, paint, inscribe, or draw the figures, letters, sigils, and other symbols to the best of your ability.

Even during the early construction stage, I maintain a mindfulness of the sacred nature of the art in which I am engaged. Magic is a love and a passion, and I have formed a deep appreciation and affection for the reality of the spiritual beings who have agreed to converse and work with me in this art. In the same way as a lover would take the time to present a heartfelt gift of their own making to his beloved, so do I conduct the making of magical tools and talismans with love and dedication.

Also, see my description above[81] regarding the use of the magical voice to intone or sing the appropriate names during the inscribing of the names and sigils.

When you have completed your talisman to the best of your ability and dedication, pass it over the incense smoke and hold it above your head, asking that it be consecrated and acceptable to the spirits whom you are about to summon.

6. Evoking the Spirit or Spirits to Consecrate the Talisman

In my experience, it should have taken about half of the specified hour to create the physical form of the talisman. Now comes the point at which the magus will evoke the proper angels or other spirits to consecrate the talisman and make it a real, living object of magical power. To reiterate the point of importance, not only are proper timing, material, effort, and knowledge necessary for talisman construction, but also a way to directly call forth the associated spirits or powers. Such magical work is nothing short of a valiant effort to bring such potent forces together at a particular time and place, creating a physical object of compatible materials during the times most auspicious to its function, and at the proper time petitioning the spirit of that talisman to imbue it with the veritable power of its nature and office.

The evocation process should be one which is familiar and practiced by the magician and one in which he or she has had success at in the past. Also, if consecrating a talisman derived from a specific grimoire or tradition, adherence to the original formulæ should be as faithful as possible.

Place the newly crafted talisman in the center of your holy table or consecration table and light the incense and colored candles if used and take a few moments to center your being. When ready, read the invocations aloud with the developed voice

---

81. In the section on "The System of the Twelve Rings."

of the magus. Wait for a sign the angels or spirits have arrived before continuing. If nothing perceivable occurs, attempt the invocation at least three more times.

When the unmistakable presence of a spirit or angel is palpable in the room and the being presents itself to you in a clear enough fashion for you to see it and hear it speak, continue with the operation. At this point, I formally ask the angels or spirits to consecrate the talisman before them, and inquire if there is anything further which is needed for the consecration and upkeep of this talisman in order for it to become the most powerful talisman possible. Listen carefully to what is said.

If and when the entities agree to consecrate your talisman, give them the time they need, as they will inform you when the act is complete. Thank them and use the remaining incense on the censers. Allow the remaining time from the hour of the operation as necessary and then formally give the spirits license to depart.[82]

7. Completing the Ceremony

> These words being said, thou shalt perfume the pentacles with the same sweet scents and perfumes, and afterwards having wrapped them in a piece of prepared silk cloth, thou shalt put them in a place fit and clean, which thou mayest open whenever it shall please thee, and close it again, at thy pleasure and according unto thy will.[83]

After the talisman has been consecrated and imbued with the spirits' power and essence, say a final blessing over it and wrap it in a piece of silk or fine linen. I also recommend that you place the wrapped talisman in a box or other protective container when it is not directly on your person. Realize this is now a fully charged and veritable talisman, an object of extreme magical potency. Treat it as such and use it only under the conditions for which it was fashioned. Follow any particular instructions the angels or spirits may have given you for its use. It is possible for a talisman to lose its effectiveness if handled or used incorrectly.

Finish the ceremony with a prayer to the Most High and formally close your working space.

A True Relation of Crafting a Jupiter Talisman
from *The Clavicles of R. Solomon*

Talisman-making was not something which captured my immediate attention and did not become a common practice of mine until later in my magical career. Although I had no trouble accepting the reality of magically charged objects, I

---

82. Unless you are performing a ritual which binds the spirit to the particular talisman.

83. Mathers and Solomon, *op. cit.*

didn't pursue crafting them until long after I was accustomed to classical magical evocation.

Of course, for the ceremonial magician conducting evocations, inscribing sigils or seals in order to evoke the proper spirits is a matter of course. The most extensive talismanic experience I had early in my magical practice was creating archangelic lamens, metal disks on which I had inscribed the seals of the seven planetary archangels, which I then wore suspended about my neck when performing magic corresponding to their planets. The importance of talismanic magic became more apparent as I began to fashion lamens or medallions with individual spirits' seals or sigils on them for use in magical evocation. It was not until after several successful evocations of the spirits that I noticed that the metal lamens I wore had begun to stimulate my recall of emotions and sensations which I had experienced when communicating previously with that particular spirit. The effect was much like that of the energy which becomes imprinted on the image of the spirit in the *Liber Spirituum*, but to a differing degree, feeling more in balance with my own personal energies.

The very first time I decided to post publicly about one of my magical workings was concerning the first talisman I made from *The Clavicles of R. Solomon*. The following is a record of my earliest attempt at making a traditional metal talisman, which I felt—and still feel—was an overall success, despite my being a beginner at the work.

As the product of the working was to be a Jupiter talisman, I looked for an auspicious upcoming Thursday. I was very pleased to find that my approaching birthday happened to fall on a Thursday, that Jupiter would be well aspected, and that several other astro-goodies would be in effect. The day in question also happened be just a couple of days away from the full moon. Naturally I saw this as an opportunity too good to pass up, and that doing some beneficial magic was a must. I planned the process ahead of time to create a powerful talisman of Jupiter.

The object of my endeavor was to create one of the Jupiter talismans (See fig. 19) from the Morissoneau *Clavicles of R. Solomon*, which had been published in *The Veritable Key of Solomon*.[84] I want to share with you my procedure for doing all of the essential work.

This operation was wonderful in every aspect, and I enjoyed the experience so immensely that even if it had produced no further results, I would have considered the whole procedure worth every ounce of work and expense that went into it. However, at the time, I had a fully confident sense that all would work according to the design of the pentacle, its ritual, and its spirits, and this proved to be true.

The *Clavicles* describes the purpose of this pentacle as follows:

---

84. Skinner and Rankine, *op. cit.*, pp. 248 ff.

> The talisman of Jupiter given here is excellent for protecting yourself against
> all evil spells, for luck in games of chance and even for luck in business....[85]

The grimoire instructs the magician to make the pentacle on the day and hour of
Jupiter, and while the Moon is waxing. Surprisingly, however, it initially says to
engrave it on a plate of copper rather than the usual Jupiter metal, tin. However, the
text soon clarifies that the reason is a necessary practicality. For most operations, the
tin disk would suffice; but for one particular function of this pentacle, an additional
ceremonial step is required, for which the copper is crucial. To use the pentacle to
overcome evil spells, it must be heated over lit charcoal, and tin melts very easily.[86]
My solution was to make the pentacle in both tin and copper, and to seal them back
to back.

Following the description of the talisman, the *Clavicles* gives a prayer in Latin
which is to be recited three times while making the talisman. The magician must
cense the pentacle with the perfume of Thursday and then rub cedar resin onto it
with wood aloes. The talisman is then to be wrapped in a lemon-colored silk cloth
and carried on the person of the magus.

The final piece of information which the grimoire provided was the incense necessary for the operation. Here is what is listed for the 'Manufacture of Perfumes for
Jupiter for the day of Thursday':

> Rowan Berry, Wood of Aloes, Storax, Benzoin, Powder of Lapis Lazuli, piec-
> es of chopped up Peacock Feathers; ground up and mixed with the blood of
> two or three Swallows or the brain of a Deer; make a paste out of this and
> make pellets for your use in the rituals of the Art on the day of Thursday
> under the auspices of Jupiter and the Spirits who rule its influences.[87]

The procuring of the correct components for the incense is one of the operations
that demonstrates the importance of thoroughly planning magical experiments
ahead of time. Gathering ingredients can take more time than you ever expected
on first reading. In the case of making the Jupiter incense for Thursday, it took
far longer than I could have ever anticipated. As I have said previously, I don't use
animal blood and flesh ingredients in my formulæ, so happily I didn't have to worry
about either swallow's blood or the brain of a deer. As to the other ingredients, I
had benzoin and lignum aloes left from an earlier purchase for magical suffumiga-
tion mixtures. However I had to order storax from an American supplier and rowan
berries from an occult dealer in England. Fortunately both arrived in time for the
chosen date. Lapis lazuli is easy to come by, but pulverizing stone into a powder

---

85. *Ibid.*

86. In fact, it melts at only 450° F (about the same temperature at which paper bursts into flame), while copper's melting point is a more respectable 1983°.

87. *Ibid.*, p. 174.

took some effort and patience. I bought peacock feathers at a local craft store. The most challenging part was finding the cedar resin which the book stated should be rubbed on the talisman with lignum aloes after you consecrate it with the incense. I looked and looked and couldn't find cedar resin for sale anywhere, locally or online. Luckily, my home state has cedar trees, and some amazing ones were located in a very auspicious place both magically and geographically. I knew of the method for collecting resin, but it was the

Fig. 19. Talisman of Jupiter from the Clavicles of R. Solomon

dead of winter here and the sap does not flow at that time. I decided to see what I could find, and was fortunate to discover that some of the trees had tiny drops of sap visible on the bark. I was pleased that I didn't need to harm any trees to collect the resin and also didn't have to expend copious amounts of time and energy. It still took me several wintry hours spread over two days to gather enough resin to fill a sizable vial. When I was finished, I decided to leave a libation offering to the nature spirits of the trees and the land in the area.[88]

All in all, the ingredients were not extraordinarily difficult to come by, but it did take a significant amount of time to obtain—whether through merchants or wild-harvesting—and prepare them all.

I set the operation for the first hour of Jupiter, which on a Thursday is the hour that begins as the sun comes to the horizon in the east. An hour or so ahead of time, I prepared myself ritually by bathing, sprinkling myself with holy water, and anointing myself with holy oil, all while repeating several Psalms and verses of cleansing, always including Psalm 51.

The creation of the talisman took almost the entire first hour of Jupiter. I cut out a disk from the copper sheet I had purchased and an equal disk of tin. During the process of cutting out the disks, I received a small nick... and on a whim, I traced

---

88. This gesture is somewhat pagan, but I continue to adhere to the practice on a constant basis in one form or another. When I can, I try to encourage beneficial interactions between all manner of spiritual beings and myself.

the glyph of Jupiter with my own blood on the backs of both metal plates before I sealed them. I adhered the two disks back to back using some of the melted cedar resin. I then etched the sigil and name of Bethor with my Solomonic awl.

I recited the Latin prayer once as I began, again after I had almost finished engraving it, and once more before I perfumed it. I also spoke the English translation of the prayer after I began sealing it with the resin.

I performed the majority of the ritual within my consecrated circle, which at the time was across from my financial altar where I do weekly rituals on Thursdays. It seemed appropriate.

After the talisman was completed, I set the incense burner on the Jupiter seal which is engraved on my Table of Art (*Ars Paulina* style). The incense is pretty amazing, and seems well suited for the operation. I sat at the altar, lit the holy candle, and meditated. I recited the Jupiter prayer, invocation, and conjuration.

The effects of the operation were immediately apparent, as I felt instantaneous energy flowing through me. Empowerment, invigoration, and other sensations that I could not completely define seemed to fill not only me but the entire room. Light seemed to radiate beyond natural luminescence, and in my peripheral vision I saw spiritual beings all around me. I kept focused on the central candle flame and let the entire experience unfold as it wished.

After several moments wrapped in this blissful experience of light and energy, I repeated an invocation for the Jupiter spirit to come forth.

I've had great success with this talisman ever since, and it has become one of my prized possessions. It sits on an altar I created and dedicated to the Jupiter current and the Archangel of Jupiter, Sachiel or Tzadkiel.

Making Magical Talismans for Others

Furthermore, my beloved Son, I order thee not to bury this Science, but to make thy friends partakers in the same, subject however to the strict command never to profane the things which are Divine, for if thou doest this, far from rendering thee a friend of the Spirits, it will but be the means of bringing thee unto destruction.

But never must thou lavish these things among the ignorant, for that would be as blameable as to cast precious gems before swine; on the contrary, from one Sage the secret knowledge should pass unto another Sage, for in this manner shall the Treasure of Treasures never descend into oblivion.

Adore and revere the most holy names of God which are found in these pentacles and characters, for without this never shalt thou be able to come to the end of any enterprise, nor to accomplish the Mystery of Mysteries.[89]

---

89. Mathers and Solomon, *op. cit.*

Since the publication of my first book and other essays, and my resulting visibility within the occult community, several people from around the world have commissioned me to create talismans as well as classical magical implements for them that they do not have the skill or time to make themselves. Despite my assurance that the best tools are ones that magicians make and consecrate themselves, I've had several people determined to own one of my magical creations. My eventual agreement was influenced less by monetary gain and more by my curiosity to learn how well the effects of the talismans would manifest once they left my hands. By this time, I was thoroughly convinced of my ability to fashion talismans for myself which would bring the effects that the spirits promised, as I had witnessed and recorded the results repeatedly. However, I wasn't sure just how well or if at all these same effects would transfer to others who had not conjured, conversed with, and worked with the spirits who actually empower the talismans. As a magician, my curiosity to see how my work would extend beyond my own immediate sphere of influence was too much to resist. To my great satisfaction, the clients who have provided feedback have consistently reported successful outcomes and pleasing results from the talismans I created for them.

In the beginning stages of deciding to craft talismans for others, I struggled with what the proper cost of such an item should be. The matter became clearer when I figured in the time, materials, effort, energy, and expertise which go into actually making a true talisman. I was of course pleased that others found what seemed to me at the time my rather amateurish engraving and metalworking jobs to be æsthetically pleasing and considered them valuable, but my main concern was creating something that worked and contributed to the intended goals of the recipients. Creating a viable magical item is not simply an art project. It is never just the time and cost of getting the proper metal and other materials and sitting down to engrave the object and to go through the form of a ritual. Those who know me and my work will affirm that I take magical pursuits very seriously, striving for unambiguous results, conducting rituals with the proper implements and paraphernalia, and determining and employing the correct and favorable astrological times for both the construction of the talisman and the evocation of the appropriate spirit or spirits to consecrate it.

I have found that I enjoy creating talismans and magical implements for individuals who truly appreciate what I do and the time and effort which goes into my magical work, and are willing to compensate me for it. Other occultists may disagree or operate differently, but as for me, I only create implements for those who see the value in my time and practice and are willing to invest in something they see as valuable and a real asset in their lives. Although it would be wonderful to have a full-time career making talismans and implements and doing spell-work for clients, I do not intend to put that sort of pressure on myself, and also do not want to risk exhausting my feeling for the sacred nature of making these treasures. There is no way I could make talismans full time while maintaining the integrity with which I construct them. I see it simply as an occasional way to fill the role of a professional magician or occultist and a way to serve the community.

Conclusion

The effects of magical talismans are such that people the world over, from antiquity to the present day, have used them and sworn by their effects and abilities. Whether this faith is truly founded or not is a matter of individual assessment by the maker and the user of a talisman. Magic is experimental. It is active and participatory, and requires a tenacious dedication. The only true way to observe the effectiveness of magical talismans is to experience it yourself. Test out the methods for yourself to see if they warrant serious consideration. This practice requires no small investment of time and resources if you are making talismans the traditional way. If you are competent to craft your own talismans and to conduct the evocations and con-secrations necessary to call the proper spirits to charge them, that is certainly the preferable route. However, if you are not at the point where you can make authentic talismans yourself, you may consider commissioning one from a reputable magus. Whichever way you obtain your talisman, meditate on it and record any sensations, feelings, and alterations in mood or behavior from yourself and others when wear-ing it or having it in your possession. Much can be learned from paying particular attention to circumstances which occur after wearing a talisman or invoking its nature.

Sometimes particular planetary aspects enhance or clash with our personal natures, and this is something which should be understood and given particular attention. Not every talisman which is described in a grimoire as having amaz-ing qualities or benefits will work well with each individual, who may have some personal karmic or other energetic opposition to the nature of the talisman. It is often not so simple a matter as gaining a good luck charm and then having good luck. Veritable charged talismans are networks of energy within a material form, much like human beings or any created life. They contain patterns and frequencies of a particular nature, and sometimes different frequencies and energy patterns just don't jive or cause unexpected reactions when they are placed in proximity to one another. There are countless variables and considerations to be mindful of when manipulating patterns of energy.

Magical working such as the evocation of spirits and the making of talismans requires much study, much practice, and much dedication, and will always be an ongoing process for the person truly on the magical path.

References

Agrippa, Heinrich Cornelius, and Joseph H. Peterson. *Heinrich Cornelius Agrippa: his Fourth Book of Occult Philosophy*, on the *Twilit Grotto—Esoteric Archives* website (http://www.esotericarchives.com/agrippa/agrippa4.htm). Last accessed 2015.

—, and Robert Turner. *Henry Cornelius Agrippa His Fourth Book of Occult Philosophy, translated into English by Robert Turner*. London: printed by J.C. for John Harrison at the Lamb at the East-end of Pauls, 1655.

—, James Freake, and Donald Tyson. *Three Books of Occult Philosophy*. St. Paul, MN: Llewellyn Publications, 1995.

—, J.F., and Joseph H. Peterson. *Of Occult Philosophy, Book I (Part 1)*, on the *Twilit Grotto—Esoteric Archives* website (http://www.esotericarchives.com/agrippa/agrippa1b.htm). Last accessed 2015.

Ashen Chassan (Bryan Garner). *Gateways through Stone and Circle: A Manual of Evocation for the Planetary Intelligences*. Timmonsville, SC: Nephilim Press, 2013.

Barrett, Francis. *The Magus, or Celestial Intelligencer*. London: Lackington, Allen, and Co., 1801.

Conybeare, F.C. "The Testament of Solomon," in *The Jewish Quarterly Review*, Vol. 11, No. 1 (Oct., 1898), pp. 1–45.

Gonzalez-Wippler, Migene. *The Complete Book Of Amulets & Talismans*. St. Paul, MN: Llewellyn Publications, 1991.

Greer, John Michael, and Christopher Warnock. *The Picatrix (Liber Atratus Edition): The Occult Classic of Astrological Magic*. [n.p.]: Adocentyn Press, 2010–11.

Hockley, Frederic, and Dietrich Bergman. *A Complete Book of Magic Science*. York Beach, ME: The Teitan Press, 2008.

Leitch, Aaron. *Secrets of the Magickal Grimoires: The Classical Texts of Magick Decyphered*. Woodbury, MN: Llewellyn Publications, 2005.

Pavitt, William Thomas, and Kate Pavitt. *Book of Talismans, Amulets and Zodiacal Gems*. 2nd and rev. ed. London: William Rider & Son, 1922.

Peterson, Joseph H. *Douze Anneaux (Lansdowne MS 1202)*, on the *Twilit Grotto—Esoteric Archives* website (http://www.esotericarchives.com/solomon/anneaux.htm). Last accessed 2015.

Roth, Harold A. *Three Books of Occult Philosophy Incense*, at the *Alchemy Works* website (http://www.alchemy-works.com/incense_agrippa.html). Last accessed 2015.

Sibley, Ebenezer, Frederick Hockley, and Joseph H. Peterson. *The Clavis or Key to the Magic of Solomon*. Lake Worth, FL: Ibis Press, 2009.

Skinner, Stephen, and David Rankine. *The Veritable Key of Solomon*. Singapore: Golden Hoard Press, 2010.

Solomon, [Mathers, S.L. MacGregor,] and Aleister Crowley. *The Book of the Goetia of Solomon the King: Translated into the English Tongue by a Dead Hand and Adorned with Divers Other Matters Germane, Delightful to the Wise: the Whole Edited, Verified, Introd. and Commented by A. Crowley.* Boleskine, Foyers, Inverness: Society for the Propagation of Religious Truth, 1904.

—, and S. Liddell MacGregor Mathers. *The Key of Solomon the King (Clavicula Salomonis)*. London: George Redway, 1889.

—, Abognazar, and Joseph H. Peterson. *The Veritable Clavicles of Solomon (Les Veritables Clavicules de Salomon) (Abognazar) (EXCERPTS)*, on the *Twilit Grotto—Esoteric Archives* website (http://www.esotericarchives.com/solomon/l1203.htm). Last accessed 2015.

Trithemius, Johannes. *The Art of Drawing Spirits into Crystals*, in Francis Barrett, *The Magus, or Celestial Intelligencer*. London: Lackington, Allen, and Co., 1801.

Waite, A.E. *The Book of Ceremonial Magic: Including the Rites and Mysteries of Goëtic Theurgy, Sorcery, and Infernal Necromancy*. London: Rider, 1911.

Zalewski, Pat. *Evocations and Talismans in the Golden Dawn*. Longborough, Leicestershire: Thoth Publications, 2002.

✣

Kalein tous Theous

Divine Invocation in
the Late Neoplatonic Tradition

JEFFREY S. KUPPERMAN

JEFFREY S. KUPPERMAN has studied Hermetics, Kabbalah, and the Western Mystery Tradition for more than 25 years, and is a hierarch of the Ekklesia Neoplatonismos Theourgia. He is the author of Living Theurgy: A Course in Iamblichus' Philosophy, Theology, and Theurgy *(Avalonia, 2014), and the founder and publisher of the* Journal of the Western Mystery Tradition *(http://jwmt.org). He is currently working on his next projects, an illuminated* Theurgist's Book of Hours *and* High Magic in the Age of Steam. *Jeffrey lives on the Mississippi River in Wisconsin, where he teaches philosophy and religious studies at local colleges, but also spends his time researching, writing, painting, and raising his two daughters. Not necessarily in that order. You may follow his blogs at* A Thirteen Petalled Rose, A Cup of Blessing *(http://cupofblessing.blogspot.com). and* The Writer's Tome *(http://jeffreyskupperman.com).*

✢

Kalein tous Theous

Divine Invocation in
the Late Neoplatonic Tradition

 INCE AT LEAST THE RENAISSANCE, and in many cases going back to the Middle Ages, western magical operations surrounding the practice of invocation have employed the ideology seemingly inherent in the word itself. From the Latin *invocare*, invocation is typically understood to mean "to call in." That is, to invoke a spirit, from soul to Gods or Goddesses, is, especially in modern ceremonial magic, understood to mean to call that spirit down, into someone, be it a priest or priestess, shaman, magician, medium, etc. This is often contrasted against evocation, from *evocare*, meaning "to call forth." We might speak of invoking a God into a magician, but evoking an angel into a specially prepared magic circle. In theurgic traditions, such as found amongst the later Neoplatonists from Iamblichus of Chalcis on, the understanding of invocation is quite different. It is not the spirit that is brought down to us, but we who are raised up to the spirit.

Iamblichus is responsible for the initial integration of the religio-ritual practice of theurgy into Neoplatonism, sometime around 280 CE. This subject is solidified in his *magnum opus* on theurgy, *De Mysteriis Ægyptiorum* or "*On the Mysteries of the Egyptians.*"[1] In this lengthy response to the critique of the subject by his former teacher, Porphyry of Tyre, Iamblichus describes *theourgia* or "theurgy," literally "God-work," as a dual-natured activity:

> On the one hand, it is performed by men [sic], and as such observes our natural rank in the universe; but on the other, it controls divine symbols, and in virtue of them is raised up to union with the higher powers, and directs itself harmoniously in accordance with their dispensation, which enables it quite properly to assume the mantle of the gods. It is in virtue of this distinction, then, that the art both naturally invokes the powers from the universe as superiors, inasmuch as the invoker is a man, and yet on the

---

1. The book was given the title *De Mysteriis Ægyptiorum* by its translator into Latin, Marsilio Ficino.

other hand gives them orders, since it invests itself, by virtue of the ineffable symbols, with the hieratic role of the gods.[2]

In this, Iamblichus is differentiating theurgy from his understanding of sorcery or magic. Theurgy engages in activities that ultimately come from the Gods, and without divine engagement, no theurgy is possible.[3] Although it is an imitation of divine activity, it is not only an imitation. By participation in that activity the theurgist engages directly in the work of the Gods, or of God, through ritual activity. Sorcery, rendered as *goēteia*[4] in *De Mysteriis*, is quite the opposite. Although sorcery may look like theurgy, its effects "have neither the energy, nor the essence"[5] of what it is trying to mimic: divine activity.

On Invocation

From the above, invocation could be understood in two ways: theurgically and goetically.[6] A goetic invocation would be an attempt to trick a spirit into obedience by mimicking divine patterns and would take the form of what is more commonly known as evocation. While this might seem impossible, especially as Neoplatonic ontology places all such beings ontologically prior to, or "higher" than, human souls, there is a class of *daimōn*, referred to as "relational daimones,"[7] somewhat akin to the Paracelsian idea of elementals, that can be called and controlled in such a way,[8] though no other beings in the Neoplatonic hierarchy can be so influenced.

Theurgic or hieratic invocation is different. Iamblichus, writing in Greek rather than Latin, uses *kalein* (καλεῖν) rather than *invocare. Kalein* means "to call or summon," with the implication of the person summoned coming to us, putting it in line with its Latin equivalent. However, Iamblichus says invocation does not incline the minds of the gods to us, as the name seems to imply, but instead "dispos[es] the human mind to participation in the gods, leading it up to the gods and bringing it into accord with them through harmonious persuasion."[9] Invocation raises the theurgist to the Gods, it does not, nor can it, bring the Gods down to the theurgist. More

---

2. *De Mysteriis* IV.2, 207. Translated by Emma C. Clarke, John M. Dillon, and Jackson P. Hershbell (Atlanta: Society of Biblical Literature, 2003).

3. Cf. *De Mysteriis* VII.5.258.5–8.

4. *De Mysteriis* III.25.160.12, VII.5.258.5. *Goēteia* is also sometimes translated as "magic."

5. *De Mysteriis* III.25.160.12–3.

6. This usage is intended to reflect Iamblichus' language and does not necessarily refer to goetic work as commonly understood today.

7. Iamblichus, *In Timæum* (Commentary *"On the Timæus"* of Plato), fr. 80.

8. Jeffrey S. Kupperman, *Living Theurgy* (London, Avalonia Books, 2014), p. 141–2.

9. *De Mysteriis* I.12.42.5–13.

specifically, though, the Gods are already here, because the Gods are everywhere.[10] Theurgy, in general, and theurgic invocation in specific, make us aware of the Gods by bringing the theurgist's mind into accord[11] with the Gods who are already pre-existing in all earthly things, as well as in everything else.[12] Nevertheless, this work is considered anagogic in nature; it raises the soul to the Gods.[13] Even though the Gods are in all things, the Gods themselves, their essences rather than their activities, exist noetically rather than in generation,[14] and the highest form of experiencing the Gods, *henōsis* or "union," occurs on that level, not this one.

Ultimately, this understanding of invocation is not surprising. All theurgic work, not just invocation, is anagogic in nature. Also, as the Gods cannot be commanded, nor can, generally speaking, any of the other "Greater Kinds,"[15] if invocation is to do anything at all, it must bring the theurgist to them, not the other way around. All this, however, only provides the underlying theory of invocation. How is theurgic invocation practiced?

There are three basic forms of invocation found in Neoplatonic practice. Here I am broadening the timeline to include not only the Neoplatonism of antiquity, but also that of the Middle Ages and Renaissance. This expansion is important for a number of reasons. First, it is thought by some scholars that upon the closing of the Athenian Academy by Emperor Justinian in 529 CE, some of its members traveled to Harran, famous for its devotion to the moon deity Sin and the *Hermetica*. From here, Neoplatonic thought would have combined with and influenced Hermetic thought, which would eventually come back into the West in the form of astral talismanry. This suggests a direct transmission of Neoplatonic practice from antiquity to the Middle Ages. Second, in the Renaissance, Neoplatonism was revived largely due to the works of the Catholic priest and humanist Marsilio Ficino, whose writings on the subject include astral talismanry and well as theurgic medicine, which was influenced by, and would influence, alchemy, which can also be interpreted

---

10. *De Mysteriis* I.8.28.4–29.3; Proclus, *Peri tēs Hieratikēs Technēs ("On the Priestly Art")*, trans. Brian P. Copenhaver, "Hermes Trismegistus, Proclus, and a Philosophy of Magic," in Ingrid Merkel and Allen G. Debus (eds.), *Hermeticism and the Renaissance* (Washington, D.C.: Folger Books, 1988), p. 104.

11. Proclus, *Ibid.*

12. See *De Mysteriis* I.8.28.4–29.3.

13. Gk. *anagōgē*, "guiding upward."

14. Neoplatonic cosmology divides reality into roughly three levels: the noetic or intelligible level, which may also include a noeric or intellective level, a psychic level corresponding to souls, and the physical level of generation.

15. All spiritual beings between the Gods and humans are termed "Greater Kinds" by Iamblichus. This category includes: archangels, angels, daimones (especially one's personal or guardian daimōn), heroes, and purified souls.

theurgically. Renaissance Neoplatonists such as Ficino also drew heavily upon Medieval traditions also influenced by Neoplatonism.

The three forms of theurgic invocation can be called *klēsis* or invocation proper, the creation of *agalmata empsycha*, and astral talismanry. The first of these, which is the focus of this paper, has two forms, which I will term cultic and theurgic. These will be discussed in detail below. An *agalma empsychon* is an "animated statue," or, more properly, "ensouled statue or shrine."[16] These statues were used both for cultic purposes as well as for oracular divination. Astral talismanry uses images, often astrologically derived and so understood as having a divine origin, and astrological timing, to create specific effects on Earth.

All three forms of invocation work by the same basic principle. An image is created in the likeness of that which is being invoked. The likeness is not limited to physical appearance, but, through the inclusion of *synthēmata* and *symbola*, divine "tokens" and "symbols," in essence as well. These tokens or signatures are unique to different Gods and Goddesses. The *Chaldean Oracles* describes them as being the "thoughts of the Father,"[17] and they may be related to the Platonic Forms on the noeric level,[18] implanted in generation in animals, plants, and minerals. Proclus discusses a number of these in "On the Priestly Art According to the Greeks," and Ficino's *De Vita* lists numerous planetary tokens and symbols and their uses. Further, the closer the token is related to a particular deity, the stronger it is. For instance, Proclus describes some solar daimones who take the form of a lion fleeing at the image of a rooster. Both are solar synthēmata, but the rooster is a more powerful representative of the sun God than the lion.[19] However, it is not always quite that simple. A particular plant, for instance, might contain tokens of multiple deities. For example, a rose is sacred to Aphroditē. However, each part of the rose plant—flowers, roots, branches, leaves, etc.—might be sacred to a different deity, even if the plant as a whole, and especially its flower, is sacred to one in particular.[20]

The more divine tokens included, the closer the image is to that which it invokes.[21] This does not occur through sympathy or likeness alone. Instead, it also occurs through "friendship and affinity," which includes notions of care and closeness

---

16. See Kupperman, *Living Theurgy*, p. 206 for more on this subject.

17. *Chaldean Oracles*, fr. 108.

18. Iamblichus only mentions the Forms at the noeric level; Proclus discusses both noetic and noeric Forms.

19. Proclus, "On the Priestly Art," p. 104.

20. Cf. Cornelius Agrippa, *Three Books of Occult Philosophy: Book One*, trans. Eric Purdue (Renaissance Astrology, 2012), p. 89.

21. *Ibid.*, p. 105.

beyond similarity.[22] In the language of late Platonism, we would describe engaging in the powers behind or above the tokens as "participating" in them. We must participate in these powers because we do not, on our own, contain them, so our only access to them is through the tokens.

Ensouled Statues and Talismans—Not as Different as You Might Think

In the case of statues—which does not necessarily need to be limited to statues of pagan deities, and which can be expanded to other depictions of divine beings such as icons—this affinity encompasses the statue's physical likeness, *eidōlon*, to the God or Goddess in question[23] but also symbols portrayed in their stories and even the inclusion of sacred animals and plants, not just in the statue's form, but actual animals and plants, appropriately sacrificed, and placed inside the statues. This similarity transforms an *eidōlon* to an *eikōn*, a true "image," not a mere reflection, and an *agalma* or "shrine." Through these, and through ritual consecration, the statue becomes a shrine of the God or Goddess, housing it, as it were, or connecting the shrine to the deity's pneumatic vehicle. Through this connection, it was understood that the deity could make oracular proclamations, which was one of the common uses of such ensouled statues by the time of Proclus.

For talismans, the various divine names, geometric shapes, and fantastic images are seen as having a divine origin, and so connect the talisman, which might have taken the shape of a small statue,[24] to a divinity or its series of Greater Kinds. As such, talismans might be likened to ensouled statues, but are created for purposes often more specific than such statues.

The divine names, whether a deity's regular name, cultic epithet, or one of the *barbara onomata* (the "barbarous names" of evocation), are especially important. Plato, in the *Cratylus*, discusses the symbolic nature of the Gods' names. Proclus, in his commentary on the same, compares divine names to ensouled statues,[25] suggesting that the divine names themselves are amongst the most powerful of divine tokens. This is especially true of the *barbara onomata*, which are given to the theur-

---

22. *De Mysteriis* v.9.209.10. This may also be an allusion to Aristotle's understanding of justice, the fullest form of which only occurs between friends. See *Nicomachean Ethics* VIII 156b5–25, 1159b25–1160a30.

23. The Neoplatonists did not believe the Gods and Goddesses actually had human form. Instead, following Plato's *Timaeus*, they held that humans were created in the likenesses of the Gods, consisting of spheres, which are seen as perfect geometrical shapes. However, if humans are in the likeness of the Gods, then, at least symbolically, we can say the Gods and Goddesses are also in the likeness of humans, so we may use anthropomorphic images to represent them. This holds true for any spiritual entity.

24. Thābit ibn Qurra, *De Imaginibus*, IX.I.62.

25. *In Platonis Cratylum Commentaria*, §46.

gists directly from the Gods.[26] These seemingly meaningless stream of vowels and consonants, which sometimes, but not always, have some correspondence to known divine names, "are all significant [to the Gods], not according to an effable mode, nor in such a way that is significant and indicative to the imaginations of human beings, but united to the gods either intellectually or rather ineffably...."[27] That is to say, these names are united to the Gods from which they come. In effect, there is no difference between the Gods and their names.

All this may make sense in the cases of statues and talismans, but what about invocations proper? In essence, they are all identical. Just as talismans are a form of ensouled statue, all of these are forms of invocation. The implications of this are important, because it means that when a theurgist invokes a divine being, that theurgist, for the time of the invocation, becomes a talisman of, and an ensouled shrine to, that being. Also, because not only the Gods and Goddesses but any of the Greater Kinds can be invoked, all of which are considered divine, a theurgist may invoke a perfected human soul, a hero, an archangel, or a deity, rather than deities alone. An invocation to Iamblichus is as legitimate as one to Hēlios or Lug; so is a shrine to him.

Cultic and Theurgic Invocation—A Distinction?

Material theurgy, the theurgic practices associated with the visible Gods who rule the heavens and are associated with celestial bodies, can take two overlapping forms. One of these forms, which is primary for most all but the advanced theurgists and purified souls, is cultic in nature, a part of one's regular worship. Theurgic *cultus*, or worship, does not necessarily take an external form different from exoteric practices. In Greek tradition there would have been sacrifices, prayers, hymns, etc., both in theurgic and common forms of worship. A theurgist could even participate in worship with non-theurgists while still acting theurgically. The theurgist would participate in the activity differently than everyone else because they would be experiencing that which is invoked in a way different from everyone else.

By purposefully engaging in such worship esoterically rather than exoterically, the theurgist, at least for themselves, transforms the practice into something theurgic and anagogic. However, nothing is necessarily added to the religious rites to make them theurgic in nature. Neither does anything need to be added; all the elements are already present. Even the famous barbarous names of evocation are not absolutely necessary. Proclus, for instance, utilized the *barbara onomata*

---

26. See *De Mysteriis* VII.4–5.

27. *De Mysteriis* VII.4.255.1–3. See also R.M. van den Berg, "The Hymns: Theurgy in Practice" in Proclus, *Hymns* (Leiden, The Netherlands: Brill, 2001), pp. 102–5.

only for deities working on levels higher than the visible Gods.[28] As already discussed, Proclus, in his commentary on the *Critias*, sees common names and titles of the Gods to be theurgic, not just the *barbara onomata*. All divine names are connected to their divinities and awaken the corresponding principles within us.[29] This awakening of the *logoi* in the soul is what differentiates theurgic *cultus* from non-theurgic *cultus*. While the *synthēmata* do this awakening or activating on their own,[30] what distinguishes the theurgist from others is the relative purity of the theurgist's soul, a purity that is accomplished through philosophical practice, cultic worship, and hieratic rites.[31] It is this which allows the external *synthēmata* to awaken those within the theurgist's soul. In cultic practice, then, we can find no disconnect between theurgic practices and the religious practices of the theurgists.[32]

What, then, distinguishes cultic and theurgic invocation? In essence, nothing. While cultic devotion and invocation can occur in public places, and take the outward form of the common worship, it can also take the form of personal devotion. Proclus is known to have prayed extensively to Aphroditē, for instance, and may have had a statue of Athēna at his own home for such purposes.[33] However, cultic invocation has, as the name suggests, cultus as its primary purpose. Theurgic invocation, outside of cultus, was often for the purpose of divination, especially oracular divination, as well as for purposes of purification, spiritual illumination, and perfection. Through these both *henōsis* and *noera gnōsis*, divine "union" and intuitive, divine "knowing," were possible. So we can see the difference between cultic and theurgic invocation to be similar to the difference between ensouled statues and talismans; the purpose of the latter is somewhat more specific than that of the former. As such, while these may be useful terms to employ in our discussion of the subject, they should not be taken as reified categories but differing aspects of the same thing: invocation.

---

28. See van den Berg, *Hymns*, pp. 103–4. Although Iamblichus said that the Gods' essences were "of a single form," their activities occurred on different levels: noetic and noeric, but also on a wide range within generation. There are transcendent invisible Gods, liminal Gods who act as bridges between the invisible and the visible, the visible Gods of the planets and stars, and even sublunar deities, called Archons in *De Mysteriis*. See Gregory Shaw, *Theurgy and the Soul: The Neoplatonism of Iamblichus* (University Park, Penn.: Pennsylvania State University Press, 1995), p. 135; Kupperman, *Living Theurgy*, pp. 128–35; and *De Mysteriis* V.14.217.5–14.

29. Van den Berg, *Hymns*, pp. 103–4. Cf. Shaw, *Theurgy*, pp. 177–8.

30. *De Mysteriis* II.2.94.7–15.

31. *Ibid.*

32. Sarah Iles Johnston, "Riders in the Sky: Cavalier Gods and Theurgic Salvation in the Second Century A.D.," *Classical Philology* 87, no. 4 (1992): p. 304.

33. Van den Berg, *Hymns*, p. 280.

Theurgic Invocation Proper—Who Ya Gonna Call?

The question as to what theurgic invocation would have looked like is more complicated. There are no surviving Neoplatonic theurgic rituals on record, nor are there descriptions of what they might have entailed. Scholars are typically of the opinion they would have looked similar to the rituals found in the *Papyri Græcæ Magicæ* *(PGM)*, which is filled with animal sacrifices and *barbara onomata*, strange-looking characters and often difficult-to-understand instructions. Hans Lewy, through a careful, though often contentious, analysis of the *Chaldean Oracles*, which were heavily influential on the Neoplatonists, has even reconstructed a ritual of invocation of Hekatē[34] which may very well have been similar to Neoplatonism theurgic rituals. Both the *PGM* and *Chaldean Oracles* will be used in constructing a ritual of invocation of Apollōn for oracular purposes later in this paper. These are not our only sources, however. While no descriptions of Neoplatonic theurgic rituals survive, there are hints about what they might contain within the writings of the Neoplatonists. These will also be employed.

Before figuring out how to invoke, some thought should be given as to what or whom to invoke. While the generalities of an invocation ritual might not be affected by this, the specifics, such as what symbols and tokens to include, are. The options for this are simultaneously broad and narrow. Broadly speaking, the entirety of the Gods and Greater Kinds are theoretical possibilities. This could include seven varieties of deities as well as archangels, angels, daimones, heroes, and purified souls. Practically, in material theurgy, we are more limited. In this regard, only one of the different ranks of Gods and Goddesses is available to us, the visible Gods, along with their attendants. In Iamblichus' system, these are the deities corresponding to the seven planets, the four elements and the fiery ether above the spheres of the planets. Sallustius, in a book on the nature of the Gods, myth, and the cosmos, gives these deities as follows:[35]

DEITY	SPHERE
Athēna	Ether / Vault of the Heavens
Dēmētēr	Saturn
Zeus	Jupiter
Arēs	Mars

---

34. Hans Lewy, *Chaldean Oracles and Theurgy*, trans. Michel Tardieu (Paris: Institute d'Etudes Augustiniennes, 2011).

35. Sallustius, *Concerning the Gods and the Universe*, trans. Arthur Darby Nock (Chicago: Ares Publishers, Inc., 1926), VI.17–23. This presumably follows Iamblichus. Cultural equivalents to these deities, acting at this level, would also be possibilities.

DEITY	SPHERE
Apollōn	Sol
Aphroditē	Venus
Hermēs	Mercury
Artemis	Luna
Hēphaistos	Fire
Hēra	Air
Poseidōn	Water
Hestia	Earth

This list might seem odd. First, two of the deities traditionally associated with the planets, Kronos and Selēnē, are absent. These deities are Titans, and Sallustius' visible Gods include only the Olympians. Artemis and Dēmētēr should not be understood as being somehow identical to Kronos and Selēnē. Instead, they are distinct entities that have overlapping spheres of influence or activity. Second, the elements would typically be considered sub-lunar in nature. As theurgy is anagogic, sublunar deities would not typically be invoked; they send us in the wrong direction. This might be a quirk of Iamblichus, who has a different set of deities ruling over the sublunar realm between the moon and our own sphere, effectively elevating the four elements to a higher rank than sublunar.[36]

The sublunar Gods are, as can be deduced from the above, already out of the question, and are mentioned but not delved into in *De Mysteriis* as they are not a proper topic for theurgy. However, all the Gods above the visible Gods are also out. Not because they do not raise us to higher spiritual heights, but because they are too high; those who must engage in material theurgy have no access to them.

From this narrowed list there are still all of the Greater Kinds in their series; *i.e.*, the various entities connected specifically to those Goddesses and Gods, from archangels to souls. This includes our own souls, which are understood to have been "sewn" into the orbit of our soul's ruling deity, following the *Timæus*.[37] As such, who we want to invoke might be our own leader God or Goddess, assuming we know who that is. We do not have to invoke this deity, though, and depending on our soul's purity, we might not effectively be able to do so anyway. Instead, we invoke one of the Greater Kinds from our series, all of whom would be "higher" up on the spiritual hierarchy than ourselves, ontologically speaking. Typically, we would start

---

36. Iamblichus, *In Timæum*, fr. 77.

37. Iamblichus, *De Anima: Text, Translation, and Commentary*, trans. John F. Finamore and John M. Dillon (Atlanta: Society of Biblical Literature, 2002), VI.26.377.16–25.

with our own "personal daimōn," the spirit set directly over us to guide our lives. Unfortunately, the specific ritual for invoking that daimōn through the Master of Daimones, tentatively identified as Haidēs or Ploutōn, is lost.

However, we're not limited to our own series, so, in practice, any of the visible Gods are a possibility. We might choose a particular deity, for instance, because of the kinds of things over which they are commonly known to rule. While there are obvious things, such as love and beauty for Aphroditē,[38] Socrates also associates particular deities with the four *maniai* or "frenzies" in Plato's *Symposium*. In this dialogue, Socrates gives prophetic *mania* to Apollōn, telestic *mania* to Dionysos, poetic *mania* to the Muses, and erotic *mania* to Aphroditē.[39] These deities could be invoked for these reasons, or for anything with which we might see them associated in their sacred stories.

Accessing a particular deity, however, might be more difficult. While we might invoke a specific Goddess or God by its name, we are not guaranteed to get that deity in return. About this, Proclus writes:

> It is not only the Greek myths that have worked this out cryptically–that is, calling both the leaders and their followers by the same names–but the non-Greek mysteries pass down the same tradition. They say that the angels in the processions of the gods especially rejoice in being called by the same names as theirs and that they put on the vehicles of those at the heads of their processions and make themselves manifest in their place to the theurgists.[40]

The above suggests that even if we have specific names, especially the names of Goddesses or Gods, we are not necessarily going to end up invoking what we intend. However, this seems to apply only to the leaders of series, *i.e.,* the Goddesses and Gods. Proclus does not suggest that if we are invoking a specific daimōn the same thing will occur. The teachings behind the invocation of the personal daimōn,[41] who is unique to every person, suggest the same.

However, we will, if successful, still invoke something from the same series, and so an attendant of the invoked deity. The notion of series can be complicated, however, as while we might see various entities, such as the Erōtes in the series of Aphroditē or the Muses in the series of Apollōn, other deities, such as Dionysos or Asklēpios, are also found in the series of the Gods and Goddesses. In this instance,

---

38. This should not be overstated. According to Iamblichus, the essences of the Gods are "of a single form," suggesting at some level they share a single essence, making the ultimate "thing" which makes up the Gods identical. We could therefore say each God and Goddess is complete and perfect.

39. Prophetic *mania* is associated with divine possession; telestic *mania* has to do with sacred ritual, sacrifice, and theurgic healing; poetic *mania* is the source of true or inspired poetry; and erotic *mania* is anagogic and allows us to contemplate the Forms and the Form of Beauty above them. *De Mysteriis* VII.14, 170.

40. *In Platonis Rem Publicam Commentarii* ("*Commentary on Plato's Republic*"), 91.19–26.

41. See, for instance, *De Mysteriis* IX.9.284.1–7.

Dionysius is in the series of Zeus and Asklēpios in the series of Apollōn. This can be confusing, because even though Zeus is the father of Dionysos, and Apollōn of Asklēpios, we do not find every divine offspring in the series of its parent. Hermēs, for instance, who is the son of Zeus, is not in the series of Zeus.

The question then becomes "how can we know what we've invoked?" Iamblichus answers this for us in book two of *De Mysteriis*.[42] The section is too lengthy to reproduce here,[43] but it describes how the various Gods and Greater Kinds manifest in appearance, their epiphanies, their divine light and fire, and so on. By observing their manifestations, we can then discern what kind of spirit has been invoked, even if not which specific entity.

Do you Want to Build a Ritual?

Determining the elements proper to a ritual of invocation is something of a challenge. As previously stated, no Neoplatonic theurgic rituals from Antiquity survive in writing. There are, however, clues left in the extant philosophical writings of these theurgists, as well as the theurgic *De Mysteriis*. These will be the primary resources used to determine what components would be requisite for such a ritual. Afterward, I will construct a ritual of invocation of Apollōn using these components, modeled around rituals such as those found in the *Papyri Græcæ Magicæ*.

The first component is that of prayer. Prayer is the efficacious underpinning of theurgic ritual. Without prayer not even the sacrifices of theurgic cultus are fully effective.[44] Prayer can consist of sung hymns, often taking the form of metered poems. Such hymns would typically begin with calling on the deity using its various names and titles. Following this is a section recalling the Goddess' or God's activities, often derived from sacred stories. Elements from the deity's myths or sacred stories are also considered theurgic in nature because the myths are also considered to have a divine origin.[45] Calling on beings from the deity's series, such as the Erōtes of Aphroditē, may also be found here. Finally there is a request, such as for purification, a vision, or an oracle.

Related to prayer are the divine names. This includes proper names, cultic titles, and *barbara onomata*. The symbolic names and titles mentioned above, as well as the *barbara onomata*, are theurgic in nature, as they contain divine tokens, giving

42. *De Mysteriis* II.3–9.90.4.

43. However, a tabulated version was created by Jonathan Henry, and is available at https://www.academia.edu/7064689/Chart_Iamblichus_analysis_of_manifestations_of_beings_by_class_from_De_Mysteriis.

44. *De Mysteriis* V.26.238.12–239.10.

45. See, for example, *Concerning the Gods and the Universe*, chapters III and IV.

them, and the prayers in which they are contained, an anagogic nature.[46] Although Proclus did not include the *barbara onomata* in his hymns, we do not know if this was common to other theurgists. These names, regardless of their form, are not only linked to the Gods, but come from them and are a part of them. As such, they are an essential part of invocation. This can be seen repeatedly in the *PGM*, where such names are not only employed in prayer but in parts specifically calling upon a deity or other divine being.

In chapter three of *De Mysteriis*, Iamblichus lambasts sorcerers who "stand on the characters." Iamblichus sees this as all that is evil in what he considers false forms of divination.[47] As such, it may seem strange for me to include magical characters as part of theurgic ritual. Iamblichus, however, commonly attacked practices not because of the practice in general, but because of a specific way it was being employed. Iamblichus makes a great deal about differentiating between a technique as having theurgic effect and the actual source of the effect, which are the Gods. In this case, Iamblichus is not necessarily attacking standing on characters for invocative and divinatory purposes. Instead, he is attacking the idea that it is standing on the characters itself that causes divine possession, *i.e.*, their sorcerous use, not their use in general.[48]

Unfortunately, we know almost nothing about what these characters might be. The *PGM* does include a number of sacred characters, but they are usually written on a piece of parchment or engraved on a talisman; they are not stood upon. Presumably, the image is derived from some divine utterance or is similar to the astrologically derived images of astral talismanry. It is possible that this tradition eventually transformed into the various magical circles found in later forms of ceremonial magic. These ideas will be used in the practical section.

All of the above have essentially been different kinds of *synthēmata*. Included amongst these might also be incense, which is mentioned in the *Orphic Hymns*, as well as precious or semi-precious stones, and sacred metals, especially those related to the planets.[49] Traditionally, as is found in the *Papyri Græcæ Magicæ*, sacrifices of sacred animals, or animals related to the invoked deity, might be offered. Other items, including incense but also possibly herbs or flowers might also have been sacrificed. Everything involved—names, colors, smells, characters, etc.—would be specific to the deity or being invoked.

---

46. Van den Berg, *Hymns*, pp. 91–9, 101, 106–7.

47. *De Mysteriis* III.13.131.3–9.

48. This can be compared to his critique of making ensouled statues, a practice common to not only sorcerers but theurgists as well. See Kupperman, *Living Theurgy*, p. 205–6.

49. Ficino, *De Vita*, III.8, 308.

A final component is something referred to as an *Iynx*. The term appears to originate in the *Chaldean Oracles*, and refers to something that connects its user to the Gods.[50] The term is specifically used of a magical wheel employed in theurgic rites.[51] This was also the name given to a tool used in theurgic rituals, which was described by the Byzantine scholar Psellus as a golden sphere or disk[52] engraved with magical symbols or names, with a sapphire in its center. It was attached to a leather strap by which it could be swung.[53] According to his biographer Marinus, Proclus used an Iynx to end a drought in Attica.[54]

Interestingly, a similar device survives in the writings of pseudo-Paracelsus in the form of a magic bell. This bell was made from a mixture of gold, silver, mercury, lead, tin, and iron, and could be used to summon the spirits of the dead. The necromancer using it would inscribe "several words and characters" inside the bell and then swing it to cause the spirits to appear.[55] The description of this bell's use, and the precious metals from which it is made, six of the seven planetary metals, is reminiscent of Psellus' gold sphere or disk and might be a survival of the Iynx. For the invocation later in this paper, an Iynx-like tool called Apollōn's Dart[56] will be employed.

Concerning the Invocation

The above components can be combined in a myriad of ways, as can be seen in the spells and rituals of the *PGM*. Our own ritual will use a number of the above components. However, it will also use other elements to round out the ritual. This will include a purification of the ritual space with *chernips* or lustral water, as commanded by the *Chaldean Oracles*.[57] Both the theurgist and the working space are so cleansed.

Following this will be a ritual of spiritual ascension derived from *PGM* XIII 760–888, the recitation of the heptagram. This rite uses the seven Greek vowels,

---

50. *Chaldean Oracles*, frr. 77–9.

51. *Chaldean Oracle*, fr. 206. See also Ruth Majercik, introduction to *The Chaldean Oracles* (Wiltshire, UK: The Prometheus Trust, 2013), p. 9.

52. Gk. *strophalos*. Ioan P. Culianu, *Eros and Magic in the Renaissance*, trans. Margaret Cook (Chicago: University of Chicago Press, 1987), p. 144.

53. Van den Berg, *Hymns*, p. 76 n. 39.

54. Majercik, *op. cit.*, p. 30.

55. Claude Lecouteaux, *The Book of Grimoires*, trans. Jon E. Graham (Rochester, VT: Inner Traditions, 2002), pp. 144–5.

56. Although based on descriptions of Iynx-like tools, Apollon's Dart is a modern construct.

57. *Chaldean Oracles* fr. 133.

which are associated with the seven directions and seven ancient planets, to raise the theurgist's consciousness, or soul, to participate in the celestial level of visible Gods. There are a couple of different ways in which the planets have been associated with the vowels. Our ritual uses this method:[58]

Vowel		Planet
A, α	A, a	Luna
E, ε	E, e	Mercury
H, η	Ē, ē	Venus
I, ι	I, i	Sol
O, o	O, o	Mars
Υ, υ	U, u	Jupiter
Ω, ω	Ō, ō	Saturn

There are two parts to recitation of the heptagram. The first part invokes the seven vowels in a downward, clockwise spiral. This serves two functions. First, it locates the ritual in space and time, creating sacred space. Second, it coils the theurgist like a metaphysical spring, readying her or him for the second part. The second half of the recitation releases the spring, invoking the vowels in an anagogic manner, spiraling counterclockwise and up. This has the effect of raising, or launching, the theurgist upwards through the seven spheres to the divine realm.

From here, the invocation of Apollōn will occur. This includes a brief prayer and a longer invocation. The prayer uses only Apollōn's common names and epitaphs and is divided into three parts: an invocation of Apollōn by his names, a brief recounting of his oracular activities, and a request for aid in the theurgic endeavor. The second invocation includes Apollōn's hieratic names and makes use of Apollōn's Dart. These two steps function to purify and elevate or illuminate the theurgist: two of the three theurgic processes. The final step, perfection, is caused by the invoked deity.[59] The end of the invocation will utilize another vowel chant. This chant replaces the vowels of Apollōn's name with the seven vowels to effect the rising up of the theurgist through the heavenly spheres to the God. This serves to fill the theurgist's consciousness with Apollōn.

The focus of this ritual is Apollōn *Thearios*, or Apollōn "of the Oracle," for the receiving of an oracular vision. Although some other deities are associated with

---

58. For a complete discussion of the relationship between the vowels and the planets, see Joscelyn Godwin, *The Mystery of the Seven Vowels* (Grand Rapids, MI: Phanes Press, 1991).

59. *De Anima*, VII.35.383.8–9.

different forms of divination, Apollōn is the most well-known for his oracular gift, and had a number of temples dedicated to oracles, the most well-known being that at Delphi. In order to achieve this, a number of *synthēmata* associated with Apollōn and the sun will be employed. Some of these are provided by ancient Platonic and Neoplatonic sources, such as Proclus,[60] while others come from the works of Renaissance Neoplatonists such as Cornelius Agrippa[61] and Marsilio Ficino.[62] Appropriate symbols and tokens are as follows:[63]

TYPE OF TOKEN	EXAMPLES
Incense	Frankincense, spikenard, rosemary
Plants, Herbs, Spices	Heliotrope, lotus, laurel, nutmeg, saffron, cinnamon, palm
Stones	Chrysolite, sun stone, red garnet, topaz
Metal	Gold
Libations	Wine, milk, honey
Colors	Golden yellow
Symbols	Sun disk, bow and arrow, lyre, spear
Animals	Rooster, lion, bull, wolf, hawk
Series	The Muses, Asklēpios
Letter	I, ι
Number	Hexad

Apollōn is also associated with a number of *barbara onomata*. For instance, in one invocation of Apollōn to gain knowledge of prophecy, divination, and other such pursuits, these two palindromic names[64] are written on linen and then placed in a lamp: ABERAMENThŌOULERThEXANAXEThRENLUOŌThNEMARAI-BAI AEMINNAEBARŌThERREThŌBABEANIMEA.[65] Another invocation

---

60. "Priestly Art," pp. 103–5.

61. *De Occulta Philosophia libri tres ("Three Books on Occult Philosophy")*, book I, ch. 23, in *Three Books of Occult Philosophy: Book One*, trans. Eric Purdue ([n.p.:] Renaissance Astrology, 2012), pp. 74–7.

62. *De Vita*, in *Three Books of Life*, trans. Charles Boer (Irving, TX: Spring Publications, Inc., 1980), pp. 12, 17, 59–60.

63. This list is not exhaustive.

64. As with several of the palindromic names in the surviving papyri, these examples are no longer truly palindromic, which speaks to the unfamiliarity of at least the final scribe with not only the particular names, but also with the very Egyptian concept of palindromic names. —APF

65. *PGM* I.294–6.

of Apollōn for oracles gives several sets of names. The first three are given in "wing formation" (See fig. 1); with each recitation of the name the first letter is dropped: AKRAKANARBA, ALLALALA, SANTALALA. These names are also included in the spell: LAĒTONION, TABARAŌTh AEŌ EŌ.[66] Another invocation of Apollōn gives him different vowel names related to his different cults: Apollōn of Klaros—EĒU,

```
Σ Α Ν Τ Α Λ Α Λ Α
Α Ν Τ Α Λ Α Λ Α
Ν Τ Α Λ Α Λ Α
Τ Α Λ Α Λ Α
Α Λ Α Λ Α
Λ Α Λ Α
Α Λ Α
Λ Α
Α
```

Fig. 1. The Barbarous Name SANTALALA in Wing Formation

Kastalian One—AĒA, Pythian—ŌAE, of the Muses—IEŌŌEI.[67] Another name, associated with a magical statue of Apollōn carved from a laurel root, is BAINChŌŌŌChŌŌŌChNIAB.[68]

The Invocation of Apollōn Thearios: Preparation

The ritual space should be clean and free of clutter. While this is always advisable, as this invocation carries with it the possibility, and even the desirability, of divine possession, this is especially important. Prepare a small altar or shrine to Apollōn with his symbols upon it, especially a sun disk, oriented to the east. Statues of the God and his sacred animals are also appropriate. An incense burner, with incense from the above list, or from the sacred plants, should be on the altar as well, to burn as an offering to the God. Take some of the lustral water, described next, and place it inside the ritual space on a side-table near the altar. Stones sacred to the God should also be placed on the altar. These will be held during the invocation. Use either a white or golden altar cloth. This may be embroidered with traditional Hellenic patterns or with images related to the God, such as his sacred animals, plants, or other symbols. For clothing, if you have regular ritual clothing, this can be worn.

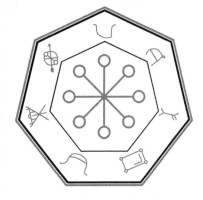

Fig. 2. Character of Apollōn

---

66. *PGM* ii.1–8.

67. *PGM* ii.139–40.

68. *PGM* xiii.101–6.

Otherwise, white clothing, representing purity, or clothing in the colors of Apollōn is appropriate.

A bowl of lustral water should be on a table or stand outside the entrance to the ritual space. To make *chernips*, have a small bowl of pure water set aside. Traditionally this would have been from a body of water, but today such water is not necessarily pure. Filtered water, or even tap water can work if necessary. Take several laurel leaves and set them on fire. Drop the burning leaves into the bowl while proclaiming *"Cherniptosai!"* or "Be purified!" The chernips is now ready to use. Alternatively, the lustral water can be made, or poured into, a small jug. In the first case, the theurgist would dip their hands, right first, into the water when purifying themselves. In the second case the water can be poured over the hands, again beginning with the right. The *chernips* should be prepared before the ritual begins.

Make a copy of the Character of Apollōn (fig. 2) on which to stand. This should be placed before the altar. It can be made of anything, such as painted on wood, canvas, or even on a shower curtain for portability. This will be placed before the altar, but with enough room between it and the altar to move between while being close enough to take something from the altar without having to step off the character. The character can be painted in gold or yellow.

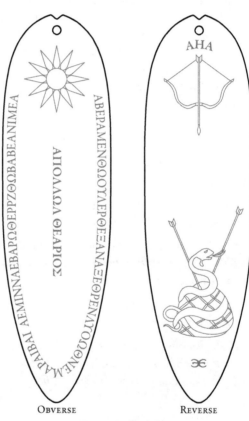

Fig. 3. Apollōn's Dart

Also make an Apollōn's Dart (fig. 3) for the altar. The dart is modeled after a bullroarer, called a *rhombos* in Greek. There is evidence of bullroarers being used in ancient Hellenic rites, especially those sacred to Kybelē. The Dart should be approximately 14 inches in length and 3 inches wide and no more than a half inch thick at the center. The edges of the Dart are like those of a double-edged blade so that when spun, the

Dart cuts through the air, making the "roaring" noise. The notch at the bottom of the Dart, below the cord hole, is to help hold the cord knots in place. The Dart should be tied to a strong cord; Proclus, for instance, used leather. The length of the cord will depend on the size and setup of the ritual space and whether you swing it horizontally overhead or perpendicular to the ground. Ideally, the Dart should be made from a wood sacred to Apollōn. If this is not possible, any sturdy, heavy wood will do. The Dart can be covered in gold leaf and the hieratic names and designs painted on top of the leaf, or the names and designs can be painted in gold on the natural wood, or even carved or burnt.

The Dart has two functions. First, it creates sound. It has been suggested that one of the kinds of sounds this type of instrument produces is that known as "infrasonic." Infrasonic frequencies, although inaudible to humans, are thought to affect the brain and influence trance states.[69] Second, the audible sound created by spinning the *rhombos* can be understood as the speaking of the divine names on the Dart. Every spin of the Dart becomes, in essence, a repetition and invocation of Apollōn.[70]

The Invocation of Apollōn Thearios: Practice

First, take a bath or shower to cleanse yourself. When ready, don your ritual clothing while saying:

For I am arrayed from head to toe with clamorous light, armed in mind and soul with a triple-barbed strength.[71]

Approach the entrance to the ritual space. In silence, purify your hands and then face with the chernips and then fumigate yourself with the incense. Enter the ritual space to stand west of the altar. Declare:

I speak to those who lawfully may hear: Depart all ye profane, and close the doors.[72]

Strongly close the door and return to the altar. If there is no door, clap loudly three times. Pick up the bowl of lustral water and sprinkle it around the room, beginning with the altar, and moving clockwise. When you have returned to altar, sprinkle the

---

69. Bethe Hagens, "Bullroarers," *Flight of Ducks*, last accessed 2015, http://www.duckdigital.net/FOD/FOD1049.html; "Timbre of the Spheres," *Mission Ignition*, last accessed 2015, http://missionignition.net/bethe/timber_of_the_spheres.php.

70. This makes the Dart similar to Tibetan prayer wheels, the spinning of which counts as prayer activity.

71. From *Chaldean Oracles*, fr. 2.

72. Porphyry, *On Images*, fr. 1, trans. Edwin Hamilton Gifford, last accessed 2015, http://classics.mit.edu/Porphyry/images.html.

water in the seven directions: Up, center, down, right, back, left, and forward. Raise the water and declare:

Be purified!

Replace the water on the side table. Light the incense on the altar while saying:

For all things have been generated from One Fire,[73] and so now, with fire, I release this token of the God from matter that it may return to its Source.

Stand upon the Character of Apollōn.

Come to me,[74] O blessed Paian, O God of Delphi, O leader of the Muses, you who are the sun, ARNEBOUAT BOLLOCh BARBARICh BAALSAMĒN PTIDAIOU ARNEBOUAT! For you are all the eye sees, bringer of light, utterer of clear oracles! Yours is the eternal heaven in which your seven-lettered name is established for the harmony of the celestial Gods. And you, Lord of Life, King of Heaven, Foreseeing One, Lord of the Oracle, you who has the truth and never lies, whom the Ogdoad attends: Ē Ō ChŌ ChOUCh NOUN NAUNI AMOUN AMAUNI. Lift my soul, enter my mind, and increase my understanding for all the time of my life.

Look upwards, place your hands on your head. Intone: **Ō.**

Continue looking upwards, place your hands over your heart. Intone: **U.**

Touch the ground. Intone: **O.**

Turn to the south. Place your hands on your stomach. Intone: **I.**

Turn to the west. Extend your hands forward, palms up. Intone: **Ē.**

Turn to the north. Raise your right hand in a fist. Intone with one breath: **E.**

Turn to the east. Stretch both arms and hands to your left. Intone: **A.**

I call on you, eternal and unbegotten, who are one, who alone holds together the whole creation of all things, whom none understands, whom the daimones worship, whose name not even the Gods can utter. Inspire from your exhalation, ruler of the pole, those who are under you that I may be raised to you.

---

73. *Chaldean Oracles*, fr. 10.

74. The following invocation is derived largely from *PGM* XIII.763ff.

I call on you as the winds call: I call on you as the dawn: A EE ĒĒĒ IIII OOOOO UUUUU ŌŌŌŌŌŌ.[75]

Turn to the north and say: I call on you as the north: E ĒĒ III OOOO UUUUU ŌŌŌŌŌŌ AAAAAA.

Turn to the west and say: I call on you as the west: Ē II OOO UUUU ŌŌŌŌŌ AAAAAA EEEEEEE.

Turn to the south and say: I call on you as the south: I OO UUU ŌŌŌŌ AAAAA EEEEEE ĒĒĒĒĒĒ.

Turn to the east, look to the ground and say: I call on you as the earth: O UU ŌŌŌ AAAA EEEEE ĒĒĒĒĒĒ IIIIII.

Look upwards and say: I call on you as the sky: U ŌŌ AAA EEEE ĒĒĒĒĒ IIIII OOOOOOO.

Looking up, see the starry heavens before you and say: I call you as the cosmos: Ō AA EEE ĒĒĒĒ IIIII OOOOOO UUUUUUU.

Pick up one of the sacred stones from the altar, hold it in right hand.

Phoibos Apollōn, Delphic Lord,
 Hear my prayer, God of Foresight!
Great Pythian God, Giver of
 Oracles, Paian and great Light!

Seated upon the omphalos
 You slew Pythōn with mighty
Arrows. You come and Pythia speaks;
 Her verses are your decree.

Most holy Apollōn, giver
 Of visions, speaker of truth,
Set your hand upon my soul, raise
 Me up, you most profound sleuth.

Put the sacred stone in your left hand. Pick up Apollōn's Dart from the altar, begin to swing it in your right hand and say:

O lord Apollōn Thearios, Apollōn Proöpsios, Apollōn Klēdonēs, whose secret names are AĒA ŌAE IEŌŌEI.

---

75. Ululate or pulse the vowel once for each character in the string over the course of a single breath, *e.g.*, the vowel ōmega should be ululated seven times in a single breath. Alternatively, all the vowels can be chanted in a single breath, again pulsing each vowel for each character in the string of vowels.

You who are called fire, and channel of fire, and dispenser of fire,[76] I call you!

You who are borne along by the eternal will of the Father, leader of the starry procession,[77] I call you!

I call on you by your oracular name: AKRAKANARBA, KRAKANAR-BA, RAKANARBA, AKANARBA, KANARBA, ANARBA, NARBA, ARBA, RBA, BA, A.

O Apollōn, giver of oracles, come, joyous one, Lētō's son, player of the golden lyre, come, sing your songs that I might know you as I know myself!

ALLALALA, LLALALA, LALALA, ALALA, LALA, ALA, LA, A and SANTALALA, ANTALALA, NTALALA, TALALA, ALALA, LALA, ALA, LA, A.

You who wear the victor's laurel, who comes with Muses and Asklēpios in your train, play your holy chords from your sacred peak that through their harmony I may become you, and you me.

Whirl the Dart faster.

Stir in me the prophetic frenzy, O mighty Apollōn, LAĒTONION and TABARAŌTh AEŌ EŌ. The sky parts at the sound of your Dart and the heavens open at the parting of your lips.

O Apollōn, mighty God, I am you and you are me! Whatever I will you will, that all shall be accomplished! I open my true eyes and see!

While swinging Apollōn's Dart, recite this chant until the God or his envoy comes to you:

APELLĒN, IPOLLUN, ŌPALLEN, ĒPILLON, UPŌLLAN, EPĒLLIN, OPULLŌN.

Once the God, or his daimōn, departs, stop spinning the Dart.

O blessed Paian, O God of Delphi, O leader of the Muses, you who are the sun, you who have perfected me in your ways and your image! I have seen you clearly and the flower of my soul has blossomed. Your seven-lettered name has been established and your sacred words have been spoken. Truthful one, Lord of Life, King of Heaven, I give thanks to you for your gift of divine knowledge, you who are mighty in heaven.

The rite is finished. Leave the incense to burn as a sacrifice to the God. You may also use this time to pray or meditate on what you have received. When ready, leave the ritual space, turning off the lights only once the incense has burnt itself out.

---

76. *Chaldean Oracles*, fr. 60.

77. *Chaldean Oracles*, fr. 107.

References

Agrippa, Cornelius. *Three Books of Occult Philosophy: Book One*. Translated by Eric Purdue. [n.p.:] Renaissance Astrology, 2012.

Aristotle. *Nichomachean Ethics*. Translated by Martin Ostwald. New York: The Bobbs-Merrill Company, Inc., 1962.

Betz, Hans Dieter. *The Greek Magical Papyri in Translation: Including the Demotic Spells*. Chicago: University of Chicago Press, 1986.

Copenhaver, Brian P. "Hermes Trismegistus, Proclus, and the Question of a Philosophy of Magic in the Renaissance." In Ingrid Merkel and Allen G. Debus, *Hermeticism and the Renaissance*, pp. 79–110. Washington, D.C.: Folger Books, 1988.

Culianu, Ioan P. *Eros and Magic in the Renaissance*. Translated by Margaret Cook. Chicago: University of Chicago Press, 1987.

Ficino, Marsilio. *De Amore: Commentary on Plato's Symposium on Love*. Translated by Sears Jayne. Dallas, Tex.: Spring Publications, Inc., 1985.

—. *Three Books of Life*. Translated by Charles Boer. Irving, Tex.: Spring Publications, Inc., 1980.

—. *Three Books on Life: A Critical Edition and Translation with Introduction and Notes*. Translated by Carol V. Kaske and John R. Clark. Tempe, Ariz.: Medieval & Renaissance Texts & Studies, 1998.

Godwin, Joscelyn. *The Mystery of the Seven Vowels: In Theory and Practice*. Grand Rapids, Mich.: Phanes Press, 1991.

Hagens, Bethe. "Bullroarers," *Flight of Ducks*. Last accessed 1/29/15, http://www.duckdigital.net/FOD/FOD1049.html.

—. "Timbre of the Spheres," *Mission Ignition*. Last accessed 1/29/15, http://missionignition.net/bethe/timber_of_the_spheres.php.

Iamblichus. *De Anima: Text, Translation, and Commentary*. Translated by John F. Finamore and John M. Dillon. Atlanta: Society of Biblical Literature, 2002.

—. *De Mysteriis*. Translated by Emma C. Clarke, John M. Dillon, and Jackson P. Hershbell. Atlanta: Society of Biblical Literature, 2003.

—. *In Platonis Dialogos Commentariorum Fragmenta*. Translated by John M. Dillon. Wiltshire, UK: Prometheus Trust, 2009.

Ibn Qurra, Thabit. *Astral High Magic: De Imaginibus of Thabit Ibn Qurra*. Translated by John Michael Greer. [n.p.:] Renaissance Astrology, 2011.

Johnston, Sarah Iles. "Riders in the Sky: Cavalier Gods and Theurgic Salvation in the Second Century A.D." *Classical Philology* 87, no. 4 (1992): pp. 303–21.

Kupperman, Jeffrey S. *Living Theurgy*. London: Avalonia Books, 2014.

Lecouteaux, Claude. The *Book of Grimoires: The Secret Grammar of Magic*. Translated by Jon E. Graham. Rochester, VT: Inner Traditions, 2002.

Lewy, Hans. *Chaldean Oracles and Theurgy*. Translated by Michel Tardieu. Paris: Institute d'Etudes Augustiniennes, 2011.

Majercik, Ruth Dorothy. *The Chaldean Oracles*. Wiltshire, UK: The Prometheus Trust, 2013.

Porphyry. *On Images*. Translated by Edwin Hamilton Gifford. Last accessed 1/26/15. http://classics.mit.edu/Porphyry/images.html.

Proclus. *Hymns: Essays, Translations, Commentary*. Translated by R.M. van den Berg. Leiden, the Netherlands: Brill, 2001.

—. *On Plato Cratylus*. Translated by Brian Duvick. New York: Bloomsbury Academic, 2014.

Sallustius. *Concerning the Gods and the Universe*. Translated by Arthur Darby Nock. Chicago: Ares Publishers, Inc., 1926.

Shaw, Gregory. "The Geometry of Grace: A Pythagorean Approach to Theurgy." In H.J. Blumenthal and E.G. Clark, *The Divine Iamblichus: Philosopher and Man of Gods*, pp. 117–37. London: Bristol Classical Press, 1993.

—. *Theurgy and the Soul: The Neoplatonism of Iamblichus*. University Park, Penn.: Pennsylvania State University Press, 1995.

✠

Evoking Zodiacal Angels

Scott Michael Stenwick

Scott Michael Stenwick is a Thelemite and ritual magician, also known as Ananael Qaa, who has been practicing for more than 25 years. He has a degree in experimental psychology from Saint Olaf College, a well-regarded Lutheran school that has a surprisingly good collection of Aleister Crowley's work, and has been involved in Ordo Templi Orientis since 1995 and Masonry since 1997. He is the author of the Mastering Enochian Magick *series, which so far includes* Mastering the Mystical Heptarchy *(Pendraig Publishing: 2011) and* Mastering the Great Table *(Pendraig Publishing: 2013), and contributed to the anthology* The Holy Guardian Angel *(Nephilim Press: 2014). He is also the author of the novel* Arcana *(Pendraig Publishing: 2009). You may follow his blogs at* Augoeides: Spiritual Technology for a New Aeon *(ananael.blogspot.com) and* Scott Michael Stenwick: Author and Esotericist *(scottstenwick.wordpress.com).*

Evoking
Zodiacal Angels

HE PRIMARY BUILDING BLOCKS of the Western Esoteric Tradition consist of the classical elements, traditional planets, and signs of the zodiac. While much information is now available on working with the planets and elements, considerably less has been compiled for working with the angels of the signs.

The terms 'angel' and 'demon' appear in the grimoires of the Renaissance as filtered through a strict Christian perspective. According to this framework, the term angel refers to those spirits who serve God in Heaven, and the term demon refers to the 'fallen angels' that rebelled and were consigned to Hell. Digging deeper into the tradition, though, it becomes clear that this is merely a gloss placed over an older and more functional schema. Generally speaking, angel is used to refer to spirits of the celestial realms, while demon is used to refer to spirits of the chthonic realms.

The term 'chthonic' refers to the underworld, while the term 'celestial' refers to the realm of the stars and planets. It is fairly straightforward to see how the Christian gloss came about; with the evolution of the underworld into Hell, a place of damnation, entities native to that realm naturally were ascribed the characteristics of archetypal evil. Likewise, with the placement of Heaven in the sky, celestial entities became associated with those of archetypal good.

Prior to the rise of Christianity, the Jewish concept of the afterlife had much more in common with the classical underworld than the celestial realms. But Jesus is portrayed in the Gospels as ascending into the sky, and Paul likewise wrote in *I Thessalonians* the passage that the King James Bible translates as:

> Then we which are alive and remain shall be caught up together with them in the clouds, to meet the Lord in the air: and so shall we ever be with the Lord.[1]

---

1. *First Epistle to the Thessalonians* 4:17 (King James Version).

Not only has a literal interpretation of this passage served as the basis for "the Rapture" in modern evangelical Christianity, the text also provides support for the idea that the Lord dwells in the Heavens and that good Christians will eventually reside there.

While I will continue to use the term angel throughout this article, it is important to keep in mind that my use of the term alludes not to some sort of good-versus-evil axis, but rather the celestial nature of the entities themselves. Furthermore, this term here has little to do with the representation of angels in popular culture as spiritual embodiments of human virtues. Not all so-called angels are necessarily friendly and good-tempered, and likewise not all so-called demons are necessarily hostile and aggressive.

When performing any sort of working with a spirit, the best practice is to at first conjure the spirit and communicate in some fashion in order to get a sense of the spirit's individual personality. Just as with individual people, you will likely find that you get along with certain spirits better than others, and there is no way to determine this simply from reading accounts of rituals performed by other magicians.

Aleister Crowley writes in *Liber O*[2] the following concerning spirits and related phenomena:

> In this book it is spoken of the Sephiroth and the Paths; of Spirits and Conjurations; of Gods, Spheres, Planes, and many other things which may or may not exist. It is immaterial whether these exist or not. By doing certain things certain results will follow; students are most earnestly warned against attributing objective reality or philosophic validity to any of them.

While it is important that as magicians we apply critical thinking to the spirits we conjure and the operations we perform, I and a growing number of modern grimoire magicians contend that the spirits are as objective as any other manifestation of consciousness. I can say with some certainty that treating them as "psychological projections" and so forth is a recipe for failure, and that treating them as independent, individual minds in their own right produces far superior practical results.

As the signs of the zodiac are represented by constellations, the angels of the signs are clearly celestial entities. However, they are not completely divorced from earthly affairs. In *Liber 777*,[3] the angels of the signs may be found under Column

---

2. Aleister Crowley, *Liber O vel Manus et Sagittæ sub figurâ VI*, in *The Equinox*, vol. 1, no. 2, September 1909 (London: Simpkin, Marshall, Hamilton, Kent & Co. Ltd.). Later republished in The Master Therion [Aleister Crowley], *Magick in Theory and Practice* ([Paris]: Lecram Press, 1929; in Aleister Crowley, John Symonds, and Kenneth Grant, *Magick* (London: Routledge & Kegan Paul, 1973); and in Aleister Crowley and Israel Regardie, *Gems from the Equinox* (St. Paul, Minn.: Llewellyn Publications, 1974). —APF

3. Anonymous [Aleister Crowley], *777: vel Prolegomena Symbolica ad Systemam Sceptico-Mysticæ Viæ Explicandæ Fundamentum Hieroglyphicum Sanctissimorum Scientiæ Summæ* (London: W. Scott, 1909). Later republished in Aleister Crowley and Israel Regardie, *The Qabalah of Aleister Crowley: Three Texts* (New

CLXXVII, where they are decribed as Geomantic Intelligences. Of these Intelligences, Crowley writes:

> The first thing to remember about Geomancy is that although the various intelligences are attributed to the twelve signs of the Zodiac they all appertain to the element of earth.[4]

Much as the god-names used in the standard pentagram and hexagram rituals are referred to as "God-Names in Assiah," this implies that the angels of the signs are those zodiacal entities which are most affiliated with Assiah, which is the most material of the four Qabalistic worlds and attributed to the element of Earth. Therefore, these angels are well-suited to all manner of practical magical operations according to their particular powers.

Liber 777 lists the magical powers appropriate to the signs of the zodiac in Column XLV: Magical Powers (Western Mysticism), which you may see in Figure 1.

While this is a modern set of attributions developed by the original Golden Dawn order and refined by Crowley, it nonetheless provides a coherent set of correspondences rooted in the structure of Hermetic Qabalah that describe how the powers of the zodiacal angels can be brought to bear.

Sign	Power
♈ Aries	Power of Consecrating Things
♉ Taurus	The Secret of Physical Strength
♊ Gemini	Power of Being in Two or More Places at One Time, and of Prophecy
♋ Cancer	Power of Casting Enchantments
♌ Leo	Power of Training Wild Beasts
♍ Virgo	Invisibility, Parthenogenesis, Initiation
♎ Libra	Works of Justice and Equilibrium
♏ Scorpio	Necromancy
♐ Sagittarius	Transmutations
♑ Capricorn	The Witches' Sabbath so-called, the Evil Eye
♒ Aquarius	Astrology
♓ Pisces	Bewitchments, Casting Illusions

Fig. 1. Table of Magical Powers (Western Mysticism)

When working with planetary spirits, the traditional grimoire method of timing rites is to use the system of planetary days and hours. For zodiacal signs, a similar

York: Weiser, 1973), reissued as *777 and Other Qabalistic Writings of Aleister Crowley: Including Gematria & Sepher Sephiroth* (New York: Weiser, 1977). —APF

4. *Ibid.*

system can be applied by taking into account the sign's ruling planet and the notion of *sect*. The proper planetary day for a zodiacal operation corresponds to the sign's ruling planet, according to the traditional rulership attributions that exclude the outer planets. Planetary days do not run from midnight to midnight, but rather from sunrise to sunrise.

Every astrological sign is also attributed to either the *diurnal* or *nocturnal* sect. As planetary hours are also grouped into day and night hours the correspondences are straightforward. The table in Fig. 2 shows the twelve signs along with their traditional planetary rulers and sects.[5]

The Sun and Moon rule one sign each. The Sun rules the day and the diurnal sign Leo, while the Moon rules the night and the nocturnal sign Cancer. Each of the other planets then rules one diurnal and one nocturnal sign, which provides some additional insight into how the rulers were allocated in ancient times and how they relate to the essential nature of the signs.

Sign	Ruler	Day	Sect
♈︎ Aries	♂	Tuesday	Diurnal
♉︎ Taurus	♀	Friday	Nocturnal
♊︎ Gemini	☿	Wednesday	Diurnal
♋︎ Cancer	☽	Monday	Nocturnal
♌︎ Leo	☉	Sunday	Diurnal
♍︎ Virgo	☿	Wednesday	Nocturnal
♎︎ Libra	♀	Friday	Diurnal
♏︎ Scorpio	♂	Tuesday	Nocturnal
♐︎ Sagittarius	♃	Thursday	Diurnal
♑︎ Capricorn	♄	Saturday	Nocturnal
♒︎ Aquarius	♄	Saturday	Diurnal
♓︎ Pisces	♃	Thursday	Nocturnal

Fig. 2. Table of Signs, Rulers, and Sects

To determine the length of day and night hours for any day of the year, take the number of minutes from sunrise to sunset and divide by twelve to get the length of each day hour, and then divide the number of minutes from sunset to the following sunrise and divide by twelve to get the length of each night hour. Then assign the day that rules the planet to the first day hour, and assign each

---

5. Note that, as this method dates back to before the era of modern astrology, the outer planetary rulers are not part of the system.

subsequent hour to the next planet in sequence according to the Chaldean Order ($\hbar \to \text{♃} \to \text{♂} \to \odot \to \text{♀} \to \text{☿} \to \text{☽}$). So, on a Sunday, the first hour would be attributed to the Sun, the second to Venus, and so forth.

To obtain the appropriate planetary hours for each sign, allocate Leo to all Sun hours and Cancer to all Moon hours, with day hours preferred for Leo and night hours preferred for Cancer. Then combine the planetary ruler and sect shown above to obtain the others. The hours of Aries are the day hours of Mars, the hours of Taurus are the night hours of Venus, the hours of Gemini are the day hours of Mercury, and so forth.

Other timing considerations concern making the sign's ruling planet as strong as possible. Renaissance astrology includes a method for calculating the strongest planet for any given moment,

PLANET	RULERSHIP	EXALTATION
☉ Sun	♌	♈
☽ Moon	♋	♉
☿ Mercury	♊, ♍	♍
♀ Venus	♉, ♎	♓
♂ Mars	♈, ♏	♑
♃ Jupiter	♐, ♓	♋
♄ Saturn	♑, ♒	♎

Fig. 3. Table of Rulership and Exaltation

referred to as *al-Mubtaz* or "the *Victor*" of the chart. Planets gain strength from being in the signs of their *rulership* or *exaltation*, according to the table of dignities in Fig. 3.

The calculation of the victor is based on the following factors in addition to the planet's rulership and exaltation, and the planetary day and hour:

→ *Sign of the Sun:* When the Sun is in the sign of a planet's rulership or exaltation the planet gains strength.

→ *Rising Sign*: When the sign of a planet's rulership or exaltation is on the horizon, the planet gains strength.

→ *Sign of the Moon:* When the Moon is in the sign of a planet's rulership or exaltation the planet gains strength.

→ *Prenatal Lunation*: This refers to the sign in which the Moon was either new or full preceding the operation. The practice of working magick on a waxing Moon may have originated with the basic fact that following a new Moon, the prenatal lunation and sign of the Sun will be in alignment until the Sun moves into the next sign or until the next full Moon.

→ *House Position*: Planets gain strength according to the House in which they fall at the moment an operation begins. The strongest house is the first, and the weakest is the twelfth.[6]

The full Victor calculation also involves triplicities, bounds, and some special considerations for Mars, Jupiter, and Saturn, but the above factors in conjunction with the day and hour will generally be sufficient to work out a time in which either the sign's ruling or exalted planet is dominant. Rulership is stronger than exaltation and is preferred, but sometimes it is necessary to make due allowance for certain operations. Likewise, there usually are trade-offs that must be made between the various factors so that the operation can be performed in a timely manner.

Planet	Detriment	Fall
☉ Sun	♒	♎
☽ Moon	♑	♏
☿ Mercury	♐, ♓	—
♀ Venus	♈, ♏	♍
♂ Mars	♉, ♎	♋
♃ Jupiter	♊, ♍	♑
♄ Saturn	♋, ♌	♈

Fig. 4. Table of Detriment and Fall

In addition to strengthening the ruling or exalted planet, you will also want to ensure that the victor of the chart is not *debilitated* in the sign with which you are working by being either in *detriment* or *fall*. An operation performed when the Victor is neither in its rulership nor exaltation can still work out fine depending upon the other factors involved. But if the Victor is in detriment or fall, the operation will very likely fail. The chart in Fig. 4 shows the signs in which the various planets are debilitated.

Finally, a couple of other factors should be kept in mind when timing your workings. A simple election for your operation can be obtained by evaluating the position of the Moon and its *final aspect*. The Moon moves through the signs very quickly, remaining in each for at most a few days. As it moves, it makes various aspects with the other planets in the chart—conjunctions, oppositions, trines, sextiles, and squares. The final aspect is the last aspect made by the Moon before it leaves the sign it is in and moves onto the next. Between the final aspect and transition to the next sign, the Moon is said to be *void of course*.

---

6. Medieval astrology uses whole-sign houses. So when the rising sign is Aries, for example, everything in Aries is treated as First House, everything in Taurus is treated as Second House, and so forth. For purposes of the Victor calculation, this is how the houses should be allocated, rather than using one of the more complex modern arrangements that can yield different results.

If at all possible, you should avoid practical magical operations when the Moon is void of course. During this time your ability to cause change is greatly diminished and will likely undermine your objective, and this is especially true for zodiacal operations. Furthermore, you should avoid times when the Moon's final aspect is a square or an opposition. These are considered negative aspects and can likewise disrupt the outcome of your work. Incidentally, this method is also applicable beyond magical work. It can serve as a quick check of the astrological landscape for just about any undertaking.

The last thing you want to check for is whether or not the planet you are working to emphasize is afflicted in some manner. A planet is afflicted if the next aspect it is moving into is an opposition or square. Note that unlike in natal astrology, though, an aspect should only be taken into account so long as it is applying to the planet—that is, the moment the aspect passes its peak it should no longer be taken into account. In electional astrology, once an aspect begins to separate from the planet it is considered passed and done.

If all of this sounds complicated, that is because taking into account all of the various astrological factors is quite a bit more involved than a simple calculation of the day and hour. Unlike Renaissance magicians, though, we have all sorts of modern astrological tools to help us out. Websites like *Lunarium* (http://www.lunarium.co.uk/), *Moon Tracks Astrology Calendars* (http://www.moontracks.com) and *AstroDienst* (http://www.astro.com) let us look up lunar aspects and create charts, and free applications like AstroLog (http://www.astrolog.org/astrolog.htm) are sufficient for doing the same on the desktop. Commercial astrology software has more available options that can speed the process up ever further.

Also, while this method is involved, understanding the basic factors is well worth it for planetary as well as zodiacal operations. A planetary evocation performed when the victor of the chart is the planet with which you are working is especially powerful, and likewise can be diminished when the victor is incompatible with the desired planet or the objective of the rite, or if the planet with which you are working is afflicted. As a related benefit, becoming familiar with how the various factors come into play provides insight into the relationship between astrological forces and other aspects of the Western Esoteric Tradition, and for that matter how they affect our daily lives.

Once an auspicious time has been chosen for your operation, you will need the name of the angel, its sigil, and the appropriate god-name for the conjuration. For any sort of mystical operation or work of illumination, you will always want to use the god-name Jah (יה) which corresponds to Chokmah, the sphere of the zodiac, in Hermetic Qabalah. For practical operations, you will want to use the permutation

Sign	Angel	Spelling in Hebrew	God-Name
♈︎ Aries	Melchidael	מלכידאל	יהוה (Yod-Heh-Vav-Heh)
♉︎ Taurus	Asmodel	אסודאל	יההו (Yod-Heh-Heh-Vav)
♊︎ Gemini	Ambriel	אמבריאל	יוהה (Yod-Vav-Heh-Heh)
♋︎ Cancer	Muriel	מוריאל	הוהי (Heh-Vav-Heh-Yod)
♌︎ Leo	Verachiel	ורכיאל	הויה (Heh-Vav-Yod-Heh)
♍︎ Virgo	Hamaliel	המליאל	ההוי (Heh-Heh-Vav-Yod)
♎︎ Libra	Zuriel	זוריאל	והיה (Vav-Heh-Yod-Heh)
♏︎ Scorpio	Barachiel	ברכיאל	וההי (Vav-Heh-Heh-Yod)
♐︎ Sagittarius	Advachiel	אדוכיאל	ויהה (Vav-Yod-Heh-Heh)
♑︎ Capricorn	Hanael	הנאל	היהו (Heh-Yod-Heh-Vav)
♒︎ Aquarius	Cambriel	כאמבריאל	היוה (Heh-Yod-Vav-Heh)
♓︎ Pisces	Amnitziel	אמניציאל	ההוי (Heh-Heh-Vav-Yod)

Fig. 5. Angels of the Signs and Corresponding God-Names (Permutations of Tetragrammaton)

of Tetragrammaton (יהוה) corresponding to the sign. The zodiacal angel names and these corresponding god-names are shown in the table in Fig. 5.[7]

The sigils of these angels can be derived by tracing the Hebrew onto the *kamea* square of the sign's ruling planet. The kamea squares are found in Agrippa's *Three*

7. The Heh with the *niqqud* (point) in it—ה—is simply to distinguish the final Heh from the medial Heh in the permutations, and does not affect the pronunciation.

Books of Occult Philosophy but are much older, and are generated from grids of numbers called 'magic squares' in which each horizontal, vertical, and diagonal line sum to the same number. The *order* of each square—that is, the number of horizontal and vertical digits—corresponds to the planet's number as allocated by Hermetic Qabalah. This arrangement follows the Chaldean sequence, beginning with Saturn as 3 and ending with the Moon as 9.[8]

These relationships are grounded in basic mathematics, and as such relate the angelic sigils to relevant principles of the material world. The Chaldean sequence arranges the planets in order of relative astrological motion, which is derived from direct observation of the physical world. Saturn is the slowest, so it is related to three, the smallest-order magic square that can be constructed. For each subsequent classical planet, then, the order is incremented by one.[9]

To derive the sigil of a zodiacal angel, employ the magic square corresponding to the sign's classical planetary ruler. The numbers on the square can be converted into letters corresponding to Hebrew gematria, so that for example 5 would be rendered as ה. You start with the first letter of the angel name, then trace a line from the cell of the magic square containing the first letter to that containing the second, then trace from the second to the third, and so forth.

When the value of a Hebrew letter is too high to be represented by one of the numbers on the particular square, it may be converted to a lower number using the *Aiq Bekar* method. This consists of reducing the number by factors of ten until you arrive at a value that can be represented. For example, the letter Resh has a value of 200 in standard Hebrew gematria. In order to represent this letter on the square of Saturn, in which the highest number is nine, it must be divided by ten twice to yield a value of two. When mapping Resh onto the square of Mars, though, it need only be divided by ten once to yield a value of 20, because the maximum value in the Mars magic square is 25.

If a name references the same number twice in a row, as, for example, Metatron (מטטרון) with its double Teth, the repetition is indicated by drawing a figure representing a double point before moving on. This figure resembles a sort of double crescent within the cell, as shown in Fig. 6.

---

8. *E.g.*, the square of Saturn is a third-order magic square, and the square of the Moon is a ninth-order magic square.

9. The outer planets are excluded from this arrangement, as they were unknown to Renaissance astrologers. While modern astrology has assigned outer planet rulers to some of the signs, this disrupts the elegant structure of planet and sect found in the classical system. Furthermore, the ongoing debate over whether to call Pluto a planet or a dwarf planet calls the modern arrangement into question. Pluto is neither the largest nor the closest of the dwarf planets (those distinctions belonging to Eris and Ceres respectively), but in the modern system it merits the rulership of a sign while the other dwarf planets do not.

There are a couple of additional methods that I make use of when constructing sigils from magic squares that are not necessarily traditional, but which I find useful nonetheless. The first is that I begin each sigil with a small circle and end it with a short perpendicular straight line. From the ren-

Fig. 6. Double-Letter Loop

derings in Agrippa this is sometimes done but often not, and there seems to be no clear pattern. Many of the sigils of the planetary spirits and intelligences both begin and end with small circles, while others begin and end in the same square and are drawn as linking back to themselves and forming a shape with no clear beginning and end.

Including the additional circle and perpendicular line encodes more information into the sigil, as it marks both the beginning and ending point. Furthermore, my use of these figures is inspired by John Dee's analysis of the circle and the straight line in the *Monas Hieroglyphica*. Dee's first theorem reads:

> It is by the straight line and the circle that the first and most simple example and representation of all things may be demonstrated, whether such things be either non-existent or merely hidden under Nature's veils.[10]

As the sigils of the zodiacal angels are intended to serve as the simplest representation of the angel's name within the corresponding magic square, it seems appropriate that the circle and straight line should be employed as markers. In a sense they denote the 'anode' and 'cathode' of the sigil, its beginning and end, as the name calls the angel from potentiality into manifestation.

The second principle that I employ is to always give preference to the exact number for each letter when tracing the name, and when using the Aiq Bekar method to give preference to the reduced number closest to the actual value. For example, even though according to the tradition the number 25 can represent either כ (20) or ה (5), I always trace ה as 5 and כ as 2 in the squares of Saturn (maximum value 9) and Jupiter (maximum value 16), and 20 in all the other squares.

The first nine letters, א through ט, are traced as their actual value in all squares, such that א = 1, ב = 2, ג = 3, and so forth. The next nine with values from 10 to 90 are represented as follows:

⇥	י	(10) =	1 on the kamea of ♄, otherwise 10
⇥	כ	(20) =	2 on ♄ and ♃, otherwise 20
⇥	ל	(30) =	3 on ♄, ♃, and ♂, otherwise 30
⇥	מ	(40) =	4 on ♄, ♃, ♂, and ☉, otherwise 40

---

10. John Dee, *Monas Hieroglyphica* (Antwerp: Gulielmus Silvius, 1564), trans. by J.W. Hamilton-Jones in *The Hieroglyphic Monad* (London: John M. Watkins, 1947), Theorem I.

⇾	נ	(50)	=	5 on ♄, ♃, ♂, ☉, and ♀, otherwise 50

⇾ נ (50) = 5 on ♄, ♃, ♂, ☉, and ♀, otherwise 50

⇾ ס (60) = 6 on ♄, ♃, ♂, ☉, and ♀, otherwise 60

⇾ ע (70) = 7 on ♄, ♃, ♂, ☉, ♀, and ☿, 70 in ☽

⇾ פ (80) = 8 on ♄, ♃, ♂, ☉, ♀, and ☿, 80 in ☽

⇾ צ (90) = 9 on all squares, as the maximum value for ☽ is 81

Finally, the remaining four letters, with values from 100 to 400, are represented as follows:

⇾ ק (100) = 1 on ♄, otherwise 10

⇾ ר (200) = 2 on ♄ and ♃, otherwise 20

⇾ ש (300) = 3 on ♄, ♃, and ♂, otherwise 30

⇾ ת (400) = 4 on ♄, ♃, ♂, and ☉, otherwise 40

What I like about this method is that it creates a mostly "reversible" or readable sigil by means of which the name can be extracted from the square. But it should also be noted that, as the tradition is more flexible, there are multiple ways to draw each sigil that could be considered correct. If you have found for yourself a sigil that follows the traditional principles and works in practice to conjure the corresponding angel, you should keep using it whether or not it conforms to the stricter set of rules that I have employed here.

The sigils that I use for the zodiacal angels are shown in Figures 7 through 18, drawn onto the corresponding magic squares.

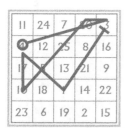

Fig. 7. *Aries—Sigil of Melchidael on the Mars Kamea*

22	47	16	41	10	35	4
5	23	48	17	42	11	29
30	6	24	49	18	36	12
13	31	7	25	43	19	37
38	14	32	1	26	44	20
21	39	8	33	2	27	45
46	15	40	9	34	3	28

Fig. 8. *Taurus—Sigil of Asmodel on the Venus Kamea*

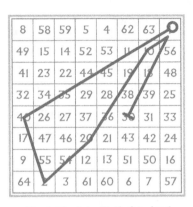

Fig. 9. Gemini—Sigil of Ambriel
on the Mercury Kamea

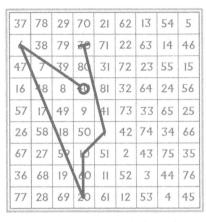

Fig. 10. Cancer—Sigil of Muriel
on the Moon Kamea

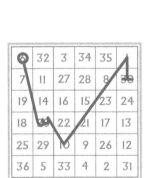

Fig. 11. Leo—Sigil of Verachiel
on the Sun Kamea

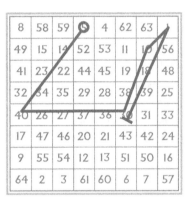

Fig. 12. Virgo—Sigil of Hamaliel
on the Mercury Kamea

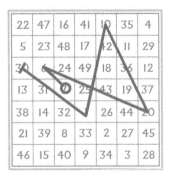

Fig. 13. Libra—Sigil of Zuriel
on the Venus Kamea

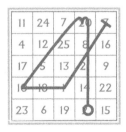

Fig. 14. Scorpio—Sigil of Barachiel
on the Mars Kamea

Fig. 15. Sagittarius—Sigil of Advachiel on the Jupiter Kamea

Fig. 16. Capricorn—Sigil of Hanael on the Saturn Kamea

Fig. 17. Aquarius—Sigil of Cambriel on the Saturn Kamea

Fig. 18. Pisces—Sigil of Amnitziel on the Jupiter Kamea

These sigils may then be used to conjure the zodiacal angels. The temple should be prepared for the ritual along Trithemian lines, based on the arrangement outlined in *The Art of Drawing Spirits into Crystals*.[11]

The Trithemian circle is drawn as shown in Fig. 19. Trithemius does not give a specific size for the circle except that it must be large enough for the magician to stand or sit in while using the crystal. Nine feet in diameter is the most common dimension given in other grimoric sources, but so long as you fit within the circle you can adapt it to your space constraints without compromising its effectiveness.

It should be noted that while it appears in many of the grimoires, the word *Tetragrammaton* is not actually a name of power. It simply means "four-letter-

Fig. 19. Trithemian Circle

11. Johannes Trithemius, *The Art of Drawing Spirits into Crystals*, in Francis Barrett, *The Magus, or Celestial Intelligencer* (London: Lackington, Allen, and Co., 1801). The full text can also be found online at Joseph H. Peterson and Johannes Trithemius, *Trithemius: The Art of Drawing Spirits into Crystals*, on the *Twilit Grotto—Esoteric Archives* website (http://www.esotericarchives.com/tritheim/trchryst.htm).

name" in Greek, and while it alludes to יהוה, it is in effect a stand-in for the name itself. When constructing my own grimoire implements, I generally replace the word Tetragrammaton with יהוה, and furthermore you can tune your circle to a particular zodiacal angel by replacing the word with the permutation shown as the God-Name in Fig. 5.

In *Liber O*, Aleister Crowley gives some additional instructions that may be used to help tune the circle. Crowley recommends painting the circle in the color corresponding to the Qabalistic sphere of the spirit being conjured, which for all zodiacal angels should be gray, the Queen Scale color of the second Sephirah, Chokmah.[12]

Within the circle, Crowley suggests inscribing the lineal figure appropriate to the spirit in the proper color, which for the zodiacal angels is the King Scale color of the associated path in *Liber 777*. The lineal figure corresponding to the zodiacal angels is the figure associated with the ruling planet. Finally, Crowley suggests placing lamps of the proper color where the points of the lineal figure contact the circle. The lineal figures and colors for the signs according to this arrangement are shown in Fig. 20.[13]

As diurnal signs are ruled by the Sun and nocturnal signs are ruled by the Moon, a hexagram may also be employed for diurnal signs and an enneagram for nocturnal signs. This may be of particular concern with the angels of Capricorn and Aquarius, as the triangle is also used as a containment structure in the Trithemian system and in some cases you may want to employ the alternates to prevent any possible resonance between the two figures that might breach the circle.

The Table of Practice is the containment structure into which the angels will be conjured. Trithemius describes it as follows:

> First, The names of the seven planets and angels ruling them, with their seals or characters. The names of the four kings of the four corners of the earth. Let them be all written within a double circle, with a triangle on a table; on which place the crystal on its pedestal: this being done, thy table is complete . . . and fit for the calling of the spirits . . .[14]

---

12. From a practical standpoint, this should be a darker gray so that the elements of the circle remain highly visible.

13. The names used by Crowley for the colors are those from the Victorian-era R∴R∴ et A∴C∴ manuscripts, and—*pace* Perdurabo—they can be somewhat misleading for the modern magician. The King Scale colors for the 12 Signs in fact comprise a standard, equal-step color wheel of primary, secondary, and tertiary colors for painters, and the names of the colors may be more simply and clearly identified as ♈ red, ♉ red-orange, ♊ orange, ♋ yellow-orange, ♌ yellow, ♍ yellow-green, ♎ green, ♏ blue-green, ♐ blue, ♑ blue-violet, ♒ violet, and ♓ red-violet. —APF

14. Trithemius, *op. cit.*

Sign	Lineal Figure	Natural Color	Complementary Color
♈ Aries	Pentagram (5)	Scarlet	Emerald Green
♉ Taurus	Heptagram (7)	Red Orange	Green Blue
♊ Gemini	Octagram (8)	Orange	Blue
♋ Cancer	Enneagram (9)	Amber	Indigo
♌ Leo	Hexagram (6)	Greenish Yellow	Violet
♍ Virgo	Octagram (8)	Yellowish Green	Crimson
♎ Libra	Heptagram (7)	Emerald Green	Scarlet
♏ Scorpio	Pentagram (5)	Green Blue	Red Orange
♐ Sagittarius	Square (4)	Blue	Orange
♑ Capricorn	Triangle (3)	Indigo	Amber
♒ Aquarius	Triangle (3)	Violet	Greenish Yellow
♓ Pisces	Square (4)	Crimson	Yellowish Green

Fig. 20. Table of Figures and Colors

Joseph Peterson adds the following with respect to the four kings:

> There is considerable variation in identification of the four kings of the cardinal directions. Here are a few: Agrippa, OP2.7 has (E, W, N, S): "Oriens. Paymon.Egyn.Amaymon", however in OP3.24 he says, "Urieus, King of the East; Amaymon, King of the South; Paymon, King of the West; Egin, King of the North, which the Hebrew Doctors perhaps call more rightly thus, Samuel, Azazel, Azael, Mahazuel," (See Cichus In Sphaeram Mundi, f. 21 apud quem: Zoroa. Fragm. O104; cf. Salom. ff. 28v–29r; sed addict. K: Reuchl. Arte 3, sig. O7r) MC has: "Bael, Moymon, Poymon, Egyn" or "Asmodel in the East, Amaymon in the South, Paymon in the West, and Aegym

in the North"; "Oriens, Paymon, Egyn, and Amaymon"; or "Amodeo [sic] (king of the East), Paymon (king of the West), Egion (king of the North), and Maimon."[15]

Some modern versions of the Table of Practice incorporate the archangels called upon in the Lesser Ritual of the Pentagram as the "kings" of the four directions. This has been the subject of some contentious online debate as to whether or not this change breaks the original system in some way. In my opinion the revised version is workable for celestial entities. However, as the four kings given by Agrippa (Oriens/Urieus, Amaymon, Paymon, and Egyn/Egin for East, South, West, and North) represent chthonic forces that complement the celestial forces represented by the planetary angels, they make the Table more complete and are therefore a better choice.

The Table of Practice may be thought of as a constructed universe in miniature in which the magician interacts with the spirits. As the universe we inhabit comprises both the celestial and chthonic poles, in order to achieve maximum resonance with the physical world this constructed universe should also include both celestial and chthonic elements. Just as an all-chthonic table misses this mark, an all-celestial one is no better. It is when both polarities are engaged that the most powerful magical effects can be conjured and sent forth.

Just as the title suggests, *The Art of Drawing Spirits into Crystals* concerns the use of a scrying crystal to contact the conjured spirits. John Dee and Edward Kelley are probably the magicians best known for using this method, but Dee was familiar

---

15. Joseph H. Peterson, note to his online edition of *Trithemius: The Art of Drawing Spirits into Crystals*, *loc. cit.*

Agrippa, OP is of course *De Occulta Philosophia libri tres ("Three Books on Occult Philosophy")*. In book II, chapter 7, Agrippa's Scale of the Quaternary lists in the Underworld both "Four Princes of the Demons (*Quatuor principes dæmoniorum*) Over the Four Angles of the Globe" (idenitfied as Oriens, Paymon, Egyn, and Amaymon) and "Four Princes of the Demons (*Quatuor principes dæmoniorum*) Wreaking Harm in the Elements" (specified as Samael, Azazel, Azael, and Mahazael, with the Hebrew spellings of their names סמאל, עזאזל, עזאל, and מהזאל). In book III, chapter 24, he explains that "Among the evil spirits, four most powerful kings are set over the rest," and again gives both sets of names as in Peterson's note. *Cichus In Sphærum Mundi* is Cecco d'Ascoli's magical commentary on Johannes of Sacrobosco's *Treatise on the Sphere*, in which Cecco discusses Oriens, Paymon, Amaymon, and Egim (spelled Orion, Pagimon, Agimon, and Egin in the copy of *Ceci Æsculani Tractatus Super Sphæram* in BnF MS lat. 7337) as the spirits of the four quarters invoked in the "Zoroastrian Art," and notes that they desire sacrifices of human blood and of flesh from the corpse of a human or a cat. Sadly but unsurprisingly, Cecco's commentary was banned, and copies were burned at the stake along with the author in 1327. *K: Reuchl. Arte 3, sig. O7ʳ* indicates the location near the end of Johann Reuchlin's 1517 dialogue *De Arte Cabalistica* where we read—after a description of Michael, Gabriel, Uriel, and Raphael as the four *antesignani* ("commanders before the banners") of the army of God—that "In like manner, in the army of Satan, the standard-bearing punishers סמאל, עזאזל, עזאל, and מהזאל (Samael, Azazel, Azael, Mahazael) carry the most wide-spread flags." Incidentally, early in his career, Agrippa taught Reuchlin's book to students, and it is almost certainly where he learned the Hebrew names of the infernal kings of the quarters. —APF

with the works of Trithemius and likely adapted his methods for use with what came to be known as the Enochian system. This crystal should be clear and spherical. It is placed on a plate of the design shown in Fig. 21.

To scry with this apparatus, the magician lights incense and a single taper candle on either side of the plate and stares into the crystal. Unfortunately, this method can be difficult to learn, and seems to require some amount of natural talent. My great-grandmother was a medium and I have no trouble "hearing" and conversing with conjured spirits, but I have never been very good at this sort of eyes-open scrying. As I understand it, the candles and incense smoke create some sort of optical effect which can induce trance in some individuals. I am not one of them. However, I did discover a simple trick that gets around my scrying problems, and while I cannot say how

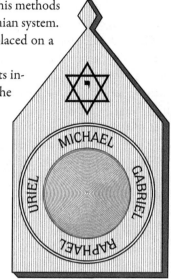

Fig. 21. Trithemian Crystal Frame

well it will work for anyone else, the first time I tried it I was surprised by its effectiveness.

This trick is to use a light and sound machine, or "brain machine," which people commonly employ to enhance meditation. The model that I use is a Photosonix Nova Pro, which is one of the more expensive ones, but the program that works best is a basic Alpha/Theta meditation program. This is a very popular program and even the economy models will have it. It works best if you have a group with one person serving as the scryer, so he or she can let the program run while the other members open the temple and conjure the spirit, but if you are using it on your own you can perform the ritual up to the conjuration and then pause to run the program for about ten minutes. After that, light the incense and candles, deliver the conjuration, and stare deeply into the crystal.

For the zodiacal angels I use the incenses attributed to the corresponding signs in *Liber 777*. These are shown in Fig. 22.

Today even the hard-to-find ones are available online, and in addition you can make substitutions so long as you keep your general attributions straight. A sign may be thought of as the combination of a planet and an element, and I remember years ago having a difficult time finding onycha for a Cancer evocation. I wound up using a mixture of incenses attributed to the Moon and Water. The incense worked fine, and the operation was successful.

When burning incense for an evocation into the crystal it is important that the incense be placed so that the smoke passes between the operator and the crystal.

This contributes to the optical effect that aids the eyes-open scrying process.

Celestials such as the zodiacal angels are usually summoned into a Table of Practice situated within the circle, unlike the setup for chthonics in which the triangle is placed outside the circle and a larger scrying mirror is generally employed rather than a crystal. For the zodiacal angels, then, the arrangement of the temple should look something like that shown in Fig. 23.

The sigil of the spirit must also be incorporated in some fashion for all these systems. It may be placed within the triangle or drawn in some (erasable) manner onto the crystal or mirror. Something like a grease pencil or dry-erase marker will work well for this purpose.

Performing practical magick with the zodiacal angels is not necessarily confined to conjuring them into crystals for the purpose of scrying. The crystal is simply a device that assists with communication, not the only viable spell focus that you can employ. When empowering a talisman, for example, so long as you can "hear" the spirit in a mediumistic sense well enough to communicate, the talisman itself can be placed on the Table of Practice in lieu of the crystal.

Sign	Incense
♈ Aries	Dragon's Blood
♉ Taurus	Storax
♊ Gemini	Wormwood
♋ Cancer	Onycha
♌ Leo	Olibanum
♍ Virgo	Narcissus
♎ Libra	Galbanum
♏ Scorpio	Siamese Benzoin, Opoponax
♐ Sagittarius	Lign-Aloes (Aloeswood)
♑ Capricorn	Musk, Civet, Myrrh
♒ Aquarius	Galbanum
♓ Pisces	Ambergris

*Fig. 22. **Zodiacal Incenses***

The spirit can then be conjured and charged to empower the device to perform some function within the entity's sphere of influence. This talisman should always bear the sigil of the entity and be constructed of materials in some fashion that are related to the nature of the angel.

Small bags work well as zodiacal talismans. They can be purchased in a variety of colors such as those shown in Fig. 20 and filled with herbs, stones, and so forth related to the nature of the angel. You can then draw the sigil on the outside with

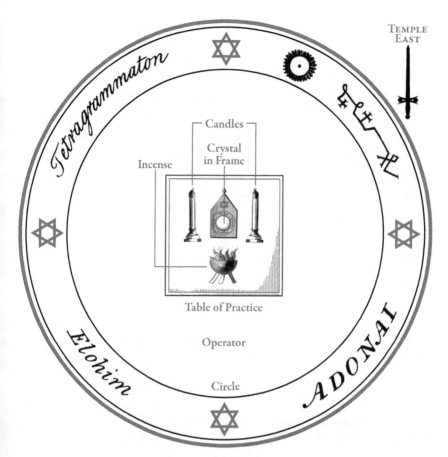

TEMPLE
EAST

Candles

Crystal
in Frame

Incense

Table of Practice

Operator

Circle

Tetragrammaton

Elohim

ADONAI

Fig. 23. The Temple Arrangement

a permanent marker. The sigil can also be engraved onto a metal appropriate to the sign's ruling planet. Some of these associations from *Liber 777* are shown in Fig. 24.

The stones shown in parentheses are those attributed to the planet ruling the sign, which may be substituted as necessary. Onyx, for example, is much easier to come by than black diamond for a Capricorn talisman. Also, it should be noted that the stones used here need not be gem quality. Raw rubies and emeralds, for example, can be obtained relatively inexpensively and will work fine for talismanic work.

A magical link may also be placed on the Table of Practice. This is for spells that are aimed at an external target. If such a spell is being anchored by a bag-style talisman it should be placed inside the bag. Otherwise, the talisman should be in contact with it while being charged.

There are two kinds of magical links, *similarity* links and *contagion* links. A similarity link is an image or representation of the external target, while a contagion

Sign	Plants	Stones	Metals
♈ Aries	Tiger lily, geranium, olive	Ruby (any red stone)	Iron, steel
♉ Taurus	Mallow, all giant trees	Topaz (emerald, turquoise)	Copper
♊ Gemini	Hybrids, orchids	Alexandrite, tourmaline, Iceland spar (opal, agate)	Mixture (all alloys)
♋ Cancer	Lotus	Amber (moonstone, pearl, crystal)	Silver
♌ Leo	Sunflower	Cat's eye	Gold, brass
♍ Virgo	Snowdrop, lily, narcissus, mistletoe	Peridot (opal, agate)	Mixture (all alloys)
♎ Libra	Aloe	Emerald (turquoise)	Copper
♏ Scorpio	Cactus, nettle, all poisonous plants	Snakestone (ruby, any red stone)	Iron, steel
♐ Sagittarius	Rush	Jacinth (amethyst, lapis lazuli)	Tin
♑ Capricorn	Indian hemp, orchis root, thistle, yohimba	Black diamond (onyx)	Lead
♒ Aquarius	Olive, coconut	Artificial glass, chalcedony (onyx)	Lead
♓ Pisces	Opium, mangrove	Pearl (amethyst, lapis lazuli)	Tin

Fig. 24. Table of Zodiacal Plants, Stones, and Metals

link is some item that has been in direct contact with the target, or even was once part of their body like hair or nail clippings. Such items form a connection to the target, and allow the talisman or spirit to act upon them. Placing them within the containment structure formed by the Table of Art insulates the magician from the conjured magical force.

Some schools of magick teach that spells cast can "rebound" in various ways. This is not a principle of the magick itself, but rather a consequence of sloppy casting that does not employ a properly constructed Table of Art. In such circumstances the conjured magical force can affect the magician just as it affects the target. With spells such as healing rituals this is not necessarily a significant problem, but for more negative magical operations it often can be. This should not be taken as license to perform such operations, but it is important to keep in mind that ethics and magical technology are completely separate concepts.

Many traditional grimoire magicians work without modern ritual forms such as pentagram and hexagram rituals. However, I employ them in my own operations because they seem to facilitate stronger magical effects than the prayers and conjurations alone. The main standard ritual forms I employ are the Lesser and Greater Rituals of the Pentagram and Hexagram found in Crowley's *Liber O*, and his Star Ruby and Star Sapphire. I also have created my own custom forms for Enochian work, found in *Mastering the Mystical Heptarchy*[16] and *Mastering the Great Table*,[17] and my magical working group makes use of a custom form of the Lesser Ritual of the Hexagram that can be found on my blog.[18]

Where my methods depart from how these rituals are generally taught is the use of what I call the *Operant Field* method. Most of the Golden Dawn orders teach that the Lesser Banishing Ritual of the Pentagram and Lesser Banishing Ritual of the Hexagram should be used to open and close all magical rites. The problem with this is that the Lesser Ritual of the Pentagram is microcosmic and the Lesser Ritual of the Hexagram is macrocosmic, and what I have found over years of testing the forms is that opening and closing this way has a tendency to "shut down" ongoing magical work. This even seems to be true when using forms like the Opening by Watchtower, which Israel Regardie wrote to facilitate practical magical work.

The main change with the Operant Field method is that for the Lesser rites you pair a Banishing Pentagram Ritual with an Invoking Hexagram Ritual. You then close your ceremony with the Banishing Pentagram Ritual alone. With this method, your magical procedure should look like this:

→ 1. Lesser Banishing Ritual of the Pentagram. This clears the mind of the practitioner and detaches his or her field of awareness from other ongoing ritual work.

→ 2. Prayers of Purification and Devotion. These further serve to clear and purify the consciousness of the operator.

→ 3. Lesser Invoking Ritual of the Hexagram. This engages the practitioner's microcosmic sphere of awareness with the macrocosmic elements of the exterior universe.

---

16. Scott Michael Stenwick, *Mastering the Mystical Heptarchy* (Los Angeles: Pendraig Publishing, 2011).

17. Scott Michael Stenwick, *Mastering the Great Table* ([n.p.]: Pendraig Publishing, 2013).

18. Scott Michael Stenwick, *Augoeides: Spiritual Technology for a New Aeon* (http://ananael.blogspot.com).

➔ 4. Preliminary Invocation. This aligns the consciousness of the operator with that of the macrocosmic divine force and confers the authority to conjure spirits.

➔ 5. Greater Invoking Ritual of the Pentagram (elements) or Hexagram (planets and signs). This tunes the working space to the appropriate spiritual force.

➔ 6. The Conjuration of the Spirit, Communication and/or Charge, and License to Depart. This portion of the operation generally follows grimoire lines, in which the spirit is called, conversed with or given a task, and finally sent on its way or sent forth to accomplish the task at hand.

➔ 7. Lesser Banishing Ritual of the Pentagram. This serves to clear and disconnect the mind of the practitioner from the magical force set in motion by the rite or the interaction with the spirit.

When using the Thelemic forms, the Star Ruby replaces the Lesser Ritual of the Pentagram and the Star Sapphire replaces the Lesser Ritual of the Hexagram. The Greater Rituals of the Pentagram and Hexagram remain the same.

Avoiding the use of the banishing forms of the Lesser Ritual of the Hexagram and Greater Rituals of the Pentagram and Hexagram allows for your magical operation to reach its full potential and operate over a longer period of time. If a ritual needs to be shut down, the practitioner can always perform the Lesser Banishing Ritual of the Pentagram and Lesser Banishing Ritual of the Hexagram together to stop the effect. I have found, though, that for the most part magical rites rarely go awry or cause problems, so it is rare that this becomes necessary, even when you are engaged in multiple ongoing operations.

One of the comments that I got from a Golden Dawn magician when I first posted this method on my blog was to the effect that the "full shutdown" problem with the Lesser Banishing Ritual of the Hexagram could be worked around by anchoring your rituals with talismans, which is true. But in that context the much greater complexity of the traditional Golden Dawn method seems more a bug than a feature. As in software design, elegance and simplicity count, especially when working with subtle forces such as those involved in consciousness. The strong practical results reported by grimoire magicians attest to the observation that in many cases a simpler, more direct ritual structure than the complex formulas of traditional lodge-style magick can get better results.

In my experience, the Operant Field method is something of a happy medium. It works better for me than the full traditional ritual sequence, but at the same time brings in just enough of the complexity and control inherent in lodge-style work. I have also experimented with omitting the forms completely, but found that my results were not as strong. At the same time, this may simply be the method most suited to my personal psychology. As such, while the ritual that accompanies this article is written with the Operant Field method forms, you should feel free to experiment as you see fit, whether that involves omitting them or adding additional components appropriate to the system that you personally practice.

Purification practices that maintain focus on the magical work at hand over an extended period of time are part of most old grimoire procedures. Generally speaking, in order to conjure a spirit the magician was expected to undergo a period of such work prior to the operation proper, lasting anywhere from a week or two to many months. Many modern magicians find value in following these instructions to the letter.

Further prayers of purification and consecration, generally written from a Christian perspective, are also part of the standard grimoire procedure. Trithemius gives the following:

> Oh, God! who art the author of all good things, strengthen, I beseech thee, thy poor servant, that he may stand fast, without fear, through this dealing and work; enlighten, I beseech thee, oh Lord! the dark understanding of thy creature, so that his spiritual eye may be opened to see and know thy angelic spirits descending here in this crystal: (*then lay thy hand on the crystal saying,*) and thou, oh inanimate creature of God, be sanctified and consecrated, and blessed to this purpose, that no evil phantasy may appear in thee; or, if they do gain ingress into this creature, they may be constrained to speak intelligibly, and truly, and without the least ambiguity, for Christ's sake. Amen. And forasmuch as thy servant here standing before thee, oh, Lord! desires neither evil treasures, nor injury to his neighbour, nor hurt to any living creature, grant him the power of descrying those celestial spirits or intelligences, that may appear in this crystal, and whatever good gifts (whether the power of healing infirmities, or of imbibing wisdom, or discovering any evil likely to afflict any person or family, or any other good gift thou mayest be pleased to bestow on me, enable me, by thy wisdom and mercy, to use whatever I may receive to the honour of thy holy name. Grant this for thy son Christ's sake. *Amen.*[19]

A similar prayer, referred to as the Prayer of Enoch, is found in the Enochian system and included as part of my Enochian evocation procedure in my *Mastering Enochian Magick* series. When I was writing the series, I included it as written because it is a "received text" that was provided to John Dee and Edward Kelley, and among Thelemites it has proven one of the most controversial portions of the procedure. It should be noted that the seemingly self-deprecating portions of these prayers serve to direct the focus of the magician's consciousness off of him or herself and onto the work at hand, which contributes to the transpersonal perspective necessary for performing the most effective magical operations. Furthermore, in the context of the Operant Field model, this augments the "microcosmic banishing" in which the

---

19. Trithemius, *op. cit.*

magician's consciousness is purified and transformed to make way for the invocation of the macrocosmic elements.

Therefore, when using modern ritual forms, such prayers should follow the Lesser Banishing Pentagram Ritual and precede the Lesser Invoking Hexagram Ritual. Also, I highly recommend that non-Christian magicians rewrite the prayers to match godforms more appropriate to their spiritual beliefs. The exact wording of the old grimoires is not where the power behind magical operations comes from, the shared roots of 'grimoire' and 'grammar' notwithstanding. This power emanates from both the practitioner and the conjured spirit, and as such it makes little sense for a magician to pray to a deity that he or she does not even recognize. On the other hand, the basic tone and function of the prayer should be preserved so that mapping the procedure onto a new pantheon or schema does not impede its effectiveness.

In my experience as a modern magician, ongoing daily practice can take the place of many of the purification practices, so long as it is adhered to diligently and includes the proper elements. The daily practice that I personally employ consists of a banishing pentagram ritual, invoking hexagram ritual, and a simple ritual such as the Middle Pillar or the Elevenfold Seal from Crowley's *Liber Reguli*[20] that serves to raise energy and identify my personal consciousness with that of the transpersonal divine. I follow that with a brief Holy Guardian Angel invocation, which you should write yourself. This invocation may be performed whether or not you have made contact with the angel, and may be employed as part of a more formal rite aimed at establishing full knowledge and conversation. If you have already made it part of your daily practice regimen, its use will be that much more natural in this context.

Trithemius follows the prayer of purification with prayers for the consecration of the circle and scrying apparatus. For the circle, he gives the following, to be said while tracing it with the wand.

> In the name of the blessed Trinity, I consecrate this piece of ground for our defence; so that no evil spirit may have power to break these bounds prescribed here, through Jesus Christ our Lord. *Amen.*

For the scrying apparatus consisting of the crystal, candles, and censer he gives the following, to be said as the incense is placed in the censer.

> I conjure thee, oh thou creature of fire! by him who created all things both in heaven and earth, and in the sea, and in every other place whatever, that

---

20. Aleister Crowley, *Liber V vel Reguli*, an appendix in The Master Therion [Aleister Crowley], *Magick in Theory and Practice* ([Paris]: Lecram Press, 1929; later republished in Aleister Crowley, John Symonds, and Kenneth Grant, *Magick* (London: Routledge & Kegan Paul, 1973); and in Aleister Crowley and Israel Regardie, *Gems from the Equinox* (St. Paul, Minn.: Llewellyn Publications, 1974). —APF

forthwith thou cast away every phantasm from thee, that no hurt whatsoever shall be done in any thing. Bless, oh Lord, this creature of fire, and
sanctify it that it may be blessed, and that they may fill up the power and
virtue of their odours; so neither the enemy, nor any false imagination, may
enter into them; through our Lord Jesus Christ. *Amen.*

When used with modern forms, these or similar prayers of consecration should
follow the invoking hexagram ritual, so that their intent may span the microcosmic
and macrocosmic realms.

The preliminary invocation follows. While much has been written regarding the
"shamanic" nature of grimoire practices, it is this step of the operation that most
clearly distinguishes grimoire magick from the sort of spiritual work generally classified as shamanism. It is during the preliminary invocation that the consciousness
of the magician identifies with that of the divine. This may be perceived as a patron
deity, Holy Guardian Angel, or even the dynamic ground of being itself. By opening up his or her consciousness in this manner, the magician takes on attributes of
this cosmic level of awareness including the authority to call and command spirits.

As I commonly work with Tahuti, I often employ the invocation from Crowley's
Liber Israfel,[21] verses 4–14, for this purpose. A preliminary invocation of this type
from any of the grimoire systems, especially one with which you have done extensive work, should also prove sufficient. The primary function here is the exaltation
and expansion of your consciousness, to "enflame thyself in prayer."

Once the ritual space is established and the preliminary invocation has been performed, modern magicians employ the Greater Invoking Rituals of the Pentagram
and Hexagram to tune the working space to the nature of the desired spirit. There is
some disagreement over whether to use a pentagram of hexagram ritual to tune the
space for a zodiacal sign. Both can be appropriate, as each sign is related to both an
element and a planet. Crowley's *Liber O* gives the hexagram ritual for zodiacal signs,
while some of the Golden Dawn orders teach that the pentagram ritual should be
employed instead. I learned the pentagram and hexagram forms from *Liber O*, and
as such use the hexagram ritual. But keep in mind that experience is always the best
teacher; if you find that for you the pentagram ritual works better, by all means
keep using it. I also have known magicians who used both, to keep all of their bases
covered.

Still, according to the Operant Field model, the hexagram ritual is the better
choice. As the pentagram represents the microcosm and the hexagram represents
the macrocosm, the pentagram ritual might be appropriate for work isolated to
your own sphere of consciousness as it calls up the sign's microcosmic manifesta-

---

21. Aleister Crowley, *Liber Israfel sub figurā LXIV*, in *The Equinox*, vol. 1, no. 7, March 1912 (London: Weiland & Co.).

tion. However, for any sort of practical work—the focus of this article—you need the sign's macrocosmic manifestation, which is more easily accessed via the hexagram ritual. This is even the case for work that is intended to affect both your sphere of consciousness and the world around you, as the microcosmic realm is a subset of the transpersonal macrocosm.

To perform the Greater Ritual of the Hexagram for a sign, the shape of the hexagram will be that of the planet that rules the sign. So, for example, for Aries the hexagram traced will be that of Mars. The planetary hexagrams are derived from the position of the relevant spheres on the Tree of Life in Hermetic Qabalah, as shown in Fig. 25.

To trace the invoking hexagram for a planet, start at the indicated point and trace clockwise. To trace the banishing hexagram for a planet, start at the same point and trace counterclockwise. The solar hexagram is a spe-

Fig. 25. The Planetary Hexagram on the Tree of Life

cial case, as it occupies the center of the figure. It is formed by tracing each of the other six hexagrams in the Chaldean order beginning with that of Saturn and ending with that of the Moon.

As the hexagram corresponds to a sign, it should be visualized in the natural color indicated in Fig. 20. As you trace, vibrate the word of power אראריתא (Ararita). Then, you trace the symbol of the sign in the center of the figure in the complementary color, again from Fig. 20. Note that the colors of the signs are set up so that the complement of each color is the natural color of the opposing sign. Finally, as you trace the symbol, you vibrate the corresponding God-Name indicated in Fig. 5.

Some groups teach that the Keyword Analysis that is used in the Lesser Ritual of the Hexagram should be repeated to open and close the Greater Ritual of the Hexagram, but I have never done this in my own magical work. My feeling is that since you have already performed it twice with the Lesser Invoking Ritual of the Hexagram, it is not necessary to perform it twice more with the Greater Ritual. Personally, I just start in the east and go clockwise, tracing the hexagram and vibrating the words of power to each direction. Finally, I return to face the east and conclude the rite with some sort of unifying statement.

For the signs of the zodiac, a very effective unifying statement can be construct-ed from *Liber 963*, also called *The Treasure-House of Images*.[22] This is a Thelemic text mostly written and compiled by J.F.C. Fuller under the guidance of Crowley, but as it calls upon "God" in the generic sense, it is suitable for practitioners of most spiritual paths. *Liber 963* was originally intended as a mystical work, in which the student would determine his or her rising sign, and then on a daily basis recite one of twelve chapters representing the state of consciousness related to the sign. For those who did not know their rising sign, a thirteenth chapter representing the "Twelvefold Unification of God and the Unity Thereof" was added to those cor-responding to the twelve signs and attributed to the Sun.

Liber 963 attributes the first line of each of the zodiacal chapters to the sign that it represents, and then attributes the next eleven to the other signs in order. Finally, a verse attributed to the Sun sums up the chapter, providing "The Unity Thereof." As practical magical work involves the shifting of consciousness through a progres-sion of states as the operation unfolds, and in the context of the zodiac, a complete movement includes all twelve signs, a highly effective invocation can be constructed by combining the line attributed to the sign with which you are working from each of the twelve chapters, starting with the "Affirmation" chapter attributed to Aries. The resulting twelve lines can then be sealed with the final line of the "Unification" chapter.

As an example, the resulting text would read as follows for Aries:

1. O Thou snow-clad volcan of scarlet fire, Thou flame-crested pillar of fury! Yea, as I approach Thee, Thou departest from me like unto a wisp of smoke blown forth from the window of my house.

2. O my God, Thou Mighty One, Thou Creator of all things, I renounce unto Thee the crimson lust of the chase, and the blast of the brazen war-horns, and all the gleaming of the spears; so that like an hart I may be brought to bay in Thine arms, and be consumed in the unutterable joy of Thine everlasting rapture.

3. O Thou flame of the horned storm-clouds, that sunderest their desola-tion, that outroarest the winds; I swear to Thee by the gleaming sandals of the stars, to climb beyond the summits of the mountains, and rend Thy robe of purple thunders with a sword of silvery light.

---

22. J.F.C. Fuller [and Aleister Crowley], *Liber ΘΕΣΑΥΡΟΥ ΕΙΔΩΛΩΝ [Liber Thesaurou Eidōlōn, "Book of the Treasure-House of Images"] sub figurā* DCCCLXIII, in *The Equinox*, vol. 1, no. 3, Special Supplement, March 1910 (London: Simpkin, Marshall, Hamilton, Kent & Co. Ltd.). Republished in Aleister Crowley and J.F.C. Fuller, *The Pathworkings of Aleister Crowley: The Treasure House of Images* (Tempe, Ariz.: New Falcon Publications, 1994). —APF

4. O Thou Sovran Lord of primæval Baresarkers, who huntest with dawn the dappled deer of twilight, and whose engines of war are blood-crested comets. I know Thee! O Thou flame-crowned Self-luminous One, the lash of whose whip gathered the ancient worlds, and looseth the blood from the virgin clouds of heaven.

5. O Glory be to Thee, O God my God; for I behold Thee in the smoke-veil'd fire of the mountains: Thou hast inflamed them as lions that scent a fallow deer, so that they may rage forth the Glory of Thy Name.

6. O Thou mighty God, make me as a white ram that is athirst in a sun-scorched desert of bitterness; I beseech Thee, O Thou great God! That I may seek the deep waters of Thy Wisdom, and plunge into the whiteness of Thine effulgence: O Thou God, my God!

7. O Thou effulgence of burning love, who pursueth the dawn as a youth pursueth a rose-lipped maiden; rend me with the fierce kisses of Thy mouth, so that in the battle of our lips I may be drenched by the snow-pure fountains of Thy bliss.

8. O Thou God of the Nothingness of All Things! Thou who art neither the fivefold root of Nature, nor the fire-crested helm of her Master: O Thou who art not the Emperor of Eternal Time, nor the warrior shout that rocketh the Byss of Space! I deny Thee by the powers of mine understanding; Raise me in the unity of Thy might, and suckle me at the swol'n breasts of Thine all-pervading Nothingness, for Thou art all and none of these in the fullness of Thy Not-Being.

9. Ah! but I rejoice in Thee, O Thou my God; Thou cloud-hooded bastion of the stormy skies; Thou lightning anvil of angled swords; Thou gloomy forge of the thunderbolt: Yea, I rejoice in Thee, Thou all-subduing Crown of Splendour; O Thou hero-souled helm of endless victory! I rejoice, yea, I shout with gladness! till the mad rivers rush roaring through the woods, and my re-echoing voice danceth like a ram among the hills, for the Glory and Splendour of Thy Name.

10. O my God, suckle me with truth and be merciful unto me, as I humble myself before Thee; for all my agony of anguish is but as a quail struggling in the jaws of an hungry wolf.

11. O woe unto me, my God, woe unto me; for all my works are as a coiled-up sleeper who hath overslept the day, even the dawn that hovereth as a hawk in the void. Yet in the gloom of mine awakening do I see, across the breasts of night, Thy shadowed form.

12. O what art Thou, O God my God, Thou eternal incarnating immortal One? O Thou wielder of life and death! Thou whose breasts are as the full breasts of a mother, yet in Thy hand Thou carriest the sword of destruction! O how can I cleave the shield of Thy might as a little wanton child may burst a floating bubble with the breast-feather of a dove?

13. O Thou Unity of all things: as the sun that rolleth through the twelve mansions of the skies, so art Thou, O God my God. I cannot slay Thee, for Thou art everywhere; lo! though I lick up the Boundless Light, the Bound-

less, and the Not, there still shall I find Thee, Thou Unity of Unities, Thou
Oneness, O Thou perfect Nothingness of Bliss![23]

While these statements may seem long to those more used to the concise statements
found in many modern magical operations, they are quite effective in terms of tuning the consciousness of the magician and the working space of the temple to the
attributes of a particular sign. If you would rather use a briefer statement, the final
line on its own embodies the fundamental nature of the primary word of power
ARARITA, which is a Hebrew *notariqon* (or acronym) for *Achad Rosh Achdotho
Rosh Ichudo Temuratho Achad*, meaning "One is His Beginning; One is His Individuality; His Permutation is One." But I recommend trying the full version a few
times and seeing how it works before you discard it in favor of a shorter statement.

It should also be noted that for planetary work, you can combine the planet
with which you are working and the sect of the hour in which the operation is being performed to yield a sign, and thus employ *Liber 963* in a similar fashion. As a
related example, if you were performing an evocation of Mars during one of the day
hours of Mars you would use the Aries (Mars–Diurnal) invocation above, but for
the same operation performed during one of the night hours of Mars you would
construct another for Scorpio (Mars–Nocturnal). For all hours of the Sun, you can
either use Leo or construct a Sun invocation from the final Sun lines of each chapter. For all hours of the Moon you can use Cancer. *Liber 963* also includes two lunar
chapters that begin and end the text, but they are not structured like the zodiacal
chapters, and I have yet to experiment with them to see how well they work in a
ritual context.

Once the space is tuned to the appropriate sign, you may proceed to conjure the
corresponding Angel by the God-Name, both of which can be found in Figure 5.
Trithemius gives the following as an example:

> In the name of the blessed and holy Trinity, I do desire thee, thou strong
> mighty angel, Michael [or any other angel or spirit], that if it be the divine
> will of him who is called Tetragrammaton, the Holy God, the Father, that
> thou take upon thee some shape as best becometh thy celestial nature, and
> appear to us visibly here in this crystal, and answer our demands in as far
> as we shall not transgress the bounds of the divine mercy and goodness, by
> requesting unlawful knowledge; but that thou wilt graciously shew us what
> things are most profitable for us to know and do, to the glory and honour
> of his divine Majesty, who liveth and reigneth, world without end. Amen.
>
> Lord, thy will be done on earth, as it is in heaven; —make clean our
> hearts within us, and take not thy Holy Spirit from us. O Lord, by thy name
> we have called him, suffer him to administer unto us. And that all things

---

23. Assembled from the chapters of *Liber 963*.

may work together for thy honour and glory, to whom with thee, the Son, and blessed Spirit, be ascribed all might, majesty, and dominion. Amen.[24]

This will work perfectly fine for a Christian magician, replacing Michael with the name of the zodiacal angel, and the word Tetragrammaton with the God-Name. As a Thelemic magician, though, I employ a much shorter conjuration that simply conjures the Angel by the God-Name, as shown in the ritual template following this commentary. I use the term 'behest' in my conjuration rather than 'demand,' because, as I noted at the beginning of this article, I treat spirits as independent individuals. The word 'behest' means "an urgent prompting," and is not the same as a command. I am inviting them by divine authority, and I do want them to appear, but I also am not attempting to force them to do anything contrary to their nature.

I state this short conjuration three times, and then vibrate the name of the angel repeatedly until I perceive its presence. One of the most common manifestations with zodiacal angels is a tangible feeling of cold emanating from the Table of Practice. I have also experimented with placing the probe of an EMF detector[25] within the Table, and in my experience, most of the time when the angel arrives, the needle will rise. The effect is small, so usually the device needs to be on its most sensitive setting for it to be very noticeable, but I have found the increase to be surprisingly reliable compared to control runs where no angel is conjured and the needle is simply observed.

The charge should always be composed by the individual magician, and as such there are few hard and fast rules for constructing it. Generally speaking, ordering the spirits around and making threats works poorly. Zodiacal angels are highly intelligent spirits and are particularly knowledgeable within their sphere of influence. In a few cases I have presented a charge that has been refused, but in those cases the angel has always been willing to tell me who I should be conjuring instead and why. I have known of magicians who push on under those circumstances and do their best to force the spirit to comply, but even if they can get their spells to work in the short term, the results never seem to last and do not turn out as well as hoped.

In order to get the best results, you should keep in mind that as the magician you are ultimately the 'boss' of your operation, but you want to be the best boss you possibly can be. Think about managers for whom you have particularly liked working. Most likely they treated you with respect, assigned you tasks appropriate to your skills, and offered a vision of success that you found appealing. If you treat the spirits in this manner, it is hard to go wrong. Not only will cultivating a deep understanding of the zodiacal signs and their attributions show the angels that you are serious about your work, it will also help you pick the right angel every time

---

24. Trithemius, *op. cit.*

25. An EMF detector or EMF meter measures variations in the ambient electromagnetic field. —APF

who will be happy to help with whatever tasks you assign or accurately answer any questions you ask.

As with most grimoire spirits, making offerings to the zodiacal angels can be highly effective. Incense is a traditional offering with a long history and should be considered as such, but other substances such as candles, essential oils, and alcohol of varying sorts can all be employed as well. My preference for offerings is to use substances that will be consumed, either by burning or evaporation. Some modern grimoire magicians have adapted techniques from traditional African systems that employ other offerings such as food that is offered to the spirit for a period of time and then consumed or disposed of in some manner, but I have little experience with those sorts of offerings and have never been asked for them. The best way to find the ideal offering for a particular zodiacal angel is of course to conjure and simply ask; as they are independent individuals, they all have their own preferences.

One important point about offerings that many sources get wrong is that humans and spirits value completely different things, and the effectiveness of an offering has nothing to do with how valuable you as a magician find it to be and everything to do with what the spirit thinks of it. You can offer the most expensive substance imaginable, but if the spirit does not like it you are wasting your money. While the psychological-only model of magick would suggest that the more money you spend and effort you exert on obtaining and offering the more effective it will be, in my experience this is just not so and presents one more piece of data supporting the existence of spirits as independent, objective entities.

In my own operations, I commonly use candles dressed with fluid condensers prepared along the lines suggested by Franz Bardon, using an alcohol base and appropriate plant materials as categorized in *Liber 777*, which the zodiacal angels all seem to appreciate.

When you have finished conversing with the angel, delivering your charge, and/or consecrating your talisman, you end the session by sending the spirit on its way with the License to Depart. This is essentially the opposite of the conjuration step, in that instead of calling up the spirit by a name of power, you release it under the auspices of that same authority. Trithemius gives the following license to depart:

> Thou great and mighty spirit, inasmuch as thou camest in peace and in the name of the ever blessed and righteous Trinity, so in this name thou mayest depart, and return to us when we call thee in his name to whom every knee doth bow down. Fare thee well, Michael; peace be between us, through our blessed Lord Jesus Christ. Amen.

Then the spirit will depart; at which point you should say,

> To God the Father, eternal Spirit, fountain of Light, the Son, and Holy Ghost, be all honour and glory, world without end. Amen.

As with the conjuration, my adaptation of this is shorter and less sectarian. The basic principle, though, is the same. The spirit should be let go in a friendly manner, without animosity or hostility. Mistreating a spirit at this point may or may not affect the operation in question, but it likely will result in less effective operations involving the same spirit from that point forward.

Finally, if you opened your ritual using pentagram and hexagram rituals, close it by repeating the Lesser Banishing Ritual of the Pentagram. As this is a microcosmic ritual, it serves to disconnect your field of awareness from the operation without shutting down the magick that you have set in motion. As you presumably want any practical effect to continue after you close the temple, you will not want to use either of the banishing hexagram rituals at this point.

This, then, provides a general but relatively complete overview of working with the angels of the twelve zodiacal signs. Adding these angels to your repertoire opens up powers and capacities above and beyond those of the elements and planets, and mastery of the zodiacal art completes the process of macrocosmic integration that begins with the planetary work. May you thus progress rapidly towards the accomplishment of this Great Work, in full alignment with the joyous company of heaven.

Zodiacal Evocation Ritual

0. Setup

The temple is arranged with the circle and the Table of Practice serving as an altar with incense and taper candles flanking the triangle (Fig. 23). In the center of the Table should be placed the focus of the rite.

➼ *If a crystal is used, a piece of paper or parchment bearing the sigil of the angel should be placed beneath it and within the triangle.*

➼ *If a scrying mirror is used, the sigil may be traced over the glass.*

➼ *If a talisman or other material basis is being employed to anchor the spell, it should bear the sigil of the angel if possible. Otherwise, it should be placed on top of paper or parchment bearing the sigil and within the triangle.*

➼ *If the ritual has an external target, a representation of that target constructed using similarity and/or contagion links should be placed within the triangle.*

A candle of the natural color appropriate to the sign (Fig. 20) dressed with oil and corresponding powdered incense (Fig. 22) and/or plant material (Fig. 24), serves as an offering to the angel and should also be placed within the triangle. The banishing dagger, invoking wand, bell chime, and any other tools should be present on the Table, outside the triangle.

The ritual shall be performed on the appropriate zodiacal day and hour derived from Figure 2, when the planet ruling the sign is as strong as possible and without affliction.

Modern ceremonial forms such as the pentagram and hexagram rituals are optional, as strict grimoire-style practitioners may wish to perform this ritual using only prayers, invocations, and conjurations. I include them here because they are what I use when performing evocation rites.

I. Opening

Perform the Lesser Banishing Ritual of the Pentagram or Banishing Star Ruby.

Perform the Purification Prayer, either that of Trithemius or an original work as you will. An original piece should serve to clarify the mind and remove any perceived "sins" or "impurities" from your sphere of consciousness.

Perform the Lesser Invoking Ritual of the Hexagram or Invoking Star Sapphire.

Perform the Consecration Prayers for the Circle and Crystal/Table of Practice. Original works should follow the basic structure of the Trithemian prayers, empowering first the circle and then the Table of Practice and crystal to ward off all uninvited spiritual forces that may seek to harm or delude you.

Bell Chime.

II. Preliminary Invocation

Perform the Middle Pillar Ritual or Elevenfold Seal from Liber Reguli.

Perform here a general invocation of the Divine or Most High, however else you conceptualize the highest manifestation of cosmic consciousness that allows you to call the spirits.

Bell Chime.

III. Tuning the Field

Perform the Greater Ritual of the Hexagram for the angel's zodiacal sign.

Perform the invocation constructed from the sections of Liber 963 associated with that sign, or other appropriate prayers, psalms, or so forth that correspond to the sign being invoked.

Bell Chime.

IV. The Conjuration

Repeat the conjuration of the angel three times:

> Come unto me, [ANGEL], angel of [Sign], by the name [God-Name]. Manifest your presence now within this Table of Practice and answer my behest.
>
> AMEN.

Vibrate the name of the angel repeatedly until the presence of the entity is sensed.

Bell Chime.

V. The Charge and Offering

Deliver your Charge and/or commune with the angel as you will.

This is followed by the statement of the offering:

> Unto you, [Angel], I offer this candle [or any other offering you are making], appropriately prepared, that my intent may be accomplished swiftly, skillfully, excellently, and with a perfect and thorough completion, if not by one means then by another.
>
> AMEN.

Bell Chime.

VI. Closing

Give the License to Depart:

> [Angel], by the name [God-Name], I hereby license you to depart unto your proper place without causing harm or danger to man or beast. May the peace of the almighty, living, and true God be ever present between us, and may you come quickly at my call when properly conjured by these sacred rites of magick.
>
> AMEN.

Bell Chime.

Perform the Lesser Banishing Ritual of the Pentagram to close the rite.

The candle should remain lit and be allowed to burn out on its own. Any talisman created or material basis employed should remain upon the altar while the candle burns.

References

Agrippa, Henry Cornelius of Nettesheim, James Freake, and Donald Tyson. *Three Books of Occult Philosophy*. St. Paul, MN: Llewellyn Publications, 1995.

Crowley, Aleister. *Liber Israfel sub figurā LXIV*, in *The Equinox*, vol. 1, no. 7, March 1912. London: Weiland & Co.

—. *Liber V vel Reguli*, in The Master Therion [Aleister Crowley]. *Magick in Theory and Practice*. [Paris]: Lecram Press, 1929.

—. *Liber O vel Manus et Sagittæ sub figurā VI*, in *The Equinox*, vol. 1, no. 2, September 1909. London: Simpkin, Marshall, Hamilton, Kent & Co. Ltd.

— (as The Master Therion). *Magick in Theory and Practice*. [Paris]: Lecram Press, 1929.

—, and Israel Regardie. *777 and Other Qabalistic Writings of Aleister Crowley: Including Gematria & Sepher Sephiroth*. New York: Weiser, 1977.

—, and Israel Regardie. *Gems from the Equinox*. St. Paul, Minn.: Llewellyn Publications, 1974.

—, John Symonds, and Kenneth Grant. *Magick*. London: Routledge & Kegan Paul, 1973.

—, and J.F.C. Fuller. *The Pathworkings of Aleister Crowley: The Treasure House of Images*. Tempe, Ariz.: New Falcon Publications, 1994.

Dee, John, and J.W. Hamilton-Jones. *The Hieroglyphic Monad*. London: John M. Watkins, 1947.

Fuller, J.F.C. [and Aleister Crowley]. *Liber ΘΕΣΑΥΡΟΥ ΕΙΔΩΛΩΝ sub figurā DCCCCLXIII*, in *The Equinox*, vol. 1, no. 3, Special Supplement, March 1910. London: Simpkin, Marshall, Hamilton, Kent & Co. Ltd.

Stenwick, Scott Michael. *Augoeides: Spiritual Technology for a New Aeon* (http://www.ananael.blogspot.com). Last accessed 2015.

—. *Mastering the Great Table: Volume II of the Mastering Enochian Magick Series*. [n.p.]: Pendraig Publishing, 2013.

—. *Mastering the Mystical Heptarchy*. Los Angeles, Calif.: Pendraig Publishing, 2011.

Trithemius, Johannes. *The Art of Drawing Spirits into Crystals*, in Francis Barrett, *The Magus, or Celestial Intelligencer*. London: Lackington, Allen, and Co., 1801.

—, and Joseph H. Peterson. *Trithemius: The Art of Drawing Spirits into Crystals*, on the *Twilit Grotto—Esoteric Archives* website (http://www.esotericarchives.com/tritheim/trchryst.htm). Last accessed 2015.

✢

Choose life. Each element in your theory is a topic for ideation. Roll it into life as needed.

CPSIA information can be obtained
at www.ICGtesting.com
Printed in the USA
BVHW061754160919
558564BV00011B/1352/P